The Ecology of Enclosure

The Effect of Enclosure on Society, Farming and the Environment in South Cambridgeshire, 1798–1850

Shirley Wittering

WIND*gather*
PRESS

Windgather Press
is an imprint of
Oxbow Books, Oxford

ISBN 978-1-905119-44-8

A CIP record for this book is available from the British Library

This book is available direct from

Oxbow Books, Oxford, UK
(Phone: 01865-241249; Fax: 01865-794449)

and

The David Brown Book Company
PO Box 511, Oakville, CT 06779, USA
(Phone: 860-945-9329; Fax: 860-945-9468)

or from our website

www.oxbowbooks.com

Printed by
Berforts Information Press

Contents

List of Figures

List of Tables

Acknowledgements

Of the many acknowledgements of help I wish to give, the first and most heartfelt is to my PhD supervisor, Professor Tom Williamson whose inspirational guidance and enthusiasm is responsible in no small measure for any success this piece of work may have. Among the many people who have been most patient and generous with their time, I should like to thank Mr Waller of the Manuscript Department of the Cambridge University Library for his help in sorting out the tithe maps and schedules and guiding me through the Commissioner's Papers; also the staff of the Official Publication Department for their help in finding various select reports in the British Parliamentary Papers, and the staff of the Rare Books Department in finding the botany notebooks and agricultural pamphlets. Mr Chris Jakes of the Cambridgeshire Collection has been most helpful in finding articles and books relating to Jonas Webb of Babraham. I should also like to thank the staff of the Cambridgeshire Record Office for their friendly and efficient help. Ann Charlton, Archivist and Ray Symonds, Collection Manager at the University of Cambridge Museum of Zoology for finding the Rev Jenyns's nature notebooks, also J. G. Murrell, Department of Plant Sciences for help with nature notebooks. I have been given much help and advice from both G. G. Crompton, Plant Recorder, Cambridge Natural History Society, who gave me her database of all the plants mentioned by Babington, and Trevor James, Plant Recorder for Hertfordshire Natural History Society, and Gareth Hughes, Curator of Audley End House.

I would also like to acknowledge the help given me by Susanna Wade-Martins on farming matters, Pat Davies and Jim Wilson of the Thriplow Landscape Research Group, for geological facts, and Peter Speak, former Director of Geography, Anglian Ruskin University for his landscape expertise. Richard Wall and Leigh Shaw-Taylor both of the Cambridge Group for the History of Population and Social Structure gave me help and advice. I would particularly like to thank Roger Lovatt, Archivist of Peterhouse, and Malcolm Underwood, Archivist of St John's College, Cambridge, for their unstinting help and guidance in researching their fascinating documents. Particular thanks go to Professor Michael Turner of Hull University and Professor Nigel Goose of the University of Hertfordshire in helping me turn my PhD thesis into, I hope, a readable book.

For financial support I am indebted to Dr Roger Schofield of the Local Population Studies Research Fund and would like to thank them for their generosity.

I am grateful to both Bill Wittering and Peter Speak for reading my thesis through and for gathering up the buckets of spare commas! My thanks go to Clare Litt, Julie Gardiner, Lizzie Holiday and Tara Evans of Oxbow Books for their unfailing patience and help.

Last but not least I should like to thank my husband Bill for his encouragement and patience at rooms undusted and meals uncooked.

List of Abbreviations

BPP = British Parliamentary Papers
NA = National Archives formerly Public Record Office
CRO = Cambridgeshire Record Office
CUL = Cambridge University Library
CUP = Cambridge University Press
OUP = Oxford University Press
VCH = Victoria Country History

On weights, measures, money and areas

The weights, areas and volumes used in this book are the ones contemporaries used. The standard unit for grain was the bushel (roughly 36 litres) of 4 pecks or 8 gallons, and 8 bushels made a Quarter. The bushel is a measure of volume so varied according to what was being weighed. The weight of a bushel of grain can vary, but a bushel of wheat weighed about 56 lb or 25 kg, a bushel of barley 48 lb and a bushel of oats 38 lb. The unit of measurement for area was the acre, about 0.4 ha, linear measurement was by the mile, still in current use. As for yield, 20 bushels per acre is roughly equivalent to half a ton an acre which is about 500 kg per acre or 1.2 tonnes per ha.

Before 1971 the English pound (£) consisted of 20 shillings (s), each shilling comprised 12 pence (d) and a penny comprised 4 farthings or 2 halfpennies.

Introduction

The word Ecology is frequently used by geographers and scientists to describe the relationship of flora and fauna to their surroundings, but man too is ultimately dependent upon the land around him, and a number of historians over the last decade or so have argued that the interaction of human societies with their environments should be an important focus of academic enquiry. Malcolm Chase, for example, has reminded the discipline that:

> 'The explicit acceptance of the view that the world does not exist for man alone can be fairly regarded as one of the great revolutions in modern western thought, though it is one to which historians have scarcely done justice.'[1]

Such an approach is not new. In the 1960s, W. G. Hoskins argued that:

> 'Ecology is that branch of science which treats of plants and animals in relation to the environment in which they live. Human beings ought to be studied in this way. We should be studying living human communities and their reaction to their environment and to change, in that environment, over the past 2000 years.'

But he also urged that we should never forget that behind all the graphs and statistics we must be able to hear 'the voices of men and women of the past'.[2] Thus 'human ecology' is an examination of the interaction of society and environment and should not lead us to ignore the experiences of individuals of all social backgrounds. At the same time, an emphasis on 'human ecology' should not obscure the fact that societies are not unitary structures, but internally fractured, divided along lines of class and sectional interest.

Although this book relies mainly on agricultural and natural history sources for its basic research, it is not intended to stand alone but to provide a select body of knowledge that will enhance the general understanding of the history of England and also of those countries to which, men and women used to our ways, moved. The study of local communities was described by Hoskins as 'a set of people occupying an area with defined territorial limits and so far united in thought and action as to feel a sense of belonging together.'[3] Within these communities, though, there was discord and disturbance as we shall see.

This study unashamedly adopts the philosophy and the agenda laid out by Hoskins some four decades ago; it seeks to investigate both the human history of a relatively limited area, although one representative of a much wider range of environments, during a period of momentous landscape change, and to trace the evolution of the modern fieldscape from before enclosure to the beginning of modern capitalist agriculture. It aims to bridge the divide between changes in agricultural production and the social framework in which that production was carried out, but most importantly it extends the study to cover the environmental effect this framework had in south Cambridgeshire.

Enclosure in the nineteenth century is a good area to investigate some of these themes. As Michael Turner has stated:

> 'Parliamentary Enclosure was possibly the largest single aggregate landscape change induced by man in an equivalent period of time, producing scattered farmsteads where once nucleated villages proliferated, walls, hedgerows and then a mosaic of geometrically shaped fields and ordered landownership patterns where once existed the relatively disorderly open fields with their complicated ownership patterns and equally complex tenurial or occupational farming patterns.'[4]

The shift from open fields to closed ones was also reflected in the mindset of those involved; the idea of privacy, of private property, went hand in hand with the privatising of the land. This did not happen all at once, some enclosed land existed well before the nineteenth century and some open field landscapes exist to this day. But enclosure was not just a social, economic and agricultural upheaval, it was also a profound environmental change and this study breaks new ground by considering, in some detail, the effects of enclosure not only on man but on other species, on biodiversity, and habitats. Some historical ecologists have taken an interest in this dimension of enclosure but usually to dismiss the process as something which was entirely negative in its effects.

Before we look at enclosure we must first appreciate the landscape which the enclosers were seeking to change. Sometime between the eighth and twelfth centuries, nucleated villages began to appear in a broad sweep of land running through the centre of England, villages where the houses were in the compact centre or nucleus of the parish and were surrounded by large open fields divided into many small strips and cultivated in common by the inhabitants of the parish, (Fig. i); Rackham calls this 'Champion' (from the French for field) land as opposed to 'ancient countryside'.[5] This area has been called the 'Central Province' by Roberts and Wrathmell.[6] The area covered by this book was on the eastern boundary, an area called the 'East Anglian Salient' (Fig. ii).[7] It was enclosed late in the timeline of Parliamentary Enclosure, between 1795 and 1850.

The history of parliamentary enclosure has been studied for centuries and debate has raged, in particular, over its social consequences. Widely-read historians such as the Hammonds have left a legacy of a common perception that enclosure deprived honest peasants of their independence and reduced working men to wage slaves, not least by robbing them of common land: semi-natural environments rich in useful resources.[8] Their ideas continue to find favour with some modern historians, such as Jeanette Neeson.[9] But others such as Leigh Shaw Taylor show that labourers had few, if any, common rights.[10] These debates are revisited here, but with one difference. For the area studied, a remarkable collection of enclosure commissioners' papers have survived,

FIGURE 1. The Central Province of mainly nucleated settlements after Roberts and Wrathmell.

containing material which can throw much new light on some old questions.[11] Enclosure also affected the wildlife of the area: the ploughing up of commons and heaths, the planting of hundreds of miles of hedges, the use of increasingly effective herbicides, insecticides and fertilisers had a dramatic affect on the plants, animals, birds and insects of this area.

Evidence only available at local level gives details of the sustainability of communities before the introduction of the New Poor law and for most of the villages in this study before enclosure:

> 'Only in both local studies and in re-analysis of published official statistics can an accurate picture be built up of parochial care before the days of the welfare state, grass roots research on original parish documents will be the final arbiter of the truth behind the debate on welfare and poor law relief in the past.'[12]

This book is divided into three sections, the first being the study of social and agricultural life before enclosure changed the landscape irretrievably in the first half of the nineteenth century. It starts with a description of the geology and climate of south Cambridgeshire as it is this that determines how men till

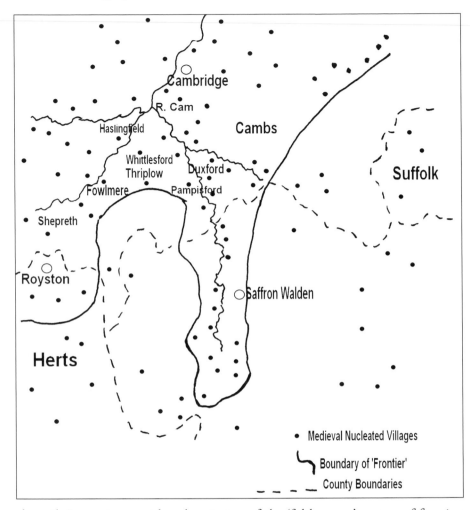

Cambridge

R. Cam

Haslingfield

Cambs

Suffolk

Whittlesford
Thriplow   Duxford

Fowlmere   Pampisford

Shepreth

Royston

Saffron Walden

Herts

• Medieval Nucleated Villages

⌐ Boundary of 'Frontier'

--- County Boundaries

FIGURE ii. The Saffron Walden Salient, after Roberts and Wrathmell.

the soil. It continues with a description of the 'fold-course' system of farming used on the light, easily drained soils of south Cambridgeshire. This ensured the fertility of the land by using the sheep as walking dung machines. Strict 'stinting' rules described how many animals were allowed on the commons and heaths and when during the year they were allowed onto the land. The open field system controlled by Manorial courts ensured a fair distribution of crops and minimised the risk of crop loss. Each open field, although divided into smaller strips, grew the same crops: the first would grow either grains (oats, wheat and barley); the second peas and beans; and the third was allowed to go 'fallow', to allow the soil to rest and recover its fertility, to grow weeds to feed the stock and be ploughed ready for the next year's crop. The following year the fields would rotate to prevent a build up of pests and to improve the fertility of the soil.

From the mid-seventeenth century enterprising farmers, by using ingenuity and co-operation, managed to grow new crops such as clover which converted atmospheric nitrogen using bacteria attached to their roots and which vastly improved the fertility of the soil: 'in Norfolk, for example, between 1700 and 1850, the doubling of the area of legumes and a switch to clover tripled the rate of symbiotic nitrogen fixation'.[13] Turnips also provided winter fodder enabling more animals to be kept and, therefore, produce more manure to fertilise the fields; unfortunately these did not fit into the pre-enclosure three-course rotation and angered the sheep masters who were expected to keep their flocks off the new crops. So the desirability of enclosure was evident, not just to enable farmers to grow new and better crops but to separate the sheep and cattle so that, by controlled breeding, farmers could improve their animals. Once the land had been improved, the owners could hope to increase their profitability by charging higher rents to their tenant farmers.

This section also studies how the village elite used their poor as a human resource to reduce the poor rates, to provide work and to enable the community to function well.

The second part describes the process of enclosure, including opposition to it, as well as the changes to both the landscape and within the village communities as industrialisation began to affect occupations. The fencing of the fields restricted the movement of people over the land and the number of paths was reduced dramatically, the new landscape reduced the 'familiar to the unfamiliar'.[14] The commons, now ploughed up, no longer provided food and fuel and space for a goose, and men became wage labourers reliant on the landowners for work and housing. This loss of independence, though, could provide stability and a steady wage as men began to work in the new occupations such as the railway and manufacturing.

The third section is an analysis of the new study of Botany which the University of Cambridge was enjoying in the eighteenth and nineteenth centuries: 'Men were becoming increasingly aware of the complex relationship between farming and wildlife.'[15] The nearness of Cambridge to the villages within this study area was ideal for professors and their students in their search for rare and unusual plants. And their resulting nature notebooks, preserved in the University Department of Zoology and the University Library, are an exciting and hitherto untapped source for the student of enclosure.

Sources available to the historian for the study of enclosure and wildlife in Cambridgeshire are second to none:

> 'Cambridgeshire ranks fifth of the fifty-four counties of England and Wales in terms of enclosure map cover …in south Cambridgeshire there is a nationally unequalled density of mapped enclosures: one 10 km National Grid square has 100 per cent enclosure map cover. Three-quarters of Cambridgeshire maps are above average in their topographical content.'[16]

And the enclosure commissioners' minutes and rate lists, applications from land owners for new allotments and compensation for loss of common rights which were originally kept by the enclosure solicitor are now safely housed in the University Library and the Cambridgeshire Record Office, a rich source indeed from which to mine the treasure of how parliamentary enclosure in south Cambridgeshire affected not only the social, economic and agricultural life of the area but the natural history as well.

A term often used in the period before the nineteenth century to describe a district to which people felt they belonged, one which could evoke sentimental feelings amongst those who had moved away was 'country'. This term never had a precise meaning, yet it nevertheless conveys:

> 'a sense of local history much wider than that of a town or rural parish, but usually smaller than a county, a sense of the district which people felt was inhabited by their relations, friends and fellow workers and which had a character all of its own.'[17]

This study covers the 'country' of south Cambridgeshire, its aim being to add to the body of local knowledge which will contribute yet one more piece of the wider, national jigsaw.

Notes

1   Chase (1992), 243.
2   Hoskins (1966), 21–2.
3   *Ibid.*, 7.
4   Turner (1980), 33.
5   Rackham (1994), 80–1.
6   Roberts and Wrathmell (2000), 15.
7   *Ibid.*
8   Hammond and Hammond (1911), 331.
9   Neeson (1993, 50.
10   Shaw Taylor (2001), 98.
11   I should like to thank Dr David Dymond for introducing me to these documents. For a wider reference see Tate (1944).
12   Thomson (1991); Marshall (1968), 20.
13   Overton (1996), 3.
14   Williamson (2000), 77.
15   *Ibid.*, 77.
16   Kain *et al.* (2004), 53.
17   Shurer (2004), 51.

CHAPTER ONE

The Character of South Cambridgeshire

'Geography makes History'[1]

The area studied in this book comprises part of the low Chalk escarpment in southern Cambridgeshire which forms the north-easterly continuation of the Chilterns Hills, often known ironically as the East Anglian Heights as, at its highest, at Melbourn, it rises to just over 265 feet (*c*.83 m). It has been an open largely treeless landscape, perhaps since the Bronze Age judging by the number of Tumuli in the area as these would have been built in an open landscape so that they could be seen from miles around. Today it is an homogeneous district of compact villages lying on light easily-cultivated soils.[2] Although supplies of water are restricted, where they do occur they are abundant in the form of springs rising through the Chalk.

The area lies at the extreme southern margins of the 'champion' region of Midland England, dominated until the eighteenth and nineteenth centuries by nucleated villages and extensive arable open fields. Only a few miles to the south and east the 'ancient countryside' begins: the landscape of more dispersed settlement which continues without interruption as far as the south

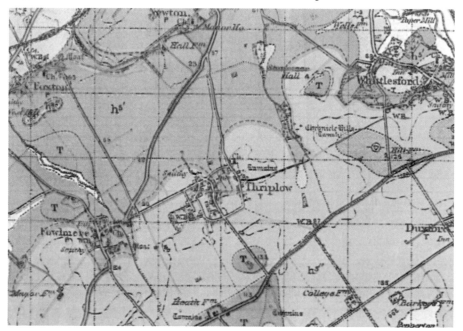

FIGURE 1.1. Geology map of south Cambridgeshire.

coast of England. The district could be said to be transitional between East
Anglia and the Midlands. While in physical terms its wide acres of intermixed
arable resembled the normal champion landscapes of the Midlands, the actual
operation of the open fields shared much in common with the areas of East
Anglia, lying to the east.[3] South Cambridgeshire is thus a boundary zone in
not one but two senses, and in 1815 William Marshall wrote with feeling of his
difficulty in placing south Cambridgeshire in the overall picture of England:

> 'The difficulty in drawing a line of separation between Midland and Southern
> departments, the clayey and chalkey lands are so intermixed. I am weary of dissecting
> County Reports.'[4]

There is little physical variation in the parishes studied; all were typical nucleated,
multi-manored villages sitting within their open fields, all with wet moors or
wastes located close to the spring line, and dry heaths on the escarpments that
were used as sheepwalks. The medieval open fields of the district were in many
respects like those found elsewhere in the Central Province: they were cultivated
in strips divided among the several manors of each parish and their tenants, the
strips being scattered fairly evenly across three or more great fields. In an area
where meadow and pasture were scarce, commoners had the right to pasture
their cattle at certain times of the year on the arable fields, usually after the hay
crop had been gathered in; they also had the use of some of the commons and
wastes although, as we shall see, not all. Perhaps the most remarkable feature
of the district is the late date at which it was enclosed. None of the parishes
studied was enclosed before 1795, and most were only enclosed after 1820. Three
were enclosed after 1840. The reasons for this late enclosure chronology will be
discussed in more detail later. Suffice to say at this point that the late transition
of a completely open landscape, to an enclosed one, created a classic 'Planned
Countryside' to use Rackham's term: a wide, rolling landscape of large fields,
defined by thinly timbered, species-poor hedges.

Figure 1.1 shows the geology of south Cambridgeshire. The geological bedrock
of the district forms part of the Cretaceous series of rocks common to south-east
England, and is overlain by drift deposits. The most significant rock horizons are
those of the Lower and Middle Chalk.[5] At the base of the Middle Chalk, there
occurs a band of harder chalk, the Melbourn Rock, and similar outcrops are found
at the base of the Lower Chalk, known as the Totternhoe Stone (Totternhoe is a
village in Bedfordshire where this stone has been quarried since Roman times).
These are not only very good aquifers, supplying pure chalk water, but can be
quarried for building stone in an area where other such stone is non-existent. These
harder bands of Chalk are known locally as 'clunch'; in the villages of this survey
there are still many remains of the 'clunch pits' from which this was extracted.
Areas of sand and gravel, various forms of glacial deposit, are found in places on
some of on the higher ground in the south of the district.

The climate of this area is relatively continental in character, with cold
winters and warm summers. The average rainfall is around 20 inches (*c.*51 cm)

but occasionally much less, providing a relatively water-stressed environment, although one – given the large number of hours of summer sun – generally good for growing cereals, both wheat but, in particular, barley, which does well on this light, freely-draining land.[6]

Not all the soils formed in Chalk have precisely the same characteristics. Those found in the district fall into three main types or 'Associations', as defined by the Soil Survey of Great Britain, namely, the Moulton series, the Swaffham Prior series and the Burwell series.[7] Soils of the Moulton series are found on the sandier, acidic land. They consist of dark brown loam and contain flint and sand. Where the land has been actively cultivated over the years, there are also significant amounts of chalk, which has worked up to the surface from lower levels. The immediate subsoil is a brown, sandy loam, changing abruptly to a more chalky texture, but still with some sand at 40–90 cm depth. Farmers traditionally described these soils as 'redlands', since arable fields have a reddish-brown tinge after rain (see Fig. 1.2). The soil is permeable, and thus has good drainage, readily absorbing rainfall.

The Swaffham Prior series is formed in chalky and loamy drift over solid chalk. On cultivated land the plough layer is a friable, dark brown loam, with a well-developed structure. At a depth of about 60 cm disturbed chalk is encountered, but the depth is sometimes variable. The soils are porous and thus have free drainage. Soils of the Burwell Association are also very chalky in character and often appear near the line of springs, which rise at the underlying boundary of Melbourn rock. Vancouver called these soils the 'whitelands' (Fig. 1.3).

All these soils probably developed their present character in prehistoric times: originally, the soils overlying the chalk would have been more moisture-retentive in character and very much thicker. These soils, being highly porous, are indeed easily leached of nutrients and need to be kept in good heart through regular inputs of manure or fertilizer. The Moulton Association, in addition, tends to be acidic in its upper layers, although this can be remedied by spreading the underlying chalk on the surface.

During the Devensian Glaciation (60,000–10,000 BC) the whole of the south Cambridgeshire area lay to the south of the principal ice-sheet and was subject for a considerable time to periglacial conditions; this produced extensive solifluction materials, drifts of sands and gravels and innumerable frost hollows and 'hummocky' ground. Today these relict small landscape features – which occur within the area of the Lower Chalk – often impede drainage and have historically had a strong influence on land use. A distinctive feature of the area are 'fossil' or 'relict' pingos, the result of a body of ice pushing up beneath the ground surface to form a mound which sometimes could be 10 m or more in height and as much as 30 m across as shown in Figure 1.4. Following post-glacial thawing, pits were formed which filled with water, and these survived into the historic period and, in some cases, to this day.[8] Some are inhabited by the 'Fairy Shrimp' *(Chirocephalus diaphanous)* whose eggs dry out and become dormant in the soil in dry years, only hatching out when the area becomes waterlogged

FIGURE 1.2. Picture of 'Redlands' Thriplow.

FIGURE 1.3. Picture of 'Whitelands' Coploe Hill, Ickleton.

again.[9] In Melbourn these pits were called 'Blind Wells'.[10] Those would have been a useful source of water for cattle. In the arable fields, 'Dispersed through the hollows of the open fields' the land would have been used as 'Half-yearly meadow land', Vancouver thought they would double in value 'by proper draining and being put into severalty.'[11] Even today they fill up with water whenever the water table rises. When these areas were cultivated, farmers, as today probably ploughed round them and accepted fewer crops; in drier years they were ploughed and grew crops with the rest of the field. Parts of this area are now Sites of Special Scientific Interest (SSSI) as wet meadow reserves.

In all periods the most important influence on where people settled has been water supply (Fig. 1.5). Water was only available on the surface at the junction

FIGURE 1.4. Fossil Pingo – Home of the Fairy Shrimp on Thriplow/ Fowlmere border.

FIGURE 1.5. Pre-enclosure map of Thriplow 1840.

of the Lower and Middle Chalk, where there was a spring line and most of the villages in the area were located here. On the higher ground to the south-east, on the escarpment proper, surface water was absent. Here, areas of open arable were found until the time of enclosure, and – on the sandier deposits – extensive heaths, of vital importance as we shall see for the local sheep-corn farming systems. The Lower Chalk was also mainly occupied by arable land, except in the poorly-draining pockets of 'hummocky ground' where the 'Moors', the areas of damp common land, could be found; it should be pointed out here that these 'moors' are alkaline not the more usual acid moorland (see Chapter 8). This essential pattern of geology, soils and hydrology was repeated in most of the parishes examined in this study.

The main environments thus lay in distinct and banded zones and the 'traditional' agrarian economy of the pre-enclosure period involved the integration of the resources which each had to offer. In particular, the leached, 'hungry' nature of most of the soils meant that they had to be intensively night-folded by sheep, which had been grazing by day on the heaths occupying the sandier, Moulton Association soils. Sheep-corn husbandry was a common – indeed, standard – feature of chalkland areas throughout England, but in this district, following East Anglian, rather than Midland practice, the flocks were the property of the lord, rather than the community, and rather than being common land, the heaths were normally sheepwalks held in severalty, the grazing of which was jealously guarded. By the sixteenth century the Lords of the Manors, who were often the Cambridge Colleges, were frequently the only owners who had the right to keep flocks of sheep, though there were some exceptions.

Sheep flocks were the 'pivot of Chalkland husbandry'[12] without sheep dung the Chalk downland of Cambridgeshire as of Hampshire and Wiltshire which were poor thin soils in their natural state, would have become rapidly exhausted and almost useless for arable farming. Ewe flocks were of central importance for breeding stores and fertilizing the ploughland. The large, lanky, downland sheep were admirably suited to a routine in which daylight was spent grazing commons and darkness folding on the arable.[13] The lateness of enclosure in Cambridgeshire and resistance to change resulted in some farmers fencing off areas of the open fields to grow the new grasses, such as sanfoin and clovers to provide winter hay for the stock. This will be discussed in more detail in Chapter 3.

Building materials

In the medieval period, and to a large extent right up until enclosure, the local environment provided not only crops, grazing and fuel but a range of raw materials, including construction material for local buildings. Eighteenth and nineteenth century commentators were generally critical of both houses and outbuildings:

> 'The farmhouse and premises are in general bad, inconvenient and of such materials
> as must subject the owners to heavy expenses in repairs. Lath and plaster or clay
> and wattle, are the most common materials; in many places clunch walls, which
> are found very warm, dry and durable, if attended to. There are many newly
> erected premises in the late enclosures, most of them defective in arrangement and
> conveniences and almost all over-barned. The barns are too low in the stud. Cottages
> are wretchedly bad, speaking generally.'[14]

Clunch from the Burwell, Melbourn and Tottenhoe stone was used, but principally for church interiors: and clay lump (locally known as clay batt), dried blocks of puddled chalky clay mixed with straw formed into blocks in moulds and air dried, was used in the area from the later eighteenth century.[15] Both materials need to be covered as they disintegrate once the rain penetrates them; so they are usually covered with plaster and walls are capped with either

FIGURE 1.6. Bacon's Manor in the 1930s showing clunch walls and dovecote.

thatch or tiles, as shown in Figure 1.6. Flint and field stones, gathered from the fields, often by the poor, were also used to a lesser extent; but most houses were timber framed, in-filled with wattle and daub or lathe and plaster or often, as time passed and houses were repaired, a mixture of both. Timber framing continued as a form of construction right through until the nineteenth century. Roofs were usually thatched with local straw until recent times when fire and the cost of insurance replaced thatch with pantiles or slate. Only high status buildings were built of brick before the nineteenth century: good-quality flint was likewise rarely employed before the mid nineteenth century, always in association with brick for corners and openings, except for churches where knapped flints were used as high quality decoration.

Before enclosure the local countryside was devoid of hedges and with very little woodland, so timber was scarce and often of poor quality, thin or second hand, and was a precious commodity; college leases always specified that the timber should remain to the owner:

'... also excepting and reserving to the said master and fellows and their successors out of the demise all timber woods and underwoods now growing ... upon the premises ... and all hedgerows quicksett lopp and cropping of all kind of trees and growth of wood there together with free liberty to the said Master to fell ... and cut down lopp and carry away the same timber wood underwood loppings of any of them in seasonable and convenient times of the yeare with men horses and cartes.'[16]

By the nineteenth century most village houses had undergone a long history of addition and change. A good example is *Anno Dom*, a Grade II listed building in Thriplow, jettied and timber framed (Fig. 1.7). This house has undergone several changes over the years; in April 2003 its new owners started extensive repairs and as the old plaster was removed the various stages of its building were revealed.

At the back, the (east) part of the end wall had probably collapsed at some stage and been replaced with clay batt. On the south side under the lath and plaster could be discerned wattle and daub filling in between the timber framing, so there were virtually two layers or skins to the building. The wattle was axe riven, and in the daub could be discerned brown animal hair. The upright wattles were tied together with hazel or willow ties. The laths that overlaid this layer were sawn and probably late Victorian.

By the time of enclosure – the mid-nineteenth century – new materials were beginning to become available to local people, largely as a result of improvements in transport: most notably Cambridgeshire brick, a yellow utilitarian brick made around the fen district of Burwell, and slates. Thriplow House was built of this brick (Fig. 1.8).

Farm buildings – ranging from large barns or granaries, to hovels for holding carts and wagons, maltings, cow sheds, stables, pig sties, hen houses, dove cotes and brew houses – were built of similar materials to houses.

Figure 1.9 shows that early structures were of timber (such as the Tithe Barn or Great Long barn belonging to the Rectory in Thriplow, built around 1320, from the scarf joints in the roof,[17] (Fig. 1.10) and from documentary evidence);[18] but later ones, from the later eighteenth and nineteenth centuries, were of clay batt, as Figure 1.11 shows.

Clay bat and clunch needs a protective coat of plaster to prevent the rain penetrating and dissolving the chalk. Repairs in 1996 allowed pictures to be taken of the clunch beneath the plaster of a barn wall in Thriplow (Fig. 1.12). Flints can be seen at the base and drainage tiles are let into the walls to provide ventilation.

The use of the local building materials reveal a community composed mainly of the 'middling' sort; and as the next chapter will show, even the village elite

FIGURE 1.7 *(left). Anno Dom,* Thriplow, with plaster removed, 2003.

FIGURE 1.8 *(right).* Thriplow House, built 1864 of yellow Cambridge brick.

FIGURE 1.9. Tithe Barn, Thriplow, in the 1930s.

FIGURE 1.10. Scarf joint in Tithe Barn, Thriplow.

FIGURE 1.11. Two barns of Bacon's Manor, built of Clay Batt, 1930s.

FIGURE 1.12. Clunch wall of the Barn belonging to Gowards, Thriplow.

who controlled the parish were only farmers, there being few aristocracy living in Cambridgeshire. The skilled use of the land before enclosure reveals a community in control of their environment within the constraints of their technology.

Having begun our study of the ecology of south Cambridgeshire by looking at the land farmed by the community before enclosure and the buildings in which they lived, we can now turn to how the community managed their social environment.

Notes

1   Paxman (1999).
2   Williamson (2003).
3   Baker and Butlin (1973), 281.
4   Marshall (1815) vol. 4, 608.
5   Perring *et al.* (1964), 23.
6   Watt (1938), 43.
7   Agricultural Research Council (1968) 'Survey No. 2 Soils of Saffron Walden, OS 1 Map.
8   I should like to thank Pat Davies and Jim Wilson of the Thriplow Landscape Research Group for the information for this section.
9   Walters (1972), 35.
10   National Archives (NA) formerly Public Record Office (PRO), (1840) IR 13609 Melbourn Tithe Files.
11   Vancouver (1794), 204, in Tate (1944), 40.
12   Jones (1960).
13   Bowie (1987).
14   Gooch, (1813), 30.
15   Conversation with George Sheldrick who remembered the last man to make 'clay batts' in Thriplow.
16   B9 Peterhouse lease of the Rectory, Thriplow to Alex Dorrington, 1663.
17   Conversation with Dr Leigh Alston, Lecturer for the University of Cambridge Departments of Archaeology and Continuing Education, 1998.
18   Hall and Lovatt (1989), 68.

CHAPTER TWO

The Village Community before Enclosure

'When the gentry are missing, the middling sort become responsible for parish affairs, and by default become the chief inhabitants.'[1]

Having looked at the type of land within which the people of south Cambridgeshire were living, and the resources available for exploitation, we can now turn our attention towards the social character of the parishes before enclosure, the dates of which stretch from 1799 to 1845.

Before 1894 when civil Parish Councils were introduced, both the church and the manor were the organising elements within each village. The reaction of both these bodies to each other, and to the conditions surrounding them, could be termed the human ecology of this period. The manorial system – in which land was held by tenant farmers in return for rents and services paid to a manorial lord – was of crucial importance in structuring agrarian forms in south Cambridgeshire as elsewhere in England and its legacy continued into the post-medieval period. In Postgate's words: 'Manorialism attained its fullest expression in Cambridgeshire and was succeeded by a society based on a landlord and tenant relationship that fostered the maintenance of traditional practices.'[2]

One of the great problems for an historian is the availability of sources. It has been said that writing history amounts to a 'dialogue between the historian and his material, he can interpret and organize only within the limits set by his materials.'[3] It is a lucky dip when researching several parishes whether they all have the sources needed. Although there are about 18 parishes in south Cambridgeshire, only five of them have records in any detail regarding enclosure and only four have tithe files. Thus the apparent anomaly regarding the sources is the reason behind the uneven and variable number of entries.

Most parishes in south Cambridgeshire had more than one manor. Indeed, by the fourteenth century the number of manors in each parish had risen from the one or two held at Domesday to as many as four or five.[4] There was usually one paramount manor and several subsidiary ones. By the sixteenth century many manors had been given or sold to found and support the colleges of Cambridge: all the parishes studied had land owned by Cambridge colleges or the Dean and Chapter of Ely, and Ickleton had one manor owned by the Dean and Chapter of Windsor. By 1874 the colleges of Cambridge owned over 26,276 acres (c.10,636.5 ha) of land in the county.[5] But most of this was not exploited directly. Instead, the manorial demesne and the manorial rights were leased to individuals who paid rent to the institutions in question.[6] Their rents were paid partly in kind and this ensured their supply of food; this was an important consideration to a non-agricultural city-based organisation:

> 'Long leases agreed by manorial tenants were controlled by a decree dating from the time of Elizabeth I which limited the length of leases made by ecclesiastical bodies and Oxbridge colleges to three lives or twenty one years (renewable every seven years) and this became the usual way by which church and college lands were held.'[7]

For example, in 1826 The Manor of Granham's in Great Shelford paid to St John's College, Cambridge, '£68 per annum plus 10 quarters of wheat and 3 quarters of malt;' the lease was for 21 years.[8] And in Stapleford the rent paid to the incumbent of the Vicarage from Manor Farm was '£22 per annum, and 2 quarters 3 gallons of Wheat and 28 quarters 3 gallons of Barley.'[9]

The rent demanded by Peterhouse for the lease of the Rectory in Thriplow in 1545 was:

> '£33 6s 4d, 19 quarters of good sweet and merchantable wheat and 19 quarters 1 bushel of good sweet and merchantable maulte, on the Feast of All Saints *(1 November)*, and also to be delivered to the Masters and Scholers of the said Colledge in the colledge dining room on the feaste of St Nicholas *(6 December)*, one goode and sufficient Boor or sixteen shillings and eight pounds in money, also one quarter of oats, good and sweet of the best on the 29th day of September at the said colledge.'[10]

In 1851 the wording and amounts had not changed, except the rent had become £22 4s 6d to be paid twice a year. As Peterhouse had owned the Rectory since its foundation in 1284, it is probable that the food rent had stayed much the same for 600 years. From 1436 until 1851 there had only been 12 tenant names and one family, the Primes, had held the Rectory for 100 years, with tenancy renewals of mostly 21 years. As Mingay has pointed out; 'These rents often bore little relationship to the economic value of the land'.[11]

Trinity Hall, Cambridge, who owned Crouchman's Manor in Thriplow, likewise had a food rent; their lease to Simon Purdue of Crouchman's dated 1782 specifies:

> 'Rent £8 to be paid twice yearly also 3 quarters of good wheat worth 6s 8d per quarter on Cambridge Market, 4 quarters malt worth 5s a quarter or money in lieu. Also every 24th December 2 couples of wholesome, good fat capons. On Eve of Trinity Sunday a wholesome, good fat capon and 1 dozen good and fat chickens and 6s 8d with the capons and 8s with the chickens.'[12]

One problem historians face is the meaning of certain words that have changed over time; terms describing land tenure, although familiar and sounding the same, have often changed their meaning, sometimes so subtly that confusion can easily arise. In the context of south Cambridgeshire, the widespread leasing of manors by colleges and other institutions can cause confusion over the term 'tenant'. There was a huge difference between a man leasing a manor from one of the Cambridge colleges, with many acres, several cottages and certain manorial rights and use of timber etc., and a labourer paying a small sum to live in one of his cottages. Yet both are often described as 'tenants' in contemporary documents, although the colleges generally used the term 'lessee' for the former. Such individuals held the manors on long leases, the terms of which were written on parchment or paper and rewritten, the wording hardly changing, each time it was renewed. In practice they became the manorial lords with all their rights, responsibilities and privileges.

The manors had numerous copyhold 'tenants' from whom some small profit could be made. In the eight parishes for which sources are available there was a total of 200 copy and 153 freeholders, which is 62% and 38% of the total number of landowners respectively. But these copyholds – which here, as elsewhere, had developed out of medieval customary tenancies – were in effect freeholds, many of which had sub-tenancies. Robert Allen found that, by the sixteenth century, copyhold of inheritance was most common in the eastern counties and in Cambridgeshire in particular.[13] Such tenants could leave their property 'to the use of their will', meaning that they could indicate in their wills to whom they wished to leave their land and this would be honoured. As long as they paid their rents their tenure was secure until either debt or death intervened, and as copyhold rents were very stable, hardly rising over the years, by the nineteenth century they had become no more than a nominal payment.[14] In 1868 the Lord of the Manor of Fowlmere enfranchised the copyholds, amounting to 380 acres (*c*.154 ha) and copyhold was eventually converted nationally to freehold in 1922.

By the nineteenth century there was thus little practical difference between copyholds and freeholds, and the rights of the former, as much as those of the latter, had to be taken into account in the enclosure process. But because the lessees of the manors were generally held on tenancies of 21 years, they too were effectively owners with almost complete autonomy of control over the use of the land, the manorial rights and ownership of the tithes. They farmed their own demesnes, collected rents and fees for enrolling new tenants and occasionally exacted fines for felling trees without permission or encroaching in a neighbour's land. Only the use of the timber was usually reserved to the corporate owners:

> 'Survey of Pittensaries Manor 1649 – 'Holds all that Manor of Thriplow called and known by the name of Pittensaries … the Dean and Chapter (of Ely) to have all trees growing upon the Manor whether it be blown down by wynd or otherwise.'[15]

This phrase was used in succeeding leases until 1840, when the estate was sold to Joseph Ellis.[16] Peterhouse leases similarly instructed that:

> 'They (the lessee) can loppe all such trees growing upon the grounde that hath afortime been lopped and to have the lopps to their own use. But not to loppe any trees for 3 yeares before the end of their lease.'[17]

Apart from the food rents and timber the rest of the profits, often including the tithes, belonged to the lessee. To the Colleges, length of tenure and food rent were more important than new techniques and profitability and were seen as a long-term hedge against inflation.[18]

	1	*2*	*3*	*4*	*5*
Parish	*No. claiming rights*	*No. Paying enclosure rates*	*Statement of property*	*Enclosure award*	*Tithe Award*
Duxford 1822–30				60	64
Gt Shelford 1834–5	99	60	52	62	-
Harston 1798–1802	42		57	53	-
Newton 1798–1802	11			25	5
Lt Shelford 1798–1802	25		25	48	
Ickleton 1810–14	63	69	45	72	
Sawston 1802–11	44	45	39	49	
Stapleford 1812–14	34	42		38	
Thriplow 1840–45			39	32	32

TABLE 2.1. Number of landowners claiming rights at enclosure. These figures are derived from three sources – the first three columns are from the Commissioners' papers, column 4 is from the enclosure award and column 5 from the tithe award. The dates are those of enclosure.

Of 18 parishes examined in south Cambridgeshire all had manors or rectories owned by colleges; they varied between one and five with most having three. Landowning structures in the south Cambridgeshire parishes were thus complex and it is possible that this very complexity may in part explain the remarkably late enclosure chronology displayed by the district. Of particular importance in this respect was the distribution of land ownership – the relative proportions of landed property held by manorial lessees, larger and smaller farmers – both freehold and copyhold. There are several sources that throw light on this, including the enclosure awards themselves and the various documents in the Commissioners' papers, which show the list of people expected to pay a rate towards the cost of enclosure, and the lists of those entitled to state whether they agreed, disagreed or were neutral regarding enclosure. The tithe awards, which are often close in date to the enclosures themselves in this district of late enclosure, also list proprietors.

Column four of Table 2.1 shows the number of people who were actually allocated land at enclosure. Those claiming and those receiving land were not necessarily the same. In Great Shelford for example, out of the 99 claims only 62 were allowed, 37% being rejected.[19] The other figures, however, are in broad agreement, and can be used to calculate that approximately 11% of the population were actually landowners (the table includes all owners however small, even those owning less than an acre).

This group can be divided into larger and smaller owners: Table 2.2 shows the parishes divided into those owning less than 50 acres (20.24 ha) and those owning more. Again the absence of source slews the figures slightly.

Although it is clear that there are more of the smaller owners (87%) than

Parish	No. owners	50 acres and under	%	Over 50 acres	%
Duxford	60	53	88	7	12
Fowlmere	42	35	83	7	17
Foxton	42	38	90	4	10
Great Shelford	58	52	90	6	10
Harston	53	48	91	5	9
Newton	25	21	84	4	16
Little Shelford	48	45	94	3	6
Ickleton	72	59	82	13	18
Melbourn	165	145	88	20	12
Sawston	49	44	90	5	10
Shepreth	41	37	90	4	10
Stapleford	38	30	79	8	21
Thriplow	32	26	81	6	19
Total	725	633	87	92	13

TABLE 2.2. Percentage owning under or over 50 acres. *Source:* Enclosure Awards and census figures nearest the date of the Award.

Parish	Total acreage	No. small owners	% total land
Duxford	3173	53	2
Fowlmere	2212	35	2
Foxton	1692	38	2
Gt Shelford	1927	52	3
Harston	1532	48	3
Newton	987	21	2
Lt Shelford	1200	45	4
Ickleton	2672	59	2
Melbourn	4567	145	3
Sawston	1817	44	2
Shepreth	1318	37	3
Stapleford	1780	30	2
Thriplow	2353	26	1
Total	27,230	633	2.5

TABLE 2.3. Percentage of small owners to total acreage by parish, 50 acres and under.

large (13%), this does not of course mean that the majority of the land was held by the smaller landowners. Far from it: holdings less than 50 acres accounted for total of only 2.5% of the land, as Table 2.3 shows.

As far as we can tell, the numbers of owners, and the distribution of land ownership, had changed little in the half century or so leading up to enclosure. In the case of Thriplow, a Field Book of approximately 1780[20] shows the number of land owners as 29: the number of people owning land in 1845 was 32. In 1780 three people owned properties extending over more than 50 acres and 26 people owned less than 50 acres; at enclosure, four owned land over 50 acres and 27 owned land under 50 acres; while the tithe schedule 1842 shows six people owning over 50 acres and 26 owning less,[21] indicating very little change over a fairly long period.

Of course, examining the social distribution of land ownership on the basis of individual parishes can be misleading. Some individuals, appearing as small owners in one place, might be large owners in another, or owners of small plots of land in several parishes; some smaller owners had inherited their property and had never lived in the parish, some had moved away and some had several

	1801 census	1821 census
Sawston, enclosed 1802–1811		
Population	466	699
Houses	94	100
Families	120	168
Families in agriculture	30	100
Proportion of labouring families	25%	59%
Whittlesford, enclosed 1809–1815		
Population	416	486
Houses	60	66
Families	100	100
Families in agriculture	14	79
Proportion of labouring families	14%	79%
Ickleton, enclosed 1810–1814		
Population	493	602
Houses	77	98
Families	121	140
Families in agriculture	75	107
Proportion of labouring families	62%	76%
Stapleford, enclosed 1812–1814		
Population	235	408
Houses	47	58
Families	64	82
Families in agriculture	46	42
Proportion of labouring families	72%	51%

TABLE 2.4. Number of agricultural workers in parishes in south Cambridgeshire enclosed before 1830.

properties and obviously could not live in them all. Of the total number of landowners, 16% were absentees leaving 84% of owners living within their parish. Most landowners, and the majority of small landowners, thus lived within their parish.

It appears from reference to 'cottagers' in contemporary documents that less than 10 acres (4.1 ha) (the size of a county council smallholding) was considered too small to be a real farm, even for a subsistence farmer; approximately 10% of the male population of the parishes studied owned 10 acres or less.

It is generally agreed that these small landowners were most at risk of losing their properties at enclosure owing to the large costs involved. What is striking is that they seem to have constituted a significant proportion of the village population, in most cases around 10%, although some of these may have possessed no more than a garden. They were, nevertheless, different from, and generally in a better economic position than, the landless poor, the numbers of which were rising: 'The Number of males aged 20 or over employed in agriculture in England increased from about 910,000 in 1811 to just over one million in 1851.'[22] This rise was nowhere as large as that in industrial towns, but it was a rise nevertheless. Table 2.4 analyses the census figures for information on the number of agricultural labourers in the period before enclosure.

Stapleford is the only parish to record a drop in agricultural workers despite the population increasing. The parish is situated between Great Shelford and Sawston and while it is possible that many labourers were walking to Sawston

TABLE 2.5. Division of
families in trade and
agriculture, Stapleford
Source: CRO P156/12/1,
2 Thriplow Overseers'
Account Books.

	Chiefly in agriculture	*Chiefly in trade etc.*	*Others*
1811	46	22	5
1821	42	14	26

to work in the paper or leather mills there, the real reason appears to be that the enumerator simply entered more people in the 'other' category than in the agricultural one: the relative proportions in the two categories certainly changed significantly between the 1801 and 1821 censuses, as shown in Table 2.4. As Edward Higgs has noted: 'The returns for the Agricultural workforce can be used for a very broad region of comparisons but their use in local studies is fraught with danger.'[23] Not until 1841 were question-forms given to each family to fill in; before then the enumerator carried out the questioning himself and then entered the final figures into his census sheets.

It is interesting to note that these questions on employment were not properly understood by the enumerators. In some cases women, children and servants were classed with the householder. And in other cases they were placed in the third category as being in neither agricultural nor commercial occupations – women were often employed in agriculture but for reasons of delicacy did not record themselves as such in the census.[24]

This led to the numbers employed being underestimated by as much as 30–40%.[25] In 1801 the heading relating to agricultural employment is '*Persons* chiefly employed in agriculture,' in the next census of 1811 the heading is '*Families* chiefly employed in agriculture' and this heading continues until 1831. So 1801 counts individuals and 1811 counts families, not the same thing at all. Table 2.5 shows the confusion in the enumerators mind over categories in Stapleford.

In spite of these anomalies, the enclosure documents and related sources give us a broad picture of the social and landowning structure of south Cambridgeshire on the eve of enclosure. In most parishes the largest landowners were manorial lords or, more usually, large farmers who leased demesne, and manorial rights, from large institutions, principally Cambridge colleges. But there were also large numbers of other small and medium-sized landowners, accounting in most villages for between a quarter and a half of the population. The upper echelons of this group, together with the lessees of manorial lands, were responsible for managing the provision for the landless poor, who in most parishes represented the majority of the population, and by examining the ways they did this we can learn much about the character of the 'community' on the eve of enclosure.

Poverty and the Poor Law

'The English village evolved as a community of responsible, self-regulating partners, with a duty not simply to the present but also to future generations.'[26] A local historian has access to many sources and by studying his particular locality acquires a strong impression of the personalities of the people who went before him. Family reconstruction and nominal record linkage can be built up by careful use of registers, manor court rolls and overseers' accounts to reveal the inter-relationships of the poor. The compounding influence of work, worship and leisure all affect a man's actions; thus poor relief can only be fully understood if it is seen as one strand among many within a small community. It is however, a strand that cannot be ignored, for how a community deals with its less fortunate members can reveal much about its underlying assumptions and attitudes. Susannah Ottoway and Samantha Williams describe the methodology of family reconstruction and nominal record linkage to provide a personalised picture of the poor, a section of the community that would otherwise be invisible to historians.[27] I have used this technique to build up a picture of the poor in Thriplow.[28]

It is not easy to discover the attitudes of the parish elite towards the poor; only those who were accepted for parish relief are shown in the overseers' books and records of refusals of help are very rarely found; one exception is the question asked by the Royal Commission into the administration of the poor laws in 1834: 'Is any attention paid to the character of the applicant or to the cause of his distress?' The answers vary but in general it is stated that 'relief is occasionally withheld but generally very little attention is given to a man's character.'[29]

In south Cambridgeshire the parish officers were usually the farmers and occupying landowners and, while the manor courts controlled the agricultural year, the fact that those running both the manor and the church were the same people meant that a certain merging of responsibilities took place. Of the 19 parishes of south Cambridgeshire studied here, only four were enclosed after the 1834 *New Poor Law Amendment Ac*t. Within the confines of source survival, this allows us to use the records of the overseers to study social conditions before enclosure; we can then draw some conclusions as to how the village landowners used the poor to the benefit not only of themselves but the rest of the village by providing work that enabled them to keep the poor rates down.

Most of the expenditure of these parishes rose steeply during the early years of the Napoleonic war but levelled out or even fell by 1821. This trend is similar to both the county of Cambridgeshire and England and Wales. Costs of providing for the poor in England and Wales between the years 1803 and 1813 (dates comparable with census population figures) rose by 63% from £4,078,000 in 1803 to £6,656,000 in 1813.[30] This drain on the poor rates was even quoted as a reason for enclosure by the Commissioners of Great Shelford:

> 'This Bill has been brought into Parliament mainly with the view of employing the surplus labourers in the Parish. This surplus is so considerable as to lay a heavy burthen on the occupiers of land, and to alleviate it, the Proprietors have agreed to enclose the Parish.'[31]

This can be further analysed to provide details of the number of poor receiving relief from the parishes in 1801 and 1811. Table 2.6 shows the percentage of the population of ten parishes in south Cambridgeshire that were receiving poor

Parish	Population	No. Relieved	Percentage
1801			
Fowlmere	420	60	14
Foxton	322	44	14
Harston	322	55	17
Hauxton	144	24	17
Newton	114	16	14
Gt Shelford	570	59	10
Lt Shelford	220	53	24
Stapleford	220	23	10
Thriplow	334	49	15
1811			
Fowlmere	448	53	12
Foxton	304	46	15
Harston	452	33	7
Hauxton	189	22	12
Newton	104	18	17
Gt Shelford	593	35	6
Lt Shelford	357	63	18
Stapleford	329	25	8
Thriplow	319	32	10

TABLE 2.6. Percentage of population receiving poor relief, by parish 1801 and 1811 (including children).

relief in 1801 and 1811, several decades before most of the parishes in the district were enclosed.

Each parish had a certain amount of autonomy within the framework of the existing laws. Under the Old Poor Law each parish could react to prevailing local conditions as it thought fit. The two overseers of the Poor within each parish decided how much would be needed each year and raised a rate, sometimes several rates, from landowners according to the value of their property.

In most south Cambridgeshire parishes, holding the position of overseer, churchwarden, surveyor of highways or constable was seen as a privilege and a position that conferred power within the parish, and was usually performed by the larger farmers. Steve Hindle points out that when gentry are missing, the 'middling sort' become responsible for parish affairs and, by default, become the chief inhabitants. This 'charisma of office' conferred status and power on the farmers and yeoman of the village; this would certainly be the case in the parishes of south Cambridgeshire where, as we have seen, resident gentry were largely absent.[32] The villages were comparatively small, the overseers would have known the claimants personally and most overseers probably perceived the holding of office as enhancing their status and authority in the community. Yet they were first and foremost farmers and husbandmen, not accountants, as their varied handwriting and idiosyncratic spelling testifies. Thomas Mowl, who in 1769 was both overseer and constable for Thriplow, writes of paying for 'tew dosen of sprows' and 'my gerny to Sheprd'[sic], his local accent coming over loud and clear. A list at the back of the Thriplow overseers' book dated 1789, names seven men as 'Overseers by turn at Triplow.' This remains the same for many years,[33] of these seven men, only one describes himself in his will as a gentleman,[34] the others use the term yeoman. An earlier overseer Gray Purdue, in his will dated 1779, describes himself as a yeoman, yet he owned land and property in several parishes and rented three large estates within Thriplow, including the Rectory and Crouchman's Manor, which would almost have given him the status of gentleman rather than yeoman.[35] Further clues to the status of the parish officers lies at the back of the account book, 'the account of the Church yard Pales and who they belong to' shows each man's financial standing, and all the men named as 'Overseers by turn' are on this list. They are all included in the Land Tax assessment of 1798, showing they were certainly of the village elite, indeed three of them were lessees of college manors. All the officers named were born within their parish, though only three, John Cowling, Simon Purdue and Richard Clements, were eligible to vote in the County elections for 1780.[36] In 1774–5 one of the overseers was Mary Tinworth widow of a previous overseer Reynold Tinworth.[37] Fowlmere, too, had a woman overseer in 1757, Mary Wedd the widow of Benjamin Wedd, overseer,[38] and in 1767 Trumpington seems to have had a husband and wife partnership as overseers, William and Mary Stacey.[39]

Overseers also played a major role in meeting the demands placed on the parishes by central government. At the outbreak of war with France, for example, there was a pressing need for soldiers and unemployed able-bodied men were urged to join the Militia. In March 1795 the Cambridgeshire Quarter Sessions under orders from Parliament set out 'a certain number of men in the several counties of England for the services of her Majesties Navy'. Within the hundred of Thriplow, each of the ten villages was ordered to supply one man.

The overseers were in a difficult position; their desire to reduce rates was balanced by the entreaties of the poor amongst whom they lived; the fact that they knew nearly all their fellow parishioners gave them an unique insight into their needs, though prejudice, either personal, moral or religious, could affect their decisions. Keith Snell points out 'the Old Poor Law allowed much scope for face to face relief between ratepayers and recipients who knew each other well and who were sometimes of comparable status.'[40]

It was in the overseers' interests to use the poor as a resource both in keeping down the poor rates by making them work the land and to provide succour to the ill and elderly poor. Henry B. Gunning of Whittlesford commenting in the Thriplow Tithe files of 1840 wrote, 'The poor rates have long been low.'[41] In 1794 Charles Vancouver listed the poor rates of the villages he visited; they varied from 2–4s in the pound. If Gunning thought that Thriplow's rates were low then at least five other villages were as low or lower. Another four villages were higher but only by 1 shilling. The provision of work for the labouring poor was to the mutual benefit of the community – the village received its necessary maintenance such as roads mended and ditches dug, and the sick and old cared for. Their wives and children were clothed and housed. The unemployed were paid, albeit a modest amount, but enough (together perhaps with what they could get from the local commons and gleaning in the open fields) to enable them to support their families. Although to modern eyes the type of work the overseers gave to the poor seems hard, at least it occupied their waking hours, kept them out of the beer houses and perhaps restored their sense of self-respect and enabled them to return to their families feeling they had earned their bread rather than having just received charity. This was not always so as one answer to the Royal Commission of Inquiry into the Poor Laws shows: Fowlmere replied to the question of whether the industry of the labourers had increased or decreased by saying that:

> 'There is general, and I believe, well founded complaint that the Labourers are not so industrious as formerly. It is the necessary effect of putting men into the gravel pits, paid so low that work is not even expected. I have known able-bodied men paid 2s 8d for digging gravel, or standing about in the gravel pit for so many hours in a day.'[42]

Yet other parishes answered that their labourers were equally as good as before.

As with all human relationships, community relationships depended on co-operation and agreement, if these were missing, then disagreement and aggression would result; an example of this concerns the overseer of Whittlesford, Ebeneza Hollick, who seemed to be rather an unpopular man; there are several contradictions to the minutes in his hand and in 1826 he issued a notice to the effect that 'There will be a Vestry meeting on Sunday afternoon October 1 1826 in the Church or directly after service to take order for setting to work all such persons married or unmarried having no means of maintaining themselves.' Below this notice are the terse words, 'N.B. *No person whatever* attended to the above notice on October 1'. He issued another notice on October 29 and the same thing happened. Although the absence could be caused by apathy, it is unlikely that every member of the Vestry should be affected at once; it would seem that Hollick was a man who had risen from poor beginnings to become a landowner of much consequence and strong opinions. He was disliked and occasions such as that described above were not uncommon.[43]

There were clear differences of interest between different levels of the farming and landowning class in the Cambridgeshire villages. In particular, smaller farmers were probably happier to lay labourers off at slack times of the year, contributing as each of them did a smaller proportion to the poor rates than their larger neighbours. This, at least, was the complaint of some of the larger proprietors. Joseph Ellis, the largest landowner in Thriplow, sent a letter to the *Cambridge Chronicle* dated 4 August 1838, replying to a letter from the Vicar of Thriplow which had accused him of sacking a boy for being confirmed:

> 'I will now lay before your readers my general conduct to my labourers. I employ on my farms, in Triplow, about 60 labourers; I find them work through winter and summer; I never turn them off except in cases of gross misconduct; they are quite secure in the continuance of their employment if they conduct themselves well, and the result is that three-fourths of the whole number of my labourers have been in my service above 30 years ... I will say to their credit I consider them the most respectable of the labourers in the Parish … Look at the smaller occupiers do they employ their proportion of labourers – and how frequently the few in their employ are sent adrift in the winter season.'[44]

This letter also gives a clue to the employment conditions of this time; that many farmers did lay off their men when there was no work for them to do knowing that the parish safety net would catch them and that their (the farmers') poor rates were subsidising the unemployed. Mr Ellis actually lived and worked in Thriplow, meeting his workers not just at work but at other social occasions within the parish. An absentee owner, employing a farm manager, could afford to be harsher, not having to rub shoulders every day with those he employed. Ellis employed many men; he (like his father before him) had been an Anglican churchwarden for more than 30 years before leaving the church to become a leading light in the local non-conformist chapel.[45]

Seasonal variation in the demand for labour was the key factor in the management of poor relief. Harvest was a time when there was plenty of work and every able-bodied person was expected to work in the harvest fields; the pay was higher and several entries in the overseers' books mention harvest pay: 'gave Joseph Salmon his wages at Harvest – £1 6s',[46] and 'John Hills Harvest Wages, £1 5s' compared with the weeks before when he was paid 6s.[47] The eagle eye of the overseer, however, caught any instance of wrong doing:

> 'Inquiry to be made into the circumstances of Robert Farnham having applied for harvest work, which E. Hollick Jun. (overseer) reports is the case, that he is claiming Parish Relief through inability to work – Inquiry also to be made respecting the capability of Samuel Rickards maintaining himself during Harvest without Relief from the parish.'[48]

It is noteworthy that when work was slack, particularly during the winter, parishes used the able-bodied poor for the benefit of the wider community, especially for maintaining the drains and ditches on the damp commons, or for mending the roads. In Thriplow the overseers employed men in ditching more than any other occupation; in 1780 they spent 234 man-days ditching.[49] Likewise the overseers' book for Fowlmere records: 'March 28 1785 – Received of Robert Adams of Foulmire the sum of twelve shillings for cleaning the River for the year at two pence a year by me, Francis Murkin.'[50] A similar amount was spent from 1790–1794 when Mr Murkin requested someone to help him as 'I cannot get the time and Mr Wallis turns the water so quick.'[51]

This last sentence is a little obscure although Fowlmere was noted for its watercress beds which needed a regular supply of fresh water. In Whittlesford similarly gravel digging and drain digging were the main forms of work for the unemployed: in January 1827 for example, the overseers agreed to employ Samuel Rickard in digging gravel at Chequer Bush Pits at 6d per load, and Samuel Nunns in Stanmore Pitt at 10d a load; the rest of the unemployed men were set to work on the drains.[52] The situation in Sawston was much the same.[53] Yet while the poor were generally used on communal works, they at times did the same kinds of work for private landowners

Apart from ditching and river cleaning, the unemployed also worked at herd-keeping, pulling thistles, picking stones, sawing and carrying of paupers' belongings to the poor house. The variety of work, and to some extent its

Year	Ditching (no. man days)	Hayward (days)	Other (days)
1765			1 work
1766		2	
1767	13	1	
1768	23	2	2 pulling thistles
1769			
1770			
1771			
1772	17	Weekly	
1773	33	1	Digging a hole
1774	127	1	Digging hole
1775	140	Weekly	3 picking stones
1776	50	Weekly	
1777	145	Weekly	
1778	17	Weekly	
1779	84	Weekly	
1780	234	Weekly	Sawing
1781	6	Weekly	
1782	5	Weekly	
1783		Weekly	
1784	10	Weekly	Keeping herd
1785	2	Weekly	
1786	17	Weekly	
1787	11	Weekly	
1788	11	Weekly	
1789	9	18	

TABLE 2.7. Work given to able-bodied unemployed men by Thriplow Overseers.

seasonality, is clearly indicated in the Thriplow overseers' accounts for the 1760s, '70s and '80s, as indicated in Table 2.7.

The large number of days spent ditching in 1780 could be accounted for by the weather; the England and Wales Precipitation charts show the 1770s and early 1780s as being very wet.[54] The wages paid for ditching work – 6s a week – can be compared with a typical non-charitable wage for agricultural work as quoted by Eden, of just below 8s per week.[55] Sometimes ditching was calculated at so much per rod (5.03 m); perhaps this was paid at a lower rate as on one occasion two men paid this way were ordered to have their pay made up to 1s a day by the JP.[56] By 1816 in Whittlesford an agreement was reached 'that weekly labourers' wages to be eight shillings and small beer – single men five shillings and small beer, six shillings per week if belonging to any benefit club.'[57]

Putting the poor to work on drainage was only one of several ways in which the overseers were involved directly in the communal agriculture of these open-field villages. The Hayward (or 'Howard' as it is spelled in the Thriplow overseers' accounts), also described as 'Field Keeper' in some accounts, had the job of regulating the cultivation of the open fields, ensuring that the boundaries of the strips were not encroached upon, and impounding any stray animals. A list at the back of the book dated 1775 states 'Howards reproved (*sic*) and put on by Vestry with the liberty to pound in the Parish of Thriplow', followed by a list of four names, all in receipt of parish relief; nor

was it just a job given to the old: John Blanks, for example, who undertook
the role in 1777, was only 26 years old. The Hayward received between 3s in
the 1770s and 6s a week in the 1780s. The overseers also provided him with
powder and shot (presumably to deter vermin) and occasionally britches and
overcoats. The last year the overseers seem to have paid the Hayward was 1786
when his pay had fallen to 3s a week, the same level as 15 years earlier, perhaps
a sign of an hardening of attitude.

The communal Herd Keeper was also often paid out of the poor rate: at
Fowlmere an agreement was reached 'between William Bird and the parishioners
of Foulmire in vestry assembled that he will keep the herd of Cows for one year
ending Christmas next at 1s'[58] (The same year he was also paid 'for cleaning the
Blind Wells on Moor – 5s').[59] One Fairchild was paid 2s 2d for 'Keeping the
Bull'. In Thriplow, and probably elsewhere, the town bull was kept by one or
other of the overseers, 'Paid Jacob Prime for keeping the Town Bull 2 weeks
6 days – 4s 8d.'[60] Perhaps he could claim a percentage of the calves born, or
more likely (in an area notoriously short of pasture land) only the large farmers
had enough meadow to keep the bull.

The Blanks family of Thriplow provide an interesting case study of a poor
family, and their interaction with the elite of farmers and landowners represented
by the overseers. The first entry relating to them is in the register of 1770 when
Thomas Blanks married Mary Smith. Three years later John Blanks married Amy
Slarter; it is possible that Thomas and John were brothers. In 1776 John was given
ditching work by the overseers at 1s a day and in July 1777 he was sworn in as
Hayward at a wage of 6s a week. He continued in this role until May 1782 when
he was paid £4 as a Militia man. The entry for November of that year reads 'pd
for signing a Bill to get Widow Blanks money', which suggests that John had
died in service. In 1783 Widow Blanks received a pension of 3s a week until May
1784 when she died and was buried by the parish. Her aunt Widow Kefford,
herself a pauper, was then paid 2s 2d for looking after the children and washing
them. Thomas Blanks senior's first and only entry in the overseers' account is on
26 January 1777 when he was buried at the parish's expense. His widow, Mary,
received fuel, and in August she was given a pint of milk. In February 1778 there
were payments 'for a quart of beer Widow Blanks had when she lay in' and in
April for 'Mr Gunning fees for bering (burying) of little Blanks';[61] his coffin cost a
mere 2s compared with 9s for an adult's coffin. In January 1780 Widow Blanks, still
aged only 39, was buried by the parish. The children from both families received
housing, clothing and, when old enough, were taken on as servants.[62]

A certain amount of fiddling and bogus claims would seem to be inevitable.
At Whittlesford in 1826: 'It was agreed at this meeting that John Gray shall
not be employed by the Parish or receive relief until he can show that he is in
absolute need of it.' And unlike the beggars of today 'it was ordered that no
person keeping a dog shall in future receive Parish Relief.'[63] Yet a certain amount
of humanity was shown as in an apprentice agreement for the same parish, and
the same year: 'John Arnold hires Thomas Hayden for a year with the express

agreement for the said Thomas Hayden to have two days to himself to go to Triplow Feast which he had.'[64]

Samantha Williams found that few paupers in the Bedfordshire parishes of Campton and Shefford lived on their own.[65] This is also true of south Cambridgeshire; daughters and husbands were often given money or medicine for their mothers or wives who were either too ill or too old to claim it for themselves, though this does not prove that these elderly people were living with their children. On 29 March 1783 the overseers of Thriplow paid 1s 'to Sarah Green for doing for her mother for a week', and this is repeated several times throughout the year. Widow Green had a weekly pension of 1s 6d but this was obviously not enough for her daughter to provide the care she needed when she was ill. It is possible that Widow Green was living with her daughter though she could have been visited by her daughter at her own house.[66] Widows who had no relatives who could accommodate them were often housed in the Poor House of the village.

Pauper women had a valuable role to play in the parish, their position as 'carers' added to the creation of closer community ties within the structure of village life. Women were mainly used to care for the sick, the dying and children, but were also given work in the fields; field work for women consisted mainly of picking stones. In May 1769 Ester Impey and Ann Searl were paid £1 11s for gathering 31 loads of stones: six months later in November of the same year Ester was dead and the parish paid for her burial. In the same year Jane Langley was paid 11s for gathering 11 'lodes' of stones, she also received fuel, relief and medicine and clothes for her children. Jane continued to receive a diminishing pension until she died and was buried by the parish in 1775. Just before her death the accounts record 'rice and half peck Barley for Jane Langleys chickens and turkeys' a charitable act by the overseers to help an old lady make a living.[67] Her goods were inventoried by the overseers in 1768 three years after her husband's death and before she became a permanent receiver of relief. Her son William was probably apprenticed when he was 12 to one Mr Prime, who was paid £2 15s in 1767. In 1775 one of Jane's twin daughters Hannah, then 13, was taken by Benjamin Prime of Horseheath, a distance of 11 miles away at 1s a week. The parish mended her petticoat and washed her shift and on 22 June, 'carried her to Horseheath to Mr Prime'. The town agreed to buy her clothes; in July they made her a new shift for 5d and in September she received 'a pair of pattens, a pair of stockings, 6 ells of Scotch Camblet and 1 yard of linen for a gown and bodice and a linen apron.' She continued to receive clothes from the parish until 1779 and Benjamin Prime received his rent up till that year; Hannah would then have been 17.[68]

The most regular payments made by the overseers were for 'sitting up with a dying pauper'; 'making the burying suit'; 'washing and laying them out'; 'carrying them to the church'; and providing 'candles, beer, cheese and bread'. Occasionally a name is mentioned in this context; in February 1776 Martha Brown and Esther Impey were paid 5s for 'sitting up, washing, waiting on Widow Slarter 1 week and 3 days', also they are paid 3s for 'laying her out and sitting up one night' and in May 1785 Rose Kefford is paid 2s 9d for 'laying

Year	Burials	Sewing and mending	Nursing and washing	Other
1766	1			
1768	2		2	
1769			1	3 picking stones
1772			2	
1774	2	1	2	
1775	4	7		
1777		1		
1778			5	
1781			3	
1782			3*	
1783	1		4	Lodging (other paupers)
1784	2		23	
1786	1			
1787			2	
1788			8	
1789				Harvest work

TABLE 2.8. Womens' work paid for by Overseers, Thriplow (No. entries).

out Widow Stubbings, Victuals & Drink and sitting up'.[69] Occasionally there is mention of wool for the shroud and a cap; the Fowlmere overseers' account for September 27 1788 records 'paid Mr Wedd, (who was a woolcomber), for a pound of wool for Elizabeth Hills and Thomas Moody – 1s 4d,'[70] Elizabeth and Thomas were buried by the parish in August of that year. Even paupers received a dignified end to their lives.

An interesting and informative entry in the Fowlmere overseers' account for October 1770 reads 'Paid Ruth Slaughter for nursing Watson at the Time of Harvest – 4/6,' presumably this higher rate of pay was to compensate for Ruth's loss of earnings in the harvest fields.[71] Thus payment to one pauper was given for helping another. Women, probably those without children to care for, were expected to undertake agricultural as well as domestic work. Table 2.8 shows the various categories of women's work.

Whilst this job lasted three weeks, Elizabeth Stubblefield was only paid 1s 6d, women's work was often of a longer duration than men's such as nursing for a week, yet was considered as one job and paid as such. The usual rate was 6d per week.

Children in the care of the parish fell into two categories, orphans and children of women who were themselves on parish relief. Orphans were cared for by relatives at the expense of the parish until they were of an age to work; sometimes this was as young as 5 years old. At the back of Thriplow's overseers' books are 13 'Agreements to take Paupers' dating from 1775–1788'. Only one concerns an adult, Widow Moule. All the rest involved orphan children or adolescents. Obviously some children are mentioned several times as their yearly contracts ended and another one started. Keith Snell, using information for settlement examinations, gives the age at which children in Cambridgeshire left home to work between the years 1700–1860 as 15.8 years for boys and 16.1 years for girls (agriculture) and 14.6 years for boys and 12.7 years for girls

Name	Gender	Date M or E	Age	Amount agreed
Ann Bonnett	Female	1776 M	?	6d per week
Hannah Langley	Female	1775 M	13	1s per week
James Farnham	Male	1775 M	14	10s paid to parish
James Farnham	Male	1775 M	15	8s paid to parish
Wm Farnham	Male	1775 M	17	15s
James Todd	Male	1782 E	7	£1 19s 0d p.a.
Thomas Blanks	Male	1782 E	5	1s per week
James Todd	Male	1785 M	10	Clothes
Thomas Blanks	Male	1785 M	8	£1 10s0d per year
Thomas Blanks	Male	1786 M	9	£1 10s0d per year
Thomas Blanks	Male	1788 M	11	10s 3d per week
Amy Blanks	Female	1788 Dec.	15	6d per week

TABLE 2.9. Children's ages when 'boarded out'. Thriplow (M=Michaelmas, E=Easter).

(apprentices).[72] Table 2.9 shows the ages of the children in Thriplow at the time of the 'agreements'; the older children do seem to reflect the ages calculated by Snell for children leaving home to become farm servants.

James Farnham's first agreement was from 10 July 1775 until 'St. Michael's next' that is 19 September 1775, when Joseph Ellis agreed to keep him. In both cases the keepers agreed to pay the parish for him, but the parish had to find him clothes; this is the only time of this happening and seems unusual.

The entry in the overseers' book for 19 September 1775 states: 'Spent at the Alehouse on Letting the Town Boys – 1/6'.[73] Michaelmas was the traditional time of year for hiring servants and the majority of the children were taken then; only the younger children were taken from Easter. The duration of the agreement varies from 'one whole year' to three years. Two specifically mention being taken as a servant. The wording for the agreement for the youngest, a 5 year old, is very specific:

> 'April 1st. 1782, Mr Benjamin Prime agrees to take Thomas Blanks as his servant from this day till Easter Monday 1783 for the sum of one shilling the week to be returned in the same condition as to Cloathing as he received him (Broken bones & small pox to be at the expense of the Parish).'[74]

The implication is that Benjamin Prime is to be responsible for Thomas's other illnesses (perhaps he thought that at a shilling a week the risk was worth it). The agreement is signed and witnessed by six parishioners, one of whom is the Lord of the Manor and the others churchwardens and overseers. I wonder whether this is the same Benjamin Prime who took Hannah Langley and her brother William as mentioned earlier.

In May 1784, Amy and John Blanks were left orphans; their cousin Thomas was already an orphan and in June 1784 the children were 'carried to Harston'. This is a puzzle as both Amy and John were from Thriplow. Harston must have been successful in denying responsibility for them, for in 1786 they were back again in Thriplow and the overseer was 'going to Harston to see after Blanks children's goods.' On 3 December 1788 the following agreement appears in the Overseers' book – 'John Faircloth agrees to keep Amy Blanks from Dec the 3

1788 to Dec 1789 at sixpence a week to find her all cloaths.' Amy was then aged
15, and although she was probably working as a servant, it must have been quite
difficult to feed and clothe a growing girl of 15 on 6d a week. Only two months
later Bennet Cranwell, overseer, was paid 9d per week to keep Amy, and in
October the parish gave her 5s to 'bur [sic] her some Cloaths.' The following
sequence of entries from the overseers' accounts gives some idea of how this
child was passed around the village.

1784	an account of the things John Adams had with the Blanks children
1787	Bennett Cranwell paid to keep Amy, 9d per week.
April 1788	John Faircloth paid to keep Amy Blanks 6d per week.
June 1788	Bennett Cranwell paid to keep girl Blanks, 13 weeks £1 9s 3d.
April 1789	Bennett Cranwell paid to keep Amy Blanks at 9d per week.

Only one apprenticeship is mentioned specifically in the accounts: 'paid part
George Isons boys Prentice Money – £7–1–6.'[75] In a survey of apprenticeships
in Cambridgeshire extracted from a return in the National Archives, only five
boys were apprenticed to shoemakers between 1765 and 1790. William Wenham,
whose name frequently appeared in the overseers' books repairing and making
shoes, is listed as taking two apprentices as cordwainers (shoemakers) in 1764 and
1765. One of Wenham's apprentices, John Hanchet, born in 1752, was the bastard
child of Mary Nunn, herself a pauper. Three years later his mother Mary married
Stephen Green; she died in 1775. A John Hanchet is noted in the overseers' books
from 1777 as making shoes for the poor. Whether this is John senior or junior
cannot be ascertained as the burial registers do not record the death of either. Of
the other apprentices listed, two are to Thomas Hayden the parish coffin-maker,[76]
one to another carpenter and one to Stephen Cowling, a tailor.[77] The Cowlings
feature largely in the overseers' records as they were related to several other pauper
families. Nine of the apprentices listed came from within the parish of Thriplow;
the tenth came from Ely yet only three are in the baptism register.

While most parishes in south Cambridgeshire thus seem to have cared well
for their paupers before the New Poor Law, Fowlmere in particular often showed
a harsher side. It is the only parish that spent more on occasional relief than
on permanent relief. One reason could be that Fowlmere was on the coaching
route from London to King's Lynn and was the last stop and parish before
Cambridge. It may have attracted beggars and vagrants hoping to obtain the
price of a meal or the fare to Cambridge or London. The overseers' accounts
are full of entries such as: 'relieved two women at the Black Horse' and 'relieved
a man upon travel with sickness.'[78] Coach travel was relatively expensive and
begging was a considerable nuisance as Alfred Kingsley recalls in an entry in
the Royston overseers' books (another coaching stop), 'ordered that notice be
given that John B- and J. B. – if they are found begging in the street from the
coaches that their pay is to be taken off.'[79] This continued drain on the parish
poor rates may have affected the Fowlmere overseers' attitude making them
particularly harsh. The entry for 27 November 27 1787 reads: 'paid Mr Fisher
for examining and the order for S. Hills to be whipped.'[80] Hills was in receipt

of parish relief several times but unfortunately there is no mention of the reason why the JP ordered her to be whipped.

Families were helped by the parish in their natural desire to support themselves, and like a pebble thrown into a pool, the ripples of aid spread outwards to include the whole community from the tradesmen who provided the clothes, shoes, fuel and food, to the farmers who were encouraged to give work to the poor to keep their own poor rates down. Once such parish-based infrastructure was broken with the setting up of the New Poor Law, this flexible form of community care could no longer function.

Occupations and 'Open or Closed' villages

The overseers' accounts and related documents provide a picture of essentially agrarian communities, and most members of the village population were, indeed, principally involved in agriculture for their living. But most villages could also boast a range of trades and occupations. Unfortunately, neither the census figures nor the trade directories cover the smaller villages until the 1840s; but the earlier censuses did record the 'those employed in Trade', and 'Other'. Once again, these figures need to be treated with caution. In Whittlesford for example 416 people are placed in these two categories, yet only 14 people were recorded as being employed in agriculture (probably farmers). Nevertheless, it is clear that in most villages a significant number of people were recorded as being involved in 'trade', although whether this was their only, or rather their primary, occupation is less apparent. Most villages presumably had one or more shops (butcher, baker, etc) and probably several publicans or beer sellers.

The question of 'open' or 'closed' villages has engendered much discussion among historians and social commentators of the Victorian era. This highly emotive term probably dates from around 1830, although the conditions that resulted in the terms were mentioned from the 1790s.[81] Contemporary writers noticed that in some parishes the poor rates were much higher than in others, so proffered various conditions that might account for this. 'Closed' parishes were considered to be those controlled by one powerful landlord, who, to lessen the number of people who might become chargeable to the parish, refused to allow new cottages to be built and even pulled down existing ones, to reduce the number of labourers living within the parish who might apply for aid. They moved pregnant single women to have their babies outside the parish so that the children would not have a settlement and become reliant on the parish for their upkeep, and they imported labour from outside when needed.[82] 'Open' parishes on the other hand, had many landowners and no restriction to the number of people living within the parish. Often labourers from 'Open' parishes had to walk many miles to find work in 'Closed' parishes that did not have enough labourers of their own. 'Open' villages also often contained chapels with their free-thinking, non-conforming members; many small shop-keepers and tradesmen who often augmented their incomes by letting properties they owned

Parish	Acreage	Houses	Acres per house
Fowlmere	2272	128	18
Foxton	1752	92	19
Gt Shelford	2258	196	12
Lt Shelford	1196	117	10
Harston	1741	155	11
Newton	994	44	23
Sawston	1898	225	8
Thriplow	2353	103	23
Whittlesford	1976	135	15

TABLE 2.10. Number of acres per house in parishes in south Cambridgeshire 1851.

Source: Census returns

to labourers (eight out of the nine parishes who answered the question,: 'what class of person are generally the owners of these cottages?' stated that they were tradesmen)[83]. Other indicators were ale houses, and the resulting drunkenness and rough behaviour; and a growing population, indicated statistically by the comparatively small number of acres per house.[84]

Holderness in his study of 'open' and 'close' villages found that the average number of acres per house in 'close' parishes in the counties of Essex, Hertfordshire and Cambridgeshire was 40 (16.2 ha) compared with 16 (6.5 ha) in 'open' parishes.[85] A comparable analysis for nine parishes in South Cambridgeshire is shown in Table 2.10.

It must be remembered that Holderness's area of study was the whole of Cambridgeshire which included the Fens, an area noted for its 'openness'. Nevertheless, the parishes studied here clearly lean more towards the 'open' than the 'closed' end of the spectrum; and not surprisingly, given the fact that all have more than one major landowner which diluted their control over the number of inhabitants within their parish.

But in reality such neat labels are problematic, and have been questioned by a number of historians. Banks for example maintains that 'parish types do not fall neatly into two mutually exclusive groups, 'open' and 'close.'[86] She points out that rather than look at each parish in isolation, a more realistic way of analysing 'open' and 'closeness' would be to look at 'clusters' of parishes which interacted with each other.[87] And in a more local context Way has suggested that 'for most of Cambridgeshire the term 'open' or 'close' is inappropriate and might better be replaced with an assessment of degree of 'social/economic control' along a continuum.'[88] It is true that south Cambridgeshire villages generally lacked resident gentry. Yet at the same time they were often dominated by a comparatively small number of large landowners, who were also farmers. They thus fit uneasily into the open/closed mode of classification. A further complication is that Sawston – although the residence of a major landowner – was in some sense semi-urban in character. It had several mills making paper, parchment, and leather; there were also seven rope makers mentioned in the 1851 census, a mineral water manufacturer and a printing works.[89] Not surprisingly, it had the lowest acreage per house for the district, as people working in factories for wages would not need so much land. Sawston also

	Enclosure date	Houses	Families	Persons	Families per house	Persons per house
Great Shelford						
1801		83	135	570	1.6	6.9
1811		123	140	593	1.1	4.8
1821		89	150	718	1.7	8.0
1831	1834	155	171	812	1.1	5.2
					Average	6.2
Little Shelford						
1801		47	61	220	1.3	4.7
1811	1813	64	66	357	1.0	5.6
1821		53	82	438	1.5	8.3
1831		95	99	483	1.0	5.1
					Average	5.9
Stapleford						
1801		47	64	235	1.4	5.0
1811	1812	52	72	329	1.4	6.3
1821		58	82	408	1.4	7.0
1831		84	87	464	1.0	5.5
					Average	5.9
Thriplow						
1801		46	73	334	1.6	7.2
1811		49	76	319	1.6	6.5
1821		50	84	371	1.7	7.4
1831		87	88	417	1.0	4.8
					Average	6.5
Sawston						
1801	1802	94	120	466	1.3	5.0
1811		87	132	603	1.5	6.9
1821		100	168	699	1.7	7.0
1831		130	182	771	1.4	5.9
					Average	6.2
Ickleton						
1801		77	121	493	1.6	6.4
1811	1810	81	126	514	1.5	6.4
1821		98	140	602	1.4	6.1
1831		133	133	682	1.0	5.1
					Average	6.0

TABLE 2.11. Number of families and persons per house 1801–1831. *Source*: Census returns. Families contain two or more people of the same name.

imported many workers from the surrounding villages; in 1851 these industries employed over 900 people, many of them coming from outside the parish.[90] It also had several Public Houses, and despite the major landowner being a Roman Catholic the first mention of nonconformity was in 1728, and the first meeting place for dissenting worshippers was a barn in 1810 with a chapel being built the following year.[91] The only anomaly is the amount of the poor rates as several parishes had lower rates than Sawston. One reason for this could be that local workers travelled to Sawston for work which would keep many from 'going on the parish'.

Further light can be shed on the character of village life by examining demographic patterns. Using the census returns a table of the number of people living in each household can be compiled as shown in Table 2.11. The years used are 1801 (when the census started) to 1831 (this includes most villages before enclosure).

All parishes with the exception of Ickleton show a rise in the number of people per house in 1821 and it is possible that this reflects the return of soldiers from the Napoleonic Wars which ended in 1815. There was no increase in families per house, however: on the contrary, the number per house drops over time, due to the gradual increase in the number of 'houses', although in many cases this was the result of the subdivision of existing dwellings, rather than the erection of new ones. Dividing a house and increasing the number of families within a dwelling must have been cheaper than building new ones.

This brief examination of the sources reveals a series of tight-knit, largely rural communities, lacking resident gentry and dominated by large and medium-sized farmers. The landless poor formed a significant proportion of the population who, within the limits of contemporary practice, were probably looked after reasonably well. The parish elite administered the poor laws and employed the poor on communal projects of use to the wider community of the village, and they were more generally involved in the appointment of the individuals necessary for the smooth running of communal agriculture. It is to the character of that agriculture that we must now turn.

Notes

1   Hindle (1999).
2   Postgate (1964).
3   Eastwood (1998), 91.
4   *VCH* 8.
5   *Op. cit.* in note 2, 149.
6   Cunningham (1909).
7   *Ibid.*, appx 1, 312; Turner (2000), 2.
8   CUL DOC 652/13 (1826).
9   CUL ADD 6069.
10 Peterhouse documents B1b (1545).
11 Mingay (1989), 2.
12 Cambridge Record Office, hereafter CRO, 413/T22.
x13 Allen (1992), 70.
14 Turner (2000), 2.
15 CUL Ely Dean and Chapter 6/2/18b.
16 CRO 413/T12.
17 Peterhouse documents B1b rental (1545).
18 Simpson (1961), 92.
19 CUL DOC 652.
20 Peterhouse Archives D4 Thriplow Field Book approx 1780.
21 CUL Tithe 1 (1842) Thriplow Tithe schedule.
22 Turner *et al.* (2001), 225.
23 Higgs (1996), 107.
24 Nissel (1987), 52.
25 *Op. cit.* in note 23, 160.

26   Turner *et al.* (2003), 124.

27   Ottoway and Williams (1998).

28   Wittering (1999).

29   BPP 30 (1834), question 26.

30   BPP (1822) Vols IX 1775, XIII, 1803–5.

31   St John's College Archives fragment headed *Case of the Promoters of the Bill* n.d.

32   Hindle (1999).

33   CRO P156/12/2.

34   CRO 413/F9.

35   CRO VC 43:251.

36   CRO Poll Lists.

37   CRO P156/12/1.

38   CRO P72/8/1.

39   CRO P158/8/2.

40   Snell (1985), 108.

41   PRO NA IR 18/13652.

42   BPP 30 (1834), Appendix B1 Vol. III.

43   Carter (2003), 75.

44   *Cambridge Chronicle* Saturday 4 August 1838.

45   Wittering (1996).

46   CRO P72/8/1.

47   CRO P72/8/2.

48   CRO P171/8/3.

49   CRO P156/12/1, 2.

50   CRO P72/12/1.

51   CRO P72/12/2 Fowlmere.

52   CRO P 171/8/3 Whittlesford.

53   CRO P136/12/9 Sawston.

54   Jones, University of East Anglia, *England and Wales Precipitation Chart Internet version.*

55   Eden (1795), 4.

56   CRO P156/12/1 (1780).

57   CRO P171/8/2.

58   CRO P72/8/2.

59   *Ibid.*

60   CRO P156/12/1.

61   CRO P156/12/1.

62   For further details see Wittering (1999).

63   CRO P171/8/3.

64   CRO P171/8/2.

65   Williams (1998).

66   For further reading on the subject of family generations living together see Spufford (1974), 111–18.

67   CRO P156/12/1.

68   CRO P156/12/1.

69   CRO P156/12/1.

70   CRO P72/8/2.

71   CRO P72/8/1.

72   Snell (1985), 324.

73   CRO P156/12/1.

74   CRO P156/12/2.
75   CRO P156/12/2 (10 July 1783).
76   CRO P171/8/2.
77   CRO Apprenticeship Books.
78   CRO P72/8/2.
79   Kingston (1893).
80   CRO P72/8/2.
81   Holderness (1972), 127.
82   Langton (1989).
83   BPP 30 (1834), question 16.
84   Way (2000), 66.
85   *Op. cit.* in note 81, 135.
86   Banks (1982), 66.
87   *Ibid.,* 65.
88   *Op. cit.* in note 84, 66.
89   Patrick (2001).
90   *Ibid.,* 56.
91   *VCH* 6, 261.

CHAPTER THREE

Farming before Enclosure

A fair field full of folk, I found there between,
Some plowed with the plow; their play was but seldom;
Some sowing, some earning, with the sweat of their brows.
Piers Plowman.[1]

This chapter looks at conditions for agriculture in the south Cambridgeshire villages before enclosure and how the farmers used the soils and climate to their advantage. The primary occupation of the majority of their inhabitants was agriculture, and as Conway and Pretty cogently argued:

'Agriculture, for most of its history, has been environmentally benign.

Even when industrial technology began to have an output in the eighteenth and nineteenth centuries, agriculture continued to rely on natural ecological processes. Crop residues were incorporated into the soil or fed to livestock, and the manure returned to the land in amounts that could be absorbed and utilised. The traditional mixed farm was a closed, stable and sustainable ecological system, generating few external impacts.'[2]

How stable and sustainable were the farms of south Cambridgeshire? The first question to address is whether the landscape of these parishes really did still consist of open fields, containing intermixed holdings, and unenclosed common land or whether forms of partial, piecemeal consolidation and enclosure had already made significant progress. The field systems of south Cambridgeshire had consisted from early medieval times of three or more large fields, often up to several hundred acres in area, divided into many narrow strips forming the units of land ownership. These strips were divided by grass baulks enabling men and horses to reach their own strips; groups of strips were divided by headlands where the ploughs turned and which now lie fossilised but still visible under the roads that were laid across them at enclosure. These subdivided fields are referred to as 'open fields'; contemporary writers called this type of landscape 'champion'.

The discovery of a Field Book in the archives of Peterhouse, Cambridge, for the whole parish of Thriplow, dating from around 1780, provides the opportunity to analyse the pattern of landholding in the open fields of one parish.[3] There were certainly three open fields in Thriplow – Heath Field, Church Field and West Field. These contained a total of 1744 strips, distributed roughly equally between the three fields; 591 in Heath Field, 624 in West Field and 529 in Church Field. Not all these unenclosed parcels, however, covered the same area

Field (acres)	0–1	1.1–5	6–10	> 10
Heath	71	28	0.5	0.5
West	77	21	1.5	0.5
Church	81	18	0.5	0.5
Total	76	22	1.5	0.5

TABLE 3.1. Number of strips as percentage of total number (Thriplow).

	No. people (acres)						Total no.
Field name	0–1	1–5	6–10	11–20	21–50	50–100	people
West	4	4	2	5	11	2	28
Heath	4	3	3	5	11	2	28
Church	5	5	3	5	9	2	29

TABLE 3.2. Number of strips per person by field (Thriplow).

Name	West Field	Heath Field	Church Field	Total
Lewis Corckran	53	52	71	176
St John's College	47	36	35	118
Wm. Benning	143	122	71	336

TABLE 3.3. Land owned by largest landowners (no. acres). *Source*: Field book 1780 (Thriplow).

as shown in Table 3.1. Nevertheless, although a measure of consolidation had taken place – so that some 'strips' now extended over as much as 10 acres (*c*.4.05 ha) – by far the greatest percentage (81% in Church Field) were of 1 acre (*c*.0.4 ha) or less. Twenty-five out of 28 landowners held land in all three fields, with a few from neighbouring parishes holding strips towards the parish boundaries. Table 3.2 shows the number of strips per person in each field.

As Table 3.2 shows, the figures are fairly consistent over the three fields. The same three names held the largest number of strips across all three. Lewis Corckran, owner of what is now known as 'Cockranes' in Lower Street, held 93, 81 and 73 pieces respectively; St John's College, who owned Barrenton's Manor and its farm house, now 'Manor Farm', held 70, 61 and 58 parcels; and the lord of the paramount manor (the Bury), William Benning, held 38, 44 and 30. But the owner of the most strips was not necessarily the owner of the most *land*, as Table 3.3 shows.

Although Wm Benning held only 112 strips, his property was mainly in larger blocks of land: whilst Lewis Corckran had 247 strips, most of which were below 1 acre in size.

Thriplow was clearly still functioning as a three field open field system, even the small amount of consolidation was still farmed under the open field system. The Tithe Award map, surveyed in 1842, shortly after the enclosure process started, suggests that there had been very little further consolidation by that date. Much the same appears to have been true of other parishes in the district. Vancouver noted that, in Duxford, only about 50 acres (*c*.2%) of arable land was held in severalty (*c*.20.24 ha); Pampisford had about 50 acres (4%) and Shepreth 100 acres (40.47 ha/8%), as did Stapleford (6%); Whittlesford had 70 acres (28.33 ha) of enclosed pasture and Thriplow 30 acres (12.14 ha) of enclosed pasture land.[4] There is thus little doubt that, throughout the district, open fields remained almost completely intact and had been only partially modified in layout since the Middle Ages.

Most of the parishes within this study also had within their boundaries areas of heath and moor. As already noted in chapter one, the heaths were dry chalk grassland eminently suitable for sheep and the moors were located in pockets of damp ground beside watercourses. Both were used principally for grazing, but their management, and the character of the rights exercised over them, were very different.

The heaths had probably all once been common, but this situation had changed over time. The Hundred Rolls of 1279 for Thriplow, for example, describe how the Bishop of Ely and 'all the other tenants of the town hold one common pasture containing 30 acres and hold one common heath (*burer*) containing 5 score (100) acres.'[5] By the seventeenth century, and probably long before, the heath here had been divided up among manorial lords and was held in severalty. The same had occurred throughout the district, probably sometime after 1236 when the Statute of Merton was enacted.[6]

These upland heaths, even in the nineteenth century, formed a wide band, extending through 15 parishes,[7] covering approximately 13% of their total acreage. Within the parishes studied, the area occupied by heath ranged from 7.5% to 27%, again averaging 13%. Chapter 8 describes the heaths in more detail.

The Fold Course system

The type of agriculture practiced in the nucleated, open field villages of south Cambridgeshire was known as sheep/corn husbandry. K. J. Allison stated that sheep/corn husbandry was unique to Norfolk and Suffolk, but this form of farming was also practised in south Cambridgeshire before enclosure.[8] The practice of dividing heaths into blocks held in severalty by manorial lords, and restricting the rights of grazing sheep over the fallows to those lords, is a common feature of field systems in Norfolk and Suffolk. In this sense, although not in others, south Cambridgeshire represents an extreme western extension of East Anglian arrangements. In other respects, such as the even distribution of holdings across two or three large open fields, the district follows more normal Midland practice.

The fold course system had developed in the early Middle Ages. The sheep were grazed on the heaths and on the stubbles and fallows by day, feeding and dunging the land: at night they were folded by wattle hurdles on the lords' land. Early breeds of sheep produced more dung at night than during the day and the lord expected to obtain the maximum fertility from his flock. Some south Cambridgeshire parishes incorporated tenants' sheep in with the lords' flocks, but for the most part – and probably, increasingly over time – sheep-keeping became a manorial privilege. Indeed, manorial rights of fold extended over the arable, as much as the heaths, at least during specified times of the year. Thus the owner of the Bury, the main manor of Fowlmere, claimed right of sheepwalk over 'all the land of the parish', while two other landowners of the same parish claimed right of sheepwalk over their own land.[9] The Enclosure Commissioners' papers reveal clearly that only lords of the manor, and the ecclesiastical foundations, who usually owned the Rectories, had the right to keep sheep; conversely, claims often made it clear that other landowners did not have such rights. David Ellis of Harston, for example, in 1798 claimed 'right of common of all kind in our several fields except sheep.'[10] This expression is repeated many times. Great Shelford seems to be the only village in which individuals claimed the right of grazing sheep: their claims were usually for two sheep but occasionally for more, though at enclosure these claims were often refused. (This is discussed in detail in Chapter six).

The expression 'sheepwalk' which frequently appears in documents thus refers not only to an area where sheep were grazed, but also to the right of grazing sheep over the land of others. The numbers grazed, however, were fixed by custom; so too were the times of year during which the right could be exercised. Charles Wale, Lord of the manor of Tiptofts, Harston, described his right of sheepwalk as:

> 'In the severalty of Harston, a right of sheepwalk for 36 score of sheep (being half the number kept in the parish) over the whole of the open field lands several to Harston when not in crop and over Red meadows and Rushams, also over the commons called Asper and Alice Dams from Candlemass (2 Feb.) to Lady Day. Also over 2 pieces of Lammas meadow called Snail's Gate and Langhams when not in crop. Also sole right of sheepwalk one half of a certain common field called the Green from Baggot to Sheep Ditch all the year round, containing 108 statute measure. Also sole right over piece of arable land belonging to the Lordship farm called Forty Acres one year in three and an equal right with the other sheep owners the other two years when in stubble.'[11]

Note the varying times of year in which animals had the right of entry. As Allison pointed out:

> 'The inclusion of open-field and heathland within a fold course was essential if a flock was to have pasturage available for the whole year. The sheep fed over all the unsown arable land (which they shared with tenants great cattle), but although this was extensive in autumn and winter after the harvest, it was severely limited during the summer months. Consequently the most important summer pasturage was that provided by the heaths and commons.'[12]

An entry in the Ickleton Enclosure claims similarly shows that William Parker Hammond, Lord of the Manor of Ickleton Priory, possessed 'a sheepwalk for 360 sheep, that is one sheep per acre of the above 18 score acres of land, that is 360 sheep'.[13] (Appendix 1).

The value of sheep cannot be over-estimated in those pre-inorganic fertilizer days: while only the manorial lands (in theory at least) benefited from the intensive night-folding, all farmers in the open fields would have received some benefit from the dung. This does not mean that sheep were valued only or simply as 'mobile muck spreaders', their meat, wool and milk (for cheese) were also valuable commodities, and probably of more value to their owners by the nineteenth century when fold-course rights were often leased out. Moreover, the sheep also trod the young grain plants, thus anchoring them more firmly in the soil, and nibbled the young grain shoots, thus causing them to sprout more stalks. Nevertheless, even on the eve of enclosure the traditional folding breeds, bred primarily for their ability to walk great distances, were still dominant in the area. Vancouver called them 'the common breed' or 'the Norfolk or Cambridge breed'; while at Shepreth he mentions 'a Derby-Cambridgeshire breed.'[14] They were short woolled, long legged and generally horned, and they could withstand dryer conditions than modern breeds and were very suitable for folding. William Marshall in his compilation of the County Reports for the Board of Agriculture mentions that there were three distinct breeds of sheep used in south Cambridgeshire before enclosure, the Norfolk, the West Country and the Cambridgeshire, but with many intermediate shades amongst them: the number of sheep per acre varied between one and 1.5.[15] They were sturdy and active, conditioned to walking miles over the commons and stubbles. In 1869 the Rev Leonard Jenyns described how 'formerly there was a breed with horns and rather long wool called the Cambridgeshire – this prevailed chiefly in the Northern part of the county whilst elsewhere the Norfolk was used – but these have now disappeared, having merged into the above from being crossed with the Leicester and Down.'[16] The Cambridge is now extinct: the Norfolk has survived and is listed as a rare breed as shown in Figure 3.1.

In most parishes the existence of fold-course rights prevented the majority of farmers from keeping sheep, but cattle and horses were of some importance to large and small farmers alike. Joseph Ellis's list of crops and stocks for 1808 includes 556 sheep, but also 39 heifers and two bulls (as well as 28 pigs and 1 boar, 120 fowls, 7 turkeys, 35 geese and 12 ducks).[17] Marshall describes how 'the suckling of calves for the London market, is carried on with great advantage.'[18] He also noted that 'Cattle were brought in for winter fattening from the North, Yorkshire and Scotland.'[19] Stock were grazed on the moors, but perhaps of more importance was the grazing afforded by the open fields themselves: stubble and

FIGURE 3.1. Norfolk Sheep.

weeds when the fields were fallow, as well as the baulks, greens and verges. At enclosure, such rights of grazing were generally claimed by commoners. In the Harston Claims Book, for example, numerous individuals claimed the same unlimited right of common 'in point of number for cow and horse kind upon the Balks and other waste lands in the common fields of Harston from May Day until Harvest, and the general right of Stray after the Harvest had been got in'.[20]

Agricultural improvers like Vancouver were unanimous in their view that open field husbandry was as bad for stock farming as it was for arable husbandry; in his description of Duxford he states, 'No improvement is possible to be made in stock or husbandry without previously laying the intermixed lands together, in the open fields and suppressing the rights of sheep-walk and shakage.' At Ickleton he similarly claimed 'that there can be no improvement made in the stock of this parish until the intermixed land, which now lies scattered through the open fields, is laid together.' At Thriplow he went further, stating, 'No improvement can be made in the breed of sheep or cow cattle, until the intermixed property is laid together, or the parish enclosed.'[21] Jeanette Neeson has argued that strict stinting rules[22] and field management meant that bulls and rams were kept separately and not allowed to run free and breed indiscriminately with the flocks,[23] though in south Cambridgeshire not all parishes had such rules, and even when they did they were not always strictly adhered to.

Livestock were an important but generally subsidiary part of the farming economy; all local farmers were primarily cereal producers, growing wheat and, in particular, barley, much of it destined for the London market. One of the main reasons contemporary writers gave for enclosing the open fields and the wastes was to improve crop yields by the use of modern methods which, they held, was not possible unless holdings were enclosed, fenced, and farmed by individuals free of communal controls. These new methods were mainly, although not exclusively, aimed at increasing the numbers of stock kept on arable farms, and thus the amounts of dung available to the farmer. Even before the discovery of coprolites from Cambridgeshire and guano from South America and the development of inorganic fertilizers in the latter part of the nineteenth century, a variety of other substances were used to increase productivity: Charles Vancouver in 1794 describes the use of oil-dust (Stapleford), cinder ashes (Whittlesford) and pigeon's dung (Stapleford);[24] Gooch includes rabbit down, soot, stickleback and street sweepings,[25] while the tithe files for Melbourne in 1840 refer to the use of bone-dust; Thriplow also had a bone mill.[26] But well into the second half of the nineteenth century dung remained the key source of fertility.

In many eighteenth century inventories 'Dung in the yard' was listed and valued; it was even sold by the parish officers when a pauper died, for instance, when Thomas Scott of Thriplow died in 1774, he was buried by the parish and the Overseers of the Poor sold his goods to recover some of the money spent on caring for him and his family: his clothes fetched £1 4s and the rest of his goods fetched £5 16s including 4s for 'The Dung'.[27] The value placed upon this form of fertilizer can also be gauged by the importance put upon it in leases of property, for instance the lease of the Thriplow Rectory from Peterhouse, Cambridge to Joseph Ellis in 1794 specifically states: 'He must live in the Parsonage for the first 19 years and till the soil in a good manner and leave upon the premises all the Compost, Manure, Dung and so forth arising from Straw and Stover.'[28] Dung in the yard, although it had to be carted to the fields, when ploughed in was said to be more effective than the droppings of grazing animals.[29] Pusey insists that 'The importance of rain or watering dung heaps in summer to keep the heaps working. Manure must be fermented, that is the urea must become ammonia before it can become the food for plants.'[30]

The main way of raising fertility and thus cereal yields was to increase manure supplies, and this could only really be achieved by increasing the amounts of manure available by using fodder crops to raise the number of stock which could be kept over winter. The principal crops which, from the seventeenth century, were used in England to do this also had other benefits, however, as Trimmer emphasised:

> 'The cultivation of fodder crops, first clover, sanfoin, lucerne and Artificial grasses, and slightly later the turnip, opened new possibilities for many lands. The leguminous crops not only increased soil fertility directly, but supported larger herds of livestock which produced more and richer manure. The turnip, when meticulously hoed as recommended by the best agricultural authorities, cleaned the fields of weeds during the fallow and supplied winter fodder for the new livestock.'[31]

An important benefit of the new crops, turnips and clover, lay in their ability either to fix nitrogen directly from the atmosphere, which the latter achieved with some success; and/or to increase the amount of fodder, and hence to recycle soil nitrogen. Nevertheless, to achieve their maximum effect these crops needed to be integrated with traditional grain crops in regular rotations, of which the Norfolk four-course – a recurrent cycle of wheat, turnips, barley and clover – is the most well known.[32] Both crops certainly provided excellent fodder. Turnips give 70% more starch per acre than the average hay crop and 40% more protein; clover hay gives 20% more starch per acre and 80% more protein.[33] Both provided vastly better feed than either the poor weeds of the winter fallows, or the heather of the heaths.

The link between the 'new husbandry' and enclosure, was frequently made by eighteenth and nineteenth-century commentators, and is often repeated by historians. In an open field community, changes in agriculture and innovations in cropping practices could only be carried out provided enough people could be persuaded of their value. Otherwise, customary forms of farming – the tried and true – were simply perpetuated:

> 'Wheat and Rye sown in the Autumn in the first year, the following year the stubble would be ploughed up in the Spring and sown with barley, oats, peas and beans and in the third year the field would be left Fallow.'[34]

Superficially, as we have seen, the open fields of south Cambridgeshire were being farmed in the traditional manner on the eve of enclosure, and the stinting rules set out for Great Shelford thus describe how the fields after harvest and before seed sowing were used:

> 'After Harvest the Herd of Great Cattle take the Wheat and Barley fields and have it exclusively for seven days. The Sheep then take the Wheat and Barley fields along with the Great Cattle for the remainder of the season.'[35]

The reason the sheep followed the cattle was that they nibbled closer to the ground, thus if they were both let into the field together the cattle would get no bite.

Nevertheless, it was possible, to some extent, to innovate within the traditional framework. Allison writes that 'Using land to grow crops that did not fit in with three course rotation began long before Parliamentary Enclosure.'[36] Allen has rightly stated that pre-enclosure farmers were not so hidebound and conservative as previously thought.[37] He has shown how, at Spelsbury in Oxfordshire in 1701, an agreement was reached between landowners to enclose land within the fields to form a sanfoin meadow.[38] He points out that as the furlong was the unit of cultivation, land could be shifted to new or experimental uses in small quantities.[39] Havinden similarly demonstrated, as long ago as 1961, that open field farmers in Oxfordshire were adopting some at least of the new crops; Williamson has likewise demonstrated how cultivators at Ashley in Lincolnshire in 1784 reorganised their field systems to allow a four-course rotation to be followed.[40]

It is not entirely surprising, therefore, to discover that in south Cambridgeshire, in spite of the gloomy comments of men like Vancouver, open field farmers also innovated. A communal agreement was thus made in Thriplow in 1789 to sow sanfoin, one of the key 'artificial grasses.' (Appendix 2) Various owners agreed to sow the crop within a fenced off area of Heath field; there was an opt-out clause for those that were unwilling to grow the crop. An area of about 50 acres was involved: Figure 3.2 is a reconstruction of its layout I made, from the document:[41] The extent to which the project was a communal one is indicated by the fact that the seed was to be provided by the overseer at a fair price.

> 'Every person to have seeds and sow the same quantity of acres with trefoil, in the same field as they have acres of sanfoin and to sow 14 pounds to every acre. Every time the sanfoin field becomes fallow the trefoil seeds are to be repeated, being sown a sufficient time before hand.'[42]

The agreement is signed by ten men, the main proprietors of the village. The terms also suggest that trefoil (clover) was being sown in the fallow field with the sanfoin.

Such arrangements appear to have been common in the area. Vancouver thus mentions that 'cinquefoil has been cultivated to great advantage at Whittlesford; the same practice prevails with similar results in the neighbouring parish of Duxford.' Of the two parishes, only the Duxford agreement has been found and it seems mainly concerned with the problem of keeping the sheep from the crop, although one sentence mentions:

'The occupiers of all such lands as are or shall be planted with Cinquefoil to have and to take the benefit of the crop in all such years as the same used to lye for Fallow and to recover satisfaction for damages or trespass according as in the other two years that the same used to be sown with Corn or Grain.'

Sheep were kept off the land until one crop of cinquefoil hay had been harvested:

'No sheep of theirs [the occupiers] shall or may be kept to feed or driven upon any of the said lands planted with Cinquefoil until one crop of it be cut or mown and made into Hay and carried off from the said lands by the occupiers. And also that for and during the term such lands lye planted for a crop of Cinquefoil no sheep shall or may be kept to feed or driven upon any of the said planted lands after the fifth day of January (commonly called Old Christmas day) yearly and every year so long as the lands lye planted with Cinquefoil as aforesaid. … And also it is granted and agreed by the said parties that as soon as all such planted lands as aforesaid shall be cut and cleared of the crop of Cinquefoil aforesaid, that then it shall and may be lawful for all those who have the Rights, Liberties and privileges to keep sheep in Duxford aforesaid for to keep and feed their sheep upon all aforesaid planted lands until the said 5th January yearly and every year. [43]

These agreements reveal an unwritten conflict between the sheep masters, who must have resented the contraction of their freedom to walk where they wanted within the stinting rules, and the farmers who were fencing off parts of the open fields to grow the new crops. It also shows an understanding of the use to which the new grasses and clovers could be put to improve fertility and the effort they made to improve their farming before enclosure.

Duxford was not enclosed until 1822, 59 years after the above agreement was drawn up; the sanfoin agreement in Thriplow was made in 1789, 51 years before enclosure. Even within the confines of the open field three-course rotation, men

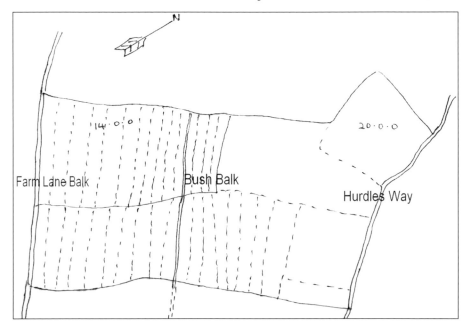

FIGURE 3.2. Map of Sanfoin meadow, Heath Field, Thriplow 1789.

were clearly capable of investing time and ingenuity to improve their profitability. Postgate has suggested that 'It is this flexibility inherent in the organization of cropping patterns may have prolonged the life of the open field system of Cambridgeshire'[44] and, while the adoption of the 'improved' crops in the open fields of the area was not specifically noted by him, these discoveries clearly confirm his opinion.

Even today Sanfoin grows along many of the roadside verges of south Cambridgeshire as shown in Figure 3.3, and in the parish of Little Shelford there is a farm called 'Sainfoins', which was probably built at the time of enclosure.

Fencing off areas of the fallow field and planting them with clover or sanfoin, was something that could be done with relative ease because it did not violate the essential rhythms of the traditional three-course rotation; it merely anticipated the new four-course rotation. The cultivation of turnips was a more complex matter, because the crop was planted in mid-summer and fed off in the fields during the winter, through to early spring. The preceding crop was wheat, harvested in the autumn; therefore the fields stood fallow before the turnip seed was planted. The crop thus took up, in effect, the whole fallow year plus nearly half of another. 'Crops that needed to stay in the ground over winter, such as turnips, were difficult on land that was pastured in common over autumn and winter.'[45] More importantly, the crop also involved more attention, in terms of hoeing and mucking, than clover. Turnips, in short, were much harder to adopt within three-course, open field systems: their cultivation on any scale usually involved the adoption of a four-course rotation, usually accompanied by enclosure. As the Tithe Commissioner for Newton pointed out as late as 1840, 'Turnips are never cultivated because of the arbitory manner in which Common sheep-rights are exercised when the land is fallow (which is every third year) by the lessee of the Dean and Chapter of Ely who alone has the right.'[46] Local farmers reportedly believed that the cost of fencing would be greater than any advantage and 'anyway turnips would not grow on their soils and would be eaten by the sheep'.[47]

Nevertheless, two local inventories from Thriplow dating from the eighteenth century, do mention turnips. The earliest, dated 1731, refers to 'Ten acres of Turnips'; the next, dated 1750, mentions 'A parcel of turnip seed worth £4.0.0.[48] By the early nineteenth century several villages were evidently growing the crop. The Enclosure Commissioners for Ickleton instructed that:

> 'All proprietors who shall sow their land with turnipseed must feed off the turnips arising therefrom notwithstanding the lands on which the same shall be growing may happen to be allotted to other proprietors.'[49]

FIGURE 3.3. Sanfoin growing on Fowlmere verge, 2012.

The Tithe Commissioner for Melbourn described the pre-enclosure farming system in 1838:

> 'The system of farming is about ⅓ fallow, 1/6th wheat, 1/6th rye and barley, 1/6th oats, 1/6th peas, tares, trefoil & clover. In order to produce a crop of turnips, both folding & manuring are frequently necessary. Seeds by the consent of the Glebe owners are sown in the fallow-field to increase the feed in some degree.' [50]

The Tithe Commissioner for Thriplow wrote in 1840, the same year as the Enclosure Act, 'The course of Husbandry is two crops and a fallow viz. Wheat and barley in the first year, afterwards on the same land barley, oats, peases and tares – third year fallow and turnips – the quantity of turnips is stated to be nearly one fifth of the arable land.' [51] By this stage, evidently, the custom of fencing off portions of the fallow field to grow turnips, both during the fallow year itself and for part of the following year, must have been well established in the district.

Other crops which necessitated fencing in part of the open fields, were also cultivated in some places. From the early sixteenth until the early nineteenth century, saffron was grown in the 'Golden Triangle', an area covering north-west Essex and south-eastern Cambridgeshire, including the villages in this study. Saffron was grown on a 6-year cycle with 20 years' break between; it was extremely labour intensive but very profitable. [52] Bundles of saffron and saffron kilns were often mentioned in inventories. In 1812 when Stapleford was enclosed, the Vicar claimed half the tithes of saffron and the lessee of the Bury, owned by the Dean and Chapter of Ely, claimed the other half. [53] The last record of saffron growing in the area was in Duxford in 1816. [54] In Figure 3.4 note the strips and headlands and the fencing on either side of the crop of saffron.

FIGURE 3.4. Gathering Saffron in Whittlesford, 1845. After painting by G. Maynard.

Crop	Acreage	% of total
Wheat	266	17 ⎫
Rye	133	8 ⎬ 38
Peas and oats	200	13 ⎭
Barley	500	31
Fallow	500	31

TABLE 3.4. Crops as percentage of total acreage the Rectory, Thriplow, 1773. *Source*: Peterhouse Archives, C5.

Parish	Wheat	Barley	Oats	Pots	Peas	Beans	Turnips	Rye
Hinxton	234	369	110	9	43	0	20	60
Histon	500	400	100	5	250	10	80	50
Melbourn	317	312	287	0	186	0	21	68
Meldreth	229	240	174	0	131	7	2	9
Whittlesford	200	426	60	2	122	0	31	90

TABLE 3.5. 1801 Crop Returns, acres.

The evidence thus shows, without much doubt, that the open fields of south Cambridgeshire could, to a significant extent, be adapted to take advantage of a range of new crops. Some local farmers were intelligent and innovative and were not hidebound by custom. This is in contrast to the picture painted by contemporary agricultural writers. Gooch in 1811, for example, claimed that several farmers had affirmed their belief in the superiority of the three-course rotation for their lands, some suggesting that turnips would rot when they reached the sub-soil. It was common currency among reformers (and some modern historians) that progressive farmers were held back by lazy and indolent workers and that the open nature of the land allowed weed seeds to blow over all men's strips:

> 'The slovenly operations of one man are often of serious consequence to his neighbours, with whose property his lands may lie and generally do lie, very much intermixed. Everyone is aware of the noxious quality of weeds, whose downy and winged seeds are wafted by every wind, and are deposited upon those lands which are contiguous to them.'[55]

Cambridgeshire farmers famously replied to the advice of Bradley, professor of Botany at Cambridge, by enquiring whether he himself could hold a plough, 'for in that they think the whole mystery of husbandry consists.'[56] The extent to which the new crops were adopted in the district was, however, clearly variable. An estimate of tithes dated 13 September 1773 for Peterhouse College, which owned the Rectory in Thriplow, gives acreages as in Table 3.4.

The wheat, rye, peas and oats form just over a third of the total and the fallow and barley just under a third each, proving they were following the three-course rotation; as yet no turnips were being grown. Such sources are not always entirely reliable, however. Figure 3.5 shows that turnips are not shown in any quantity until 1836 though other sources show turnips were being grown at an earlier date.

A more reliable source is perhaps the 1801 Crop Returns although few of these survive from south Cambridgeshire.[57] These indicate that turnips were a small but significant crop in all the parishes for which returns survive. No record was ever made in this source of the use of 'artificial' grasses but, as noted, their use locally was undoubtedly extensive (Table 3.5).

Acres	Roods	Perches	Crop
93	3	0	Trefoil and red clover seed,
5	3	0	Cole seed,
1	3	0	Turnip seed
3	3	0	Clover mown in the common field
18	2	20	Green Tares
	2	0	Potatoes in common field
87	2	20	Turnips
3	2	1	Cabbage
214	1	1	Total

TABLE 3.6. Crop Returns Thriplow 1814.

Although in many cases the absence of turnips may be a clerical error, in others it clearly is a reliable guide to farming practice reflecting the policy of individual farmers. Among the Ellis papers for Thriplow in the Cambridgeshire Record Office, are two documents dated 1808 and 1814. They seem to be Mr Ellis's own figures by which he calculated his tithes and include crops by type, acreage, amount and value, livestock, buildings, rents and tithes.[58] On page 1 under the title 'LIST OF CROPS AND STOCK OF MR ELLIS 4–7–1808', he lists one acre each of coleseed and turnip seed, 55 acres of sanfoin, some for hay and some for seed, seven acres of trefoil and 30 acres of grass. The 1814 list of the same document shows only 3 roods of turnip seed but trefoil and tares much increased.

The last five crops can be classed as artificial grasses and total 95 acres (38. 45 ha) in 1808 and 148 acres 59.90 ha) in 1814: Ellis evidently made much use of these, but little of turnips. Against this, however, we need to consider the report drawn up by the vicar of Stapleford for the enclosure commissioner in 1812, which lists the crops that affected his tithes.[59] In short, the sources suggest that both 'artificial grasses' and turnips were widely cultivated on the pre-enclosure farms of the district (Table 3.6).

Use and Value of the Commons

The word 'common' is an emotive and potentially confusing one. It is often thought to indicate an area belonging to everyone, yet this was rarely true; most commons although often open to all, were owned by someone. The rights of common, moreover, did not belong to everyone either; they were a particular privilege, evolving over time, relating to a particular category of person. A useful distinction can also be made between the commons themselves, their physical characteristics, where they were and of what soils they consisted, and common 'rights', which also applied to the land in the arable open fields at certain times of the year.

A strong historical tradition, running from Arthur Young writing in the early nineteenth century (many years after his initial enthusiasm for enclosure) through the Hammonds writing in 1911 to such recent writers as Jeanette Neeson writing in the twenty-first century, has emphasised the benefits of common land to the poor and the negative impacts of its enclosure. As Leigh Shaw-Taylor has

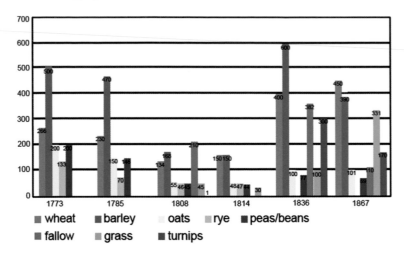

FIGURE 3.5. Crops as percentage of total acreage of 1773–1867, Thriplow.

pointed out, contemporary writers did little to actually quantify the value of the commons.[60] George Sturt, writing under the name of George Bourne (the village near Farnham in Surrey in which he lived), talked about the independence of the poor tenants before enclosure: 'Those living under the old system subsisted on what their own industry could produce out of the soil and materials of their own countryside. Their wellbeing depended on their knowledge of its resources.'[61] Neeson has shown that the right to keep a cow in open-field villages was very common, and that half the villages she studied in Northamptonshire enjoyed common pasture rights.[62] She concluded her study with the words:

> 'Commoners are not labourers. Their defenders and critics agreed on this. Some laboured, some earned wages, but even they were independent of the wage. Their lands and common rights gave them a way of life quite unlike that of the agricultural labourers, outworkers and smallholders they might become at enclosure.'[63]

To the owner of a cottage with a small amount of land, the common land within each village might thus have been a valuable resource, each season bringing its bounty to be gathered and used. 'The land was not the commoners but the use of it was.'[64] Cobbet commented on the enclosure of Horton Heath in Dorset:

> 'The Cottagers produced from their little bits, in food, for themselves, and in things to be sold at market, more than any neighbouring farm of 200 acres … I learnt to hate a system that could lead English gentlemen to disregard matters like these! That could induce them to tear up 'wastes' and sweep away occupiers like those I have described! Wastes indeed! …Was Horton Heath a waste? Was it a 'waste' when a hundred, perhaps, of healthy boys and girls were playing there of a Sunday, instead of creeping about covered in filth in the alleys of a town?'[65]

According to such a view, the commoners were as much part of their landscape as it was part of them; they used their environment to gather nuts, blackberries or mushrooms in season. Such occasions would have been a social event, an expedition for whole families, a chance to forge bonds, to teach the children the intricacies of the landscape as they had been taught by their parents. Small gifts of kind could be brought back for those unable to make the outing. In fact, Jeanette Neeson even goes so far as to suggest that relationships of obligation with the gentry could be built up by selling them blackberries or woodland strawberries, nuts, wild birds or herbs.[66]

These are powerful and evocative arguments, but how far they are true in particular cases will depend on three things: the extent of the commons; their condition and the kinds of resources which they were able to provide; and the numbers and kinds of people who were able to exploit them.

The enclosure awards themselves can provide an answer to the first of these questions. Given that the south Cambridgeshire heaths were held in severalty, it might be thought that there was little actual common land in the district. But most parishes possessed significant areas of damp 'Moors' and to these should be added the grazing offered by the greens and baulks within the open fields, as well as the fallows. The percentage of moors to total acreage is a little over 8%, quite a sizeable amount of land. Sawston is the one exception with 16% of the land being low lying and wet. As Enclosure in southern Cambridgeshire included both the moors and the heaths, this was quite a large area of land no longer accessible to the commoner.

The second question – about the character of the grazing and other resources offered by the commons – is more complex. We have little way of knowing how abundant in fruits and herbage the commons were. Babington and his fellow botanists who visited the villages give no clue as to how extensive the vegetation was as he was really only looking for rare and interesting plants. Nevertheless, Vancouver at least was of the opinion that the moors were of no value, being too wet and boggy to be of any value to stock and only suitable for grazing cattle during the summer, he commented time and time again on the improvement that could be made if only these moors were drained and cultivated, 'The Moor commons contribute little to the support of the stock, though greatly to the disease of the rot in the sheep and cows; they are capable of very great improving.'[67] Vancouver almost certainly exaggerated, in his support for enclosure and 'improvement'.

As we have seen, the documentary evidence shows that the common moors were often well looked after and drained; between 1775 and 1782 the moor at Thriplow was mentioned as being drained 42 times, totalling 131 days.[68] But in some places the quantity and quality of the feed was probably poor. The people of Pampisford complained that:

> 'The meadow land consists of about 20 acres, inter-commoned with Whittlesford, from the end of hay harvest until Lady Day, (with a bite on Easter Sunday); this bite formerly destroyed the whole crop of hay; for although Whittlesford's cattle were only allowed from six o'clock in the morning on Easter Sunday, till the end of morning church service, still the multitudes that were driven on to this common, during this time, either eat up, or destroyed every prospect of a hay crop; at present, as Easter falls so much earlier, this custom is not so injurious.'[69]

Other parishes complained of overstocking resulting in the land becoming thin and overgrazed with nothing left, such as shrubs that could be used for firewood or for gathering fruit.[70] On the other hand, the damp condition of the commons did ensure that some provided another source of fuel – peat – and this was widely dug. Leigh Shaw Taylor found, in Buckinghamshire, that the loss of fuel rights was more damaging than the loss of cow keeping at Enclosure, as not every commoner could afford a cow, yet all could collect fuel.[71]

Further light can be shed on this question – and on that of who actually used the commons – by examining the enclosure Commissioners' papers. Once the principal landowners had decided to enclose their parish and appointed the officers, notice of their intentions were pinned on the church doors of the parish and of those adjoining and were published in the local papers. Those with claims for allotments of land and compensation for common rights which would be abolished were invited to attend a meeting and present their claims. At the first meeting of the Commissioners for Great Shelford, held at the *Eagle Inn*, Cambridge, on 1 October 1833, a committee was formed to look into various matters including the question of the 'Trees planted by the Poor on the Common and to be claimed by them.'[72] These trees were probably planted to provide firewood for the poor, or maybe they were fruit trees such as greengages or apples.

The Hammonds made great play of the inability of the poor unlettered inhabitants to set out a sufficiently legible claim,[73] but John Barrell found no evidence in Helpston, Northamptonshire, that any owners of land or common rights, were unable to submit claims to the commissioners,[74] and the bundles of claims in the Cambridge University Library show that most claimants were able to write. Some asked a friend or agent to apply on their behalf, and even the Lord of a Manor claimed on behalf of an absentee landowner 'as he may not know about the meeting.'[75] Christopher Pemberton the solicitor acted as agent for many claimants; whether he charged for this service we do not know. After that, objections to claims were heard and judged relevant or not. Many local inhabitants claimed rights of grazing on the commons, and also the right to pasture animals on the fallow fields once the harvest has been gathered, and the right to lead cattle on the baulks and keep geese, turkeys and hogs on the greens. In some parishes, commoners could enjoy the grazing available on Lammas meadows after hay harvest and, above all, the right to glean or gather the fallen heads of grain after harvest which could sometimes last them the winter.

Evidence for the number of cows allowed on the common fields and wastes can be obtained from the claims made by individuals for compensation for their lost rights. In Hauxton, Great Shelford, Sawston, Stapleford and Harston, all claims were for the right to put unlimited numbers of cattle on the common. As Henry Driver put it:

> 'Each cottage in Harston has right of Common in the fields of Harston, on commons, meadows, common Balks, lammas grounds from Lammas Day to Lady Day and on the entire common to cows, horses and what stock I please to put on – and on the Green what Hogs, Turkies etc. I please.'[76]

Charles Wale, Lord of the manor of Tiptofts, Harston claimed for right of
common for an unlimited number of cattle but added a note that his tenant
usually kept 27 cattle.[77]

The evidence for Ickleton is rather confusing; some individuals, like John
Hanchet who owned three dwellings claimed 'Right of common and shakage after
harvest for cows and horses without stint for all the above houses', while others
such as Thomas Hopwood who owned one cottage claimed for two cows, as did
Richard Soole, and one man, Benjamin Jeffrey, who also owned one cottage,
claimed for three cows; Thomas Wiskin who owned one copyhold messuage
claimed for seven cows, though claims applied for were not always granted.[78] In
most places the commons thus seem to have been quite heavily stocked. Indeed,
stinting rules varied from place to place and were often lax. The vicar of Harston
stated that 'the custom of this parish has always been for every house to stock
without stint,' meaning there was no limit to the number of animals allowed on
the commons: the Rector claimed the 'Great and Small tithes and also unlimited
right of leading cows over all the Balks in Mount Field.'[79] Many claims have similar
wording, implying that the balks as well as the commons themselves must have
been fairly intensively grazed, at least during the summer months.

A most important question concerns how far the commons were exploited
by the poorer members of society. A pamphlet published in 1785 described the
importance of common rights for the cottager:

> 'Besides the farmers there were other village people, such as the cottagers, the
> mechanic, the inferior shopkeeper, to whom common rights are an incitement to
> industry. Their children, sent out to yearly service among the farmers, manage in
> time to scrape together £20 or £30, marry a young woman possessed of an equal
> sum, obtain a cottage, and purchase cows, calves, sheep, hogs and poultry. Then
> while the husband hires himself out as a day labourer, the wife stops at home and
> herds the live stock on the common. Out of the former's wages the rent of cottage,
> orchard, and two or three acres of meadow ground is paid, which save for the rights
> of common, would be insufficient to support the beasts and poultry of which his
> property exists.'[80]

In reality, the statements of claims make it clear that the use to which the
poor could make of the common was more limited. In south Cambridgeshire
a common right was attached to a particular dwelling, and the owner of that
dwelling was owner of the common right. At enclosure such individuals would
be given land to compensate them for the loss of that right. Mr Bridge Littell,
owner of over 300 acres (121.4 ha) in Harston and many cottages, stated:

> 'All of which right of common are considered to attach to the Houses of respective
> parishes. As such only and to go to the exclusions of all others excepting the owners
> of established flocks.'[81]

Newton Tithe schedule states that:

> 'Each ancient house in the parish has the right of running two cows upon the
> commons and upon the open fields after harvest two years of the three. The Dean
> and Chapter of Ely has exclusive right of Sheepwalk, William Hurrell their lessee
> has 300 sheep.'[82]

Parish	No. households	No. claiming common rights	%	No. without common rights	%
Newton	29	8	28	21	72
Harston	90	52	57	38	43
Hauxton	44	21	48	23	52
Sawston	120	74	62	46	38
Ickleton	120	87	72	33	28
Stapleford	72	49	68	23	32
Lt Shelford	61	35	57	26	43
Gt Shelford	140	75	54	66	46
Total	676	401	59	275	41

TABLE 3.7. Percentage of those claiming common rights to total population by Parish.

The owner of several cottages could thus claim for the rights of common attached to each. The list of cottagers whose claims were objected to in Great Shelford and those who had their claims agreed were all listed as having 'Ancient Houses'.[83] In spite of the rather romantic descriptions of pre-enclosure society found in the works of some writers, very few labourers in south Cambridgeshire possessed houses with common rights attached (Table 3.7). Shaw-Taylor found the same to be true in Buckinghamshire: 'In the late eighteenth century labourers who owned common-right dwellings were rare and the labourers who rented or occupied such dwellings were in the minority'.[84]

Indeed, relatively few labourers actually owned houses of any kind; the Royal Commission of 1834, inquiring into the Administration of the Poor Laws, questioned how many labourers owned cottages and nearly all those parishes that answered said 'very few' or 'not many' or 'about two or three'.[85] That is not to say that the poor did not use the commons and this may have been encouraged as a means of keeping down the poor rates. The Claims for Thriplow mention that the baulks were used by the poor to feed their cattle, 'there being a great deficiency of meadow and pasture in this parish.'[86]

It is important to emphasise that 59% of householders in south Cambridgeshire *did* claim common rights. These figures correspond closely with those produced by others, particularly Neeson and Shaw-Taylor, who also found that about 60% of householders could claim common rights.[87] Of the remaining 41% who did not, some may possibly have used the commons to some extent, and exploited other common rights in the fields. Some of the claims of the 59% were rejected, but this does not mean that rights had not been exercised. The communal use of the moors for grazing by a large community is also attested by Robert Maynard in his diary of 1866, recording a story about an old oak:

'It is the finest oak in Whittlesford, and has lived in time when the fields were divided into small strips of land separated from each other by narrow green baulks, with its common moors surrounding the village. Upon these moors the parish cows come, driven every morning to graze, by the herdsman, who as he went round the village to collect them blew his horn to testify his approach to their respective owners.'[88]

In short, we should not underestimate the significance of commons in south

Cambridgeshire before Enclosure. But how far common rights were exercised by the *poor* is less certain. Indeed, the Enclosure records reveal that even people who legally possessed common rights were often unable to afford to keep a cow because of poverty.[89] Documents relating to the contested claims in the Great Shelford Commissioners' papers are particularly informative in this respect. The commissioners questioned the oldest inhabitants as to the length of time the owners had kept cows upon the commons. The main witness in Shelford was one Crisp, 'who kept the herd for 50 years but ceased keeping it 16 years ago'. One claimant was Robert Edwards, whose house Crisp describes as an 'Ancient one'. He stated that:

> 'John Gunner who occupied this House 60 years ago kept several cows for about 9 years, after this Ward became the occupier and lived there 20 years and all the time kept cows, sometimes 3, 4 and 5 – after Ward, then Jennings became the Occupier for 2 or 3 years and kept several cows being a jobber – after him Joseph Senby and one Graves became tenants and both are there now, they have lived there only 2 years, and from Poverty have been unable to keep cows.'

Another claim was made by John Careless:

> 'About 60 years ago his Grandfather lived in it (the house) and kept one cow always; then the claimant's father became the owner and kept a white cow for some years, he died about 20 years ago – then the claimant succeeded but has never kept a cow because it was not convenient to him to purchase one. This will be proved by Crisp.'[90]

Landless labourers living in small cottages were even less likely to have been able to afford a cow, and therefore less able to exercise grazing rights, even if they had been permitted to do so by the community.

The evidence from south Cambridgeshire thus suggests that commons and common rights were of some significance in the pre-Enclosure landscape. Well over half the population seem to have been involved in the exploitation of the commons in some way, and communities acted to maintain them in a reasonable condition. However, it was the small or medium-sized farmers who gained most from the grazing, as they generally received some compensation at enclosure for their lost rights. The majority of the poor, unable to afford a cow and usually renting property, were probably only marginally involved in the exploitation of the commons, beyond being allowed to cut peat and other fuel, and to glean across the open arable – the latter a custom which continued after enclosure (there are still local people today who can remember going gleaning for grain to feed chickens when they were children).[91]

One way local communities helped the poor provide for themselves, and thus reduce the poor rates, was to provide land for them to cultivate. A scheme was set up under an Act of 1832 to enclose areas of common land for the use of the poor in the form of allotments to grow potatoes and other crops. The land was to be controlled by the overseers of the poor; a small rent was charged and the cultivation was to be by spade husbandry only.[92] In the north of Cambridgeshire, outside the area studied here, the importance of such allotments was emphasised by John Denson of Waterbeach in a letter dated 1830. He complained that the practice of spade husbandry had been discontinued in his neighbouring parish of Willingham for fear that the poor rates should rise, for as he commented, the churchwardens and landlords were afraid that they might lose their profits if the tenants did not pay; he wrote:

> 'I can inform the landlords that, on arable land, at Waterbeach, not superior to the arable land in the neighbourhood of Ely, 200 bushels of potatoes, and sixteen bushels of wheat, on an average per acre, are annually grown, on land cultivated by the spade, by labourers; and that a labourer, with the assistance of his family, would at his leisure hours, annually till an acre in this manner, and with this good result.'[93]

Similar forms of allotment were occasionally provided by charities, or even individual landowners. The lords of the manors and the overseers of Shepreth, for example, put aside just over 18 acres for small cottagers as an:

> 'Allotment for the use of occupiers of Cottages on L Moor held by the Lords and overseers for the sole and proper use of such occupiers of cottages in Shepreth of less than 10 acres in their respective tenures. The said Common to be stocked from the 1st May to 31st December every year with one cow or bullock for the occupiers of each cottage.'[94]

Whatever their origin, such plots were evidently well-established in south Cambridgeshire by the time of enclosure for in 1834, when a Royal Commission into the Administration of the Poor Laws enquired whether any land was let to the poor, the following parishes answered:

> **Fowlmere** – 'Yes, commenced very lately, about half an acre, rent varies according to the soil, from penny farthing per rod to twopence.'
> **Melbourn** – 'Some of the best land in the vicinity is let to labourers in pieces of a quarter to half an acre at £1 10s per annum, free of tithes and rates.'
> **Meldreth** – 'We have 4 acres of parish land let to the poor, about 20 roods each, at low rent.'
> **Sawston** – About 20 have allotments from 1 rood to half an acre according to their wish at 30 shillings an acre.'[95]

Such provision was evidently increasing rapidly for by 1847 the tithe schedule for Fowlmere shows three pieces of such land, two of 14 acres (5.67 ha) and one of 3 acres (1.21 ha), owned by the churchwardens' and overseers and let to the poor on a regular basis.[96] The Newton labourers also had rent free allotments to grow potatoes,[97] but a study of the Newton Enclosure Award merely shows 1 acre allotment for 'Exercise and recreation the fences of which were to be mended by the churchwardens and overseers.'[98] It was in the interests of the landowners to keep their farms profitable and their outgoings low, so that providing land for the poor to cultivate reduced their poor rates, which was of benefit to both owners and cultivators. Such provision was by no means universal, however: a search through other Awards reveals that neither Harston, Ickleton, Great Shelford nor Stapleford had any allotments for the poor.[99]

Gardens and Orchards

Other possible sources of food for the poor were gardens and orchards; but in some cases the poor were denied even these. The Royal Commission of 1834 asked how many cottages had gardens; Fowlmere replied that 'Very few have any garden or land let with them.' The other parishes said 'few', or 'not many'. The tithe schedules give a better breakdown of the actual figures (Table 3.8).[100]

With the exception of Thriplow and Shepreth, the parishes were remarkably similar in their percentage of gardens and orchards being about 43%. Both Thriplow and Shepreth had far larger percentages with Shepreth having 72% of all properties, but even this leaves 28% without a garden. Thriplow had 38 gardens mentioned in the Tithe Schedule of 1842 compared with 41 gardens mentioned in the Enclosure Award completed in 1845, perhaps indicating problems of definition.[101] Of these 41 gardens, 33 belonged to tenants. No record has been found of what was grown but an intelligent guess can be made from what was *not* mentioned in the list of food provided by the overseers to the poor.[102] There is no record of cabbages, onions, beans, potatoes and salads, all everyday items of diet, so it may be assumed that these were grown by cottagers, perhaps also some corn for the chickens and the pig. It is impossible to calculate the acreage of gardens from the tithe schedules as they were often combined in the list with tenements, yards and orchards. Occasionally a garden is mentioned individually and then the size is always under an acre, often less than a rood (¼ acre). In Newton mention is made of 'Gardens of small cottagers = 1acre 1rood 2perch;'[103] a very small area in total. As the population rose and houses were divided and more and more families were crowded into the space once occupied by one family, the gardens either became split into smaller pieces or the new tenant received no garden at all.

Orchards provided not only fruit, a useful addition to the diet, but perhaps space for a pig (to eat fallers in the autumn) and chickens. Melbourn is still noted for its orchards and within living memory several acres of the ground on either side of the Fowlmere Road, Thriplow was full of greengage trees, and Peck's Close, a piece of charity land, later the football field, was ringed with Walnut trees. But it was the farmers who had the benefit of such spaces, not the poor. In 1889, Joseph Ellis sued E. Garner from Harston for refusing to pay the agreed price for a crop of greengages and walnuts and for not collecting the crop when agreed.[104] It would seem from this that fruit was not only useful for personal use but formed part of the commercial crop of the farmers.

TABLE 3.8. Number of properties with gardens and orchards, south Cambridgeshire.

Parish	Total no. properties	Gardens	Orchards	% of total
Foxton	88	25	1	30
Fowlmere	124	37	4	33
Newton	44	16	–	36
Melbourn	351	60	48	35
Shepreth	76	36	19	72
Thriplow	92	38	14	56

The numbers of orchards varied from parish to parish, to judge from the Tithe Schedules, but once again some of this is due to variations in practices and definition. The contrast between Melbourn with 48 orchards and Newton with none at all, does not mean that Newton had no orchards: the rules for the tithe commissioners were fairly flexible and often orchards were simply added in with arable.[105]

To sum up, the landscape of south Cambridgeshire in the nineteenth century provided a range of resources, and these were exploited by local populations in diverse ways. But not everybody had equal access to them. The small and medium sized farmers cultivated the open fields and grazed the commons; the larger farmers, usually lessees of manors, had more substantial open-field holdings, and also grazed the heaths and fallows with their sheep flocks. All these cultivators appear to have been more innovatory in their farming – and the open fields more flexible in their organisation – than contemporary commentators often allowed, and the cultivation of the 'new crops' was well-established in the area by the time of enclosure. The landless poor, who formed the majority of the population, possessed no land in the open fields and the extent to which they benefited from the commons, and common rights, is less certain. Most had no rights to use the commons and even when they had they would, in some cases at least, probably have found little of use there. Few could probably afford to keep a cow. In many cases, the lowest strata of the population even lacked a garden in which to grow food. Nevertheless, the ties of community described in Chapter 2 – together with a strong desire to keep the poor rates down – did encourage some parishes to create 'spade husbandry' allotments on the commons, as well as to allow more general use of the commons for peat cutting, and the fields for gleaning.

Notes

1   Skeat (1905), 4.
2   Conway and Pretty (2003), 991, quoted in Turner *et al.* (2003), 124.
3   Peterhouse Archives, D4, *Survey of the Parish of Triplow*, although the field book is undated, the names of the landowners have been compared by the author with the manor court rolls and other documents and compare favourably with those for the 1780s.
4   Vancouver (1794); Board of Agriculture, Duxford p. 72, Pampisford p. 66, Shepreth p. 77, Stapleford p. 53, Thriplow p. 22, Whittlesford p. 75.
5   *The Hundred Rolls, 1279* (1818).
6   S. Harrison (2002), 186.
7   Postgate (1964), 13.
8   Allison (1957), 14.
9   CRO 317/T1.
10 CUL ADD 6011c, Harston and Hauxton Claims (my italics).
11 *Ibid.*
12 Allison (1957), 16.
13 CUL DOC 640/32.

14   Vancouver (1794), 77.

15   Marshall (1815), 621.

16   Jenyns (1869), 5. I am indebted to Ann Charlton, Museum Archivist and Ray Symonds, Collections Manager, Museum of Zoology, University of Cambridge, for their help and assistance in enabling me to access their archives and the Rev Jenyns's notebooks.

17   CRO 413/E8.

18   Marshall *op. cit.* in n.15, 618.

19   *Ibid.*, 642.

20   CRO ADD 601c, 'shakage' is the right to gather fallen grain after harvest, in other words gleaning.

21   Vancouver (1794), 72, 22, 1.

22   Stinting – the number and time animals were allowed on the commons.

23   Neeson (1993).

24   Vancouver (1794), 53, 75.

25   Gooch (1813), 263.

26   CRO 296/B855/11 (1855) Crocket and Nash Sale of Bone Mill.

27   CRO P156/12/1–2 Thriplow.

28   CRO 413/T21. 'Stovers' is straw from any plant other than grain.

29   Shiel (1991), 59.

30   CUL LO.28.5; Pusey (1851), 41.

31   Timmer (1969), 375.

32   Shiel (1991), 59.

33   Overton (1996).

34   Seebohm (1952), 101.

35   CUL DOC 652/113

36   Allison (1957), 28.

37   Allen (2001), 56. Other authors inclined to the same view include Kerridge and Havenden.

38   *Ibid.*, 56, 57.

39   *Ibid.*, 62.

40   Williamson (2003), 155.

41   CRO 413/04 (1789).

42   CRO 414/04, (1789); see Appendix 2.

43   CRO P62/28/1.

44   Postgate (1964), 272.

45   Ernle (1912), 199; see also Allison (1957), 27.

46   NA PRO IR 18/13615.

47   Gooch (1813), 92.

48   CRO VAC 2:4 and 2:80, Thriplow.

49   CRO 107 (31 August 1810).

50   CRO NA IR 18/13609.

51   PRO NA IR 13652.

52   Saffron Walden Museum (1997).

53   CUL ADD 6069c, Excerpt from Inclosure Commissioners Claims book for Stapleford.

54   Saffron Waldon Museum (1997).

55   Ernle (1912), 234.

56   Trow-Smith (1967), 110.

57   Turner (ed.) (1982), 58–68.

58 CRO 413/E8–9.
59 CUL ADD 6069c (1812).
60 Shaw-Taylor (1999), 8–9.
61 Bourne (1912), 78.
62 Neeson (1993), 296.
63 *Ibid.*, 297.
64 *Ibid.*, 1.
65 Quoted in Hoskins and Stamp (1963), 61.
66 Neeson (1993), 181.
67 Vancouver (1794), 203.
68 CRO P156/12/1.
69 Vancouver (1794), 66.
70 *Ibid.*
71 Shaw Taylor (2001), 125.
72 UL DOC 652/3.
73 Hammond and Hammond (1911), 63.
74 Barrell (1972), 193.
75 CUL ADD 6011c, 27 August.
76 CUL ADD 6011, 25 August.
77 *Ibid.*, 5 November.
78 CUL DOC 640.
79 CUL ADD 6011.
80 *A Political Enquiry into the Consequences of Enclosing*, 1785, quoted in Hoskins and Dudley Stamp (1963), 61.
81 CUL ADD 6011.
82 CUL EDR T, Newton (1840).
83 CUL DOC 652/110.
84 Shaw-Taylor (1999), 225.
85 BPP 30 (1834), Appendix B1, vol. 1, question 17.
86 PRO NA IR 13652.
87 Neeson (1993); Shaw-Taylor (1999).
88 CRO R58/5, Vol. 12, 54.
89 CUL DOC 652/47 Great Shelford.
90 CUL DOC 652/110/8.
91 Conversation with Bill Wittering and Peter Speak (2003).
92 CRO 292/03 8–2–1845.
93 Denson of Waterbeach (1830), 55.
94 CRO Q/RDz10, Shepreth Enclosure Award.
95 BPP 30 (1834), question 20.
96 CUL EDR T Fowlmere (1847).
97 BPP 30 (1830), 328–9, quoted in *VCH* 8.
98 CRO Q/RDc 73.
99 CRO Q/RDc 3, Harston, Q/RDz 27, 129–87, Ickleton, Q/RDc 50, Gt Shelford, Q/RDz7, 84–128, Stapleford.
100 BPP 30 (1834), question 19.
101 CUL EDR T (1842) Tithe Schedule and Map, CRO (1845) Thriplow Enclosure Award.
102 CRO P156/12/1, 2.
103 CUL EDR T, Newton.
104 *Royston Weekly News*, 20 December 1889, Cambridgeshire Collection Cambridge.
105 Kain and Prince (2000).

CHAPTER FOUR

The Enclosure Process

....

I have put my sickle into other men's corne, and
have laid my building upon other mens' foundations.

John Speed's *Atlas of Great Britain*, 1612

The subject of enclosure and the means whereby it was achieved has interested historians for many years; in the 1940s W. E. Tate mentioned those who had preceded him, but it was he who really introduced us to the enormous amount of material available for study.[1] He points out:

'The outstanding feature ... is, I think, the lateness of the movement in this county (*Cambridgeshire*). The first Act is dated 1770, and there are only three before 1796, by which time the movement for Parliamentary enclosure in many counties was half completed. Similarly Cambridgeshire is one of the few counties having much enclosure by private Act after *c.*1830 ... There are many counties without any.'[2]

The wealth of documentation available for south Cambridgeshire allows us to chart the process of enclosure in considerable detail.[3] It is certainly our good fortune that the papers of Christopher Pemberton, enclosure solicitor for some 35 parishes in Cambridgeshire, were preserved and eventually found their way into the Cambridgeshire University Library and the Cambridgeshire Record Office. Of these 35 parishes six cover the chalk villages of south Cambridgeshire.[4]

When enclosure was first mooted a notice was usually placed in the newspapers to test the waters, to see how much opposition there would be. Attempts were made to canvas interested parties; Mr Pemberton, the commissioners' solicitor, certainly travelled many miles a year persuading and explaining the process to landowners as the example below shows. It is reproduced in full to give some idea of the many and varied journeys a commissioner of enclosure's secretary undertook and covers only the parish of Ickleton:

'February 16 1812 – Journey to Chesterford to attend a meeting, Attending Mr Gunning to get the Petition signed by him.
February 6 to 8 – Journey to Town to get petition presented, out three days,March 3 to 8 – Journey to Town to get the Bill printed, various attendances upon the proprietors to explain Clauses in the Bill.
March 13 – Attending at Trinity College near 2 hours to procure the seal testifying their consent to the Bill.
April 14 – Attending twice at Clare Hall to procure the consent of the College to the Bill.

April 16 and 17 – Journey to Shelford, Hinxton, Duxford, Ickleton, Stapleford, Babraham and Walden to obtain consents to the Bill.
April 25 to 28 – Journey to Windsor, Sunbury and Kensington to obtain the consents of the Dean and Canons, Mr Wyndham and Mr Fuller, 4 days.
April 28 and 29 – Journey to Pulham in Norfolk and Holbrook in Suffolk to obtain the consents of Mrs Brooke and Mrs Pytches but Mrs Pytches refused to sign.
May 1 to 4 – Journey of myself and 2 clerks to Town to witness approval of consents before the House of Commons.
May 8 – Journey to London, the Bill being read the third time in the House of CommonsMay 22 – Journey to Walden to inspect the Court Rolls of Mr Wyndham's Manor.
May 23 – Journey of myself and 2 clerks to town to prove the consents in the House of Lords, out 4 days.'[5]

Pemberton was acting for three other parishes in south Cambridgeshire during this year. Apart from pointing to the fair number of absentee owners the document is an example of the type of activity behind the official face of enclosure. Many of these documents will be examined in this chapter as they are so vital to a good understanding of what went on behind the scenes.

The commissioners' papers reveal much of the inner workings of the enclosure process. Many of the records start at the first meeting with the Commissioners, but one, Great Shelford, includes a record of: 'A meeting of the proprietors of Lands in the parish of Great Shelford in County of Cambridge, this day held, to consider the propriety of inclosing the said parish.'[6] There are 13 names listed as present 'and others.' Those named include Samuel Prest Esq, in the chair, the Master and Bursar of Jesus College, the Bursar of St John's College and the Vicar, the Rev Henry French. The first action they agreed upon was to apply to Parliament for an Act to inclose Great Shelford and commute the tithes of the parish. Other agreements made were that the owner of the Manorial Rights of Soil should receive a twentieth part of the commons and wastes in lieu of those rights, and that the impropriators should receive compensation of one-fifth part of the value of all arable lands and one-eighth part of the value of all meadow lands subject to payment of tithes. They appointed Mr Edward Curning of Great Shelford as Surveyor, Messrs Pemberton and Hayward as Solicitors and agreed to have two commissioners, one appointed by the impropriators and the other by the proprietors, and that the commissioners should appoint an umpire. At this stage no commissioners' names were mentioned. The last agreement was a list of names including the Bursars of the three colleges – major landowners in this as in other neighbouring parishes – be nominated as a committee for:

'Settling the details of measure and to confer with the Trustees of Hobson's Conduit (a water-way bringing fresh water from Great Shelford to Cambridge built around 1614) as to the preservation of the water at Nine Wells and to make such agreement as shall seem fit respecting the trees alleged to have been planted by the poor on the common and to be claimed by them.'[7]

Once agreement to enclose a parish had been reached by the principal landowners, the next step was to appoint the Commissioners who would oversee and manage the whole process. The *General Enclosure Bill* of 1796 stated that one Commissioner should be chosen by the lord of the manor, one by the tithe owner and a third by the major part in value of the proprietors,[8] though this was not always adhered to. A short note to John Ingle, one of the manorial lords of Shepreth, from Charles Ware of Grey's Inn, solicitor, thanks him for a brace of birds and submits his bill; Ingle had fought against only having one commissioner, and had applied to the Commons with the help of Charles Ware.[9]

Commissioners, who in this period were often surveyors, farmers or lawyers, are always named in the enclosure award and a small group of men became almost professional commissioners, often covering several enclosures at a time. John Chapman found 24 commissioners who acted for 50 or more enclosures, three of whom were involved in over 100.[10] An analysis of commissioners' names for south Cambridgeshire reveal a similar pattern, a few names covering many parishes as shown in Table 4.1.

Of the 18 commissioners' names covering the seven parishes studied, four were mentioned twice and one, three times. Three parishes had three commissioners; Great Shelford enclosed in 1833 and Fowlmere 1845, had two commissioners and an umpire, and Stapleford (1812) had only one. Within south Cambridgeshire as a whole Alexander Watford was responsible for surveying 20 maps and Edward Gibbons for ten.[11]

At the first meeting a solicitor and a surveyor would also be appointed, and a banker into whose bank monies would be paid and upon whom cheques could be drawn. As mentioned before, Christopher Pemberton was solicitor to the first five parishes listed in Table 4.1. As will be noticed, sons often followed in their father's footsteps and became surveyors then commissioners. Newton is such a case, having father and son as surveyor and commissioner.

TABLE 4.1. Names of enclosure officers by parish in south Cambridgeshire. Sources: CUL ADD 6013; CRO 107; CRO R72/54; CUL ADD 6065; CUL ADD 6068; CRO Q/RDc 73; CRO Q/RDc 65.

Parish	Commissioner	Solicitor	Surveyor	Banker
Harston/Hauxton/ Little Shelford and Newton	Geo. Maxwell Alex Watford Edward Hare	Christopher Pemberton	Thomas Thorpe, Gt Barford, Essex	
Ickleton	Chatles Wedge Martin Nockold William Custance	Pemberton and Hayward	Thomas Wakefield Chambers, Ickleton	Searle and Son, Saffron Walden
Great Shelford	Thomas Utton Edward Gibbons	Pemberton and Hayward	George Cumming, Great Shelford	Mortlock and Son, Cambridge
Sawston	Edward Hare William Custance Charles Wedge	Christopher Pemberton	Thomas Thorpe, Gt Barford, Essex	Thomas Fisher, Cambridge
Stapleford	William Custance	Christopher Pemberton	Edward Gibson	Thomas Fisher, Cambridge
Newton	Marion Welstead, Kimbolton Martin Nockold, then William Noel Jackson	John Bridges Nathaniel Mason	Arthur Henry Welstead, Kimbolton	
Thriplow	John Isaacson Anthony Jackson, then William Noel Jackson	Henry Turnall	Alex Watford Simeon King	

Landowners did not always agree over the choice of a Commissioner, as happened at Sawston: Ferdinand Huddlestone, the main landowner wrote to Mr Pemberton that: 'Mr Martindale says that Gosling is willing to come into this Enclosure business provided he is able to nominate a Commissioner.'[12] In fact things did not go well as a second letter from Ferdinand Huddlestone to Christopher Pemberton begged to be excused from attending a meeting, 'especially as this dispute about Commissioners has hurt me much and am not at present well able to come so far – I heard Gosling was in a furious taking last night and rode over to Cambridge to stop all proceedings in the Bill.'[13] Such a radical change in the village geography was bound to engender some disagreement even among the principal landowners who stood most to gain from the process.

Edward Humphrey Green Esq., one of the principal landowners in Great Shelford, wrote in 1833 that he felt he had a right to nominate a Commissioner, but Mr Pemberton, the solicitor, replied that Mr Green had not been at the first meeting at which the Commissioners were chosen, and that Mr Gibbon whom he wanted to replace 'was well known, had done many inclosures and was not known to any colleges.'[14] This last point was important in an area where much of the land was owned by the Cambridge colleges. It rather looks as though the colleges were not beyond putting some pressure upon the commissioners in order to get their way.

Generally the meetings were held within the village or in Cambridge, but sometimes they could be many miles away: in one case, the inhabitants of Harston and Hauxton had to go to the *Angel* Inn, Peterborough, a distance of 40 miles (*c*.64 km). Edward Hare, one of the commissioners, lived near Peterborough so maybe the meeting was held there at his request, or more likely the commissioners were involved in several parishes within the area at that time. The public meetings were always held in public houses, presumably because they were the only secular places large enough to hold all those wanting to attend. As the meetings sometimes stretched to two or three days, the availability of food and drink and stabling for horses was important. The officials must have stayed at the inn, while those villagers with their claims probably went home once their case was heard. If the commissioners were hearing several enclosure cases, the jostling of people and horses coming and going must have been quite an occasion.

Commissioners could also cause meetings to be postponed if they did not turn up when expected; the Sawston minute book records: '4 November 1803, Eagle and Child Inn, Cambridge. Adjourned as only one Commissioner present.'[15] On 4 September 1804 Mr Wedge, one of the commissioners to Sawston wrote to say that he could not come to the meeting on Friday as: 'they do not start until the afternoon and I am busy with the harvest.' On 21 of the same month he wrote to say he could not attend the meeting as the Commissioners did not meet until the evening and he was busy with the harvest.[16] Great Shelford's first meeting with commissioners was held only seven months after their first meeting, over three days from 18–20 June: the meeting was held at the *Eagle* Inn, Cambridge and details were circulated to all those interested, notices were inserted in the *Cambridge Chronicle* newspaper, and a copy was affixed to the church door. But the time taken from the first meeting until the Act was presented to Parliament could be several years. Sawston's first meeting with the commissioners was on 16 January 1802 at the *King's Arms*, Bournbridge, and the second was on 10 October 1803 at the *Queen's Head*, Sawston, 20 months later. Harston posted a notice of intent in the *Cambridge Chronicle* originally for 5 August 1796 but another notice announcing its postponement until 18 October of that year appeared in the Cambridge Chronicle for October 8;[17] their first actual meeting was not held until 28–29 August 1798,[18] a gap of two years. Ickleton first posted their notice of intent to inclose in the *Cambridge Chronicle* on 9 September 1800;[19] their first meeting with the Commissioners was held on 10 July 1810, a gap of 10 years.[20] And Thriplow put its first notice in the Cambridge Chronicle in 1819 but enclosure did not start until 1840, 21 years later.

Some glimpse into what had been happening all that time is given in the solicitor, Mr Pemberton's, statement of accounts for Ickleton:

> '1806, various attendances upon several of the principal Proprietors to advise respecting the Inclosure of the parish and it was at last determined to call a Meeting for the purpose of ascertaining the opinion of the Proprietors at large.'[21]

The rest of the years seemed to be spent in travelling to see proprietors and sending out advertisements. Three years later he wrote:

> '1809, several Proprietors being desirous of the expediency of the Measure should be reconsidered and being instructed to give the usual notice of an Application to Parliament in the ensuing session for an Act to inclose the Parish – drawing notice accordingly.'[22]

Landowners had a legitimate means of stating their opposition to enclosure. One of the first things the solicitor did was to produce a 'Statement of Property' which listed all landowners and put them into three categories, Assent, Neutral or Dissent. These documents were often based on the Land Tax assessments and give the amount each landowner held, whether he agreed, was neutral or disagreed to the proposed enclosure, and included notes regarding the status of various people and sometimes interesting information as to how they changed their mind (Appendix 3). Even quite substantial landholders' opinions could be manipulated by a resolute and powerful group determined that enclosure should go through.

Not everyone approved of the move to enclose their parish; fear of losing common rights; fear of the costs involved, coupled with a reluctance to change a system of agriculture which seemed to be working, added to the fact that some landowners were concerned that the poor would be ignored, resulted in some opposition to the proposed changes. It required great optimism to risk such a dramatic upheaval in the hope that profits might increase. Vancouver mentions the fact that farmers in Pampisford were 'apprehensive regarding the practicability of raising and supporting light fences on these thin soils'.[23]

Parish	No.*	0–10 acres			No.	11–50 acres			No.	Over 50 acres		
		A	D	N		A	D	N		A	D	N
Newton	2	2	0	0	5	5	0	0	3	2	1	0
Harston	27	5	16	6	10	3	6	1	5	5	0	0
Hauxton	13	4	3	6	2	0	1	1	2	2	0	0
Ickleton	24	10	14	0	11	8	3	0	13	12	1	0
Lt Shelford	10	3	5	2	3	3	0	0	2	1	1	0
Gt Shelford	45	23	8	14	32	31	0	1	10	8	2	0
Total	121	47	46	28	63	50	10	3	35	30	5	0

TABLE 4.2. Numbers of peope Assenting, Dissenting or Neutral, by parish. * = Total no. landowners asked.

From the surviving records we can analyse how many landowners were opposed to enclosure in south Cambridgeshire. The Statement of Property divided all those holding land into those who consented, those who dissented and those who were neutral (Table 4.2).

Table 4.2 shows that the smaller landowners seemed to be equally divided, although if the neutral and dissenting were added they would far outnumber the assenters; those with 11–50 acres (4.45–20.23 ha) were mainly for enclosure and the majority of those with over 50 acres were in favour of enclosure.

Although the large landowners who held a majority of the land could initiate the enclosure process, parliament insisted that all landowners should have the opportunity to dissent by placing their names in the 'dissenting' column of the Statement of Property; if enough opposed enclosure the process might be delayed or even cancelled altogether. As already noted, the 1836 legislation authorized enclosure if two-thirds of the owners of open field rights in number and value agreed.[24] Bearing in mind it was a legal requirement that the solicitor should show that all interested parties had been consulted, some persuading obviously went on behind the scenes. Evidence that a certain unease at the outcome is found in statements made in the 'Notes' column. Pemberton, the solicitor to the Commissioners, worked hard to persuade people to agree to enclosure; as solicitor to so many enclosures, much of his income depended on a successful outcome. Of those owning over 50 acres and dissenting, Mr Littell of Harston finally decided that he would be Neutral; Pemberton wrote:

> 'Mr Littell having signed the petition to be heard against particular parts of the Act, is put down as dissenting, but as he has offered to consent to the Act if he is permitted to name a Commissioner and has declared that he considers himself as a Mediator between the proposers and opposers of the Bill, it is presumed the Committee of the House of Lords will consider him as Neuter.'[25]

Mr Edward Green of Great Shelford must have changed his mind as at the first meeting on 1 October 1833 he wrote expressing agreement to enclose, yet in the Land Tax list, used to show agreement or otherwise, he is put in the 'dissenting' column.

While many saw only the profit to be made from enclosing their land, there were some who felt disquiet regarding the loss of privileges to the poor. Edward Gillam Esq, owner of Hauxton Mill, first declared himself Neutral, but then signed a petition against enclosure saying 'that he did not think the rights of the poor were considered enough, but if this was not the case, he had no objection to the Act', against Gillam's name Pemberton noted:

'Mr Gillam before the Act went before the House of Commons declared Himself Neuter, after the Act passed the House of Commons he signed a petition against it and upon being asked his reason since he signed, he told the solicitor for the Act, that he did not understand the subject but that it was represented to him that the rights of the poor were not properly stated in the Act consequently they would be much injured; in consequence of his having said this the solicitor considers himself authorised to place him with the Neutral, notwithstanding he has signed the Petition.'[26]

As all parishes had to have a Statement of Property before Parliament would sanction enclosure this juggling with the results must have happened many times. The final result was that one way or another, the majority agreed and the Act was presented to Parliament.

Small owners probably had most to lose by enclosure. Their common rights may have supplemented their incomes to quite a large degree. Moreover, compared with the larger landowners, smaller proprietors' enclosure rates, fencing costs and other expenses were proportionally higher; so it is not surprising that many of them were unhappy about enclosure. Many of their claims for common rights were contested by the Commissioners, as we shall see, but such opposition was not universal, as Mingay has noted in the case of Cumbria, where:

'Small subsistence farmers welcomed enclosure as it would result in enfranchisement, the conversion to legal certainty of their existing customary rights. For them enclosure was the means of improving their status while at the same time maintaining their livelihood as small producers.'[27]

Before the *Reform Act* of 1832, only people with property worth more than 40s a year could vote; the extra land allotted to common right holders in recompense for losing those rights would for some, for the first time, enfranchise them. Moreover, many small owners probably relished the increased value of their land which enclosure would bring, even when the various costs of the process had been taken into account. Chapter 8 shows that many trees were felled at enclosure both for fencing and to provide income towards the costs of enclosure.

The regulations regarding the numbers who needed to acquiesce to an enclosure by act seem to have been fairly flexible; the Hammonds quote the Parliamentary Commission of 1801, saying that there was no fixed rule, that in some cases the consent of three-fourths was required; in others the consent of four-fifths. This of course was in value of land owned, not the numbers of proprietors. In the Hammonds' oft quoted words: 'The suffrage was not counted but weighed'. Furthermore the value was calculated sometimes by acres, sometimes in Annual Value, sometimes in assessment in Land Tax and sometimes in assessment in Poor Rate.[28] The 1801 Act is described by Mingay as 'a dismal half-measure', being not specific enough in its instructions to commissioners regarding the process of enclosure.[29] This was remedied by the 1836 and 1840 *Acts of Enclosure by Consent* which specified that enclosure could proceed if two-thirds of the interested parties (again, by value) agreed.[30]

It is frequently stated that complexity of landowning structures was a major factor in determining the chronology of enclosure:

> 'The presence of numerous landlords in the same parish had a delaying effect for the complex system of intermingled demesnes and conflicting sheepwalk claims militated against mutual agreement necessary for the replacement of existing cultivation practices by more advanced systems.'[31]

Michael Turner has suggested that this was, indeed, the case in south Cambridgeshire: 'In south Cambridgeshire where the greatest density of enclosure took place the delay was more likely due to large number of small proprietors.'[32] Postgate, however, has suggested that parishes dominated by college land were more likely to be enclosed late,[33] and this would be in line with Cunningham's more general observation about the economic management of the colleges: that they were inclined to maintain a policy of land management which was unenterprising and traditional.[34] Several decades before enclosure took place an official of Peterhouse College neatly expressed the Fellows' views on the matter: 'They think Inclosures injurious to open field property and there are no circumstances under which they would think an Enclosure beneficial'.[35] So a combination of small landowners and traditionally minded colleges would certainly delay enclosure by several years. The average length between Act and Award was six years, ranging from only one (Great Shelford) to 12 years (Shepreth).

Much of the time was taken up with the meetings held by the Commissioners to hear the various claims to common rights made by interested parties, from major landowners to small cottagers, and investigating those claims rigorously but, so far as it is possible to tell, fairly. The rights claimed varied from parish to parish and between classes. The lords of the manors claimed '*Right of Soil*' (ownership of all minerals on their land even if it is rented out), '*Right of Fold*' (the right of the lord to demand that all sheep be folded over-night on his land thus ensuring greater fertility), and '*Right of Sheepwalk*' (the sole right to keep a sheep flock). Other farmers could claim '*Right of Stray*' (the right to keep straying animals). They were all compensated for the loss of these rights. Many, as described in the previous chapter, claimed more general rights of common grazing. These rights were investigated by interviewing claimants and hearing the testimony of long-established residents. As already discussed, claims were not always successful but there is no evidence for outright chicanery and those whose claims were recognised seem to have been dealt with fairly, if not generously, when land was allotted to them.

Labourers who had no land, and thus no legal rights of common to claim compensation for, may have had less to lose; even if they rented a commonable tenement they are unlikely to have been able to afford a cow or other stock.

They had no voice in the decision-making process, their opposition was ignored. They could write letters but often these carried little weight, though the labourers of Fowlmere, as we shall see, wrote to good effect. So they were left with two alternatives, passive acceptance or active opposition. It is not easy to simplify the choices of the disenfranchised; so many aspects of position and employment influenced such choices. Men were aware that they owed their living to the farmers who employed them and any resistance could risk them being turned off and even prosecuted for violence. Yet desperate men will seek desperate remedies and the unemployed, relying on the pittance from the parish with no job to lose, might not feel so constrained. The fact that so few parishes rioted perhaps indicates, clearly enough, that the poor were not very much affected by enclosure. Indeed, a range of other pressures – over-population, unemployment and inflation – impacted on those living in enclosed as much as in unenclosed parishes.

It has nevertheless been suggested that enclosure caused much unrest and uprising, certainly between 1830 and 1833 there were 13 riots and acts of arson in Cambridgeshire. Yet most of these were attributed to the influence of a certain 'Captain Swing' whose activities had resulted in a spate of burning ricks and breaking machines throughout most of the Home Counties in 1830.[36] Like the Littleport riots of 1816 most of these later uprisings were driven by hunger and fear of unemployment, not directly by enclosure.[37] Low wages, high bread prices and unemployment made men insecure and they feared the introduction of threshing machines which would put them out of work during the winter months. Between 1815–20 and 1830–35 attitudes hardened and poor law expenditure per head of the population was reduced by almost a third. The Cambridgeshire magistrates thought that a working man could subsist on a 'two gallon' loaf compared with a 'three and a half gallon' loaf in 1795, this reduction in calories resulted in a corresponding drop in productivity: between 1832–33 12 counties reported declining productivity in 50% and 76% of their parishes. Men were also aware that even by working harder they could not earn any more as the system of topping up wages by the parish meant that wages remained static thus removing the incentive to do so.[38]

One riot that was caused by the fear of enclosure occurred in 1797 when Harston was preparing to enclose. The *Cambridge Chronicle* describes in great detail a group of labourers led by one Nordon refusing to let the Constable pin the notice regarding enclosure to the church door:

> 'He called out 'We have been waiting for you, and if you attempt to put up the Notice you shall suffer for it'. Very soon after this, Nordon caught hold of Brand (the constable), kicking his horse violently, and attempted to pull him off; but after tearing his coat nearly from his back, he quitted him, and as many of the other persons who had collected to prevent the Notice being put up, made use of very violent language. Brand found it necessary to get away as fast as he could, without making any attempt to put up the Notice; and he was pelted out of the parish.'[39]

The local magistrate Mr Andrew Pern decided that this sort of behaviour could not be overlooked and issued a warrant for Nordon's arrest but as he was 'Guarded from the harvest field to his own house by a number of persons armed with scythes,'[40] he decided to gather a number of Yeoman Cavalry under the command of Mr Pemberton and ride out to Harston to arrest Nordon and affix the notice to the church door:

> 'Nordon was found in the harvest field, and as Mr Pemberton had long known him, he attempted to convince him of the impropriety of his conduct, and strongly recommended to him to submit quietly. This he refused and some others that were with him encouraged him to resist; he was therefore taken by force out of the cart that he was in. By this time a great number of people who were at work in the field began to assemble about Nordon with pitchforks and other weapons of like description, and declared they would resist anyone who attempted to carry him off. Presently Nordon broke away from the constable and got amongst the Rioters, but was very soon secured. By this time two more of the Cavalry had joined, but as the rioters were increasing in number, and several were observed coming from the town to join them, it was thought necessary to order the Cavalry to load their pistols with ball. Nordon was then led off towards Cambridge by Mr Pern and the constable, the former having very spiritedly jumped off his horse when Nordon broke away, to assist in securing him, and continued to lead him till all chance of his being rescued was at an end. Many of the rioters followed even to Cambridge, armed with their pitchforks etc., making use of the most violent language and evidently watching for an opportunity to rescue Nordon. Fortunately they did not attempt it; if they had, the consequence must have been fatal for many of them, as the cavalry were determined to proceed to the last extremity rather than suffer a rescue.'[41]

By August 1798 the required notices had been affixed to the church doors and the process of enclosure started. The riot was over; although it was never stated exactly why the rioters objected to enclosure, the landowners had prevailed by using superior force rather than by addressing the cause of the problem.

The Swing Riots started in 1830 and in December of that year the Fowlmere labourers went on strike for more wages; they refused to disperse for three days. Eventually a troop of mounted constables came out from Royston, read the *Riot Act* and after some skirmishing arrested five men who were sent to Cambridge Goal.[42] As Fowlmere was not enclosed until 15 years later, enclosure could not have been the reason for this unrest. The same month the men of Great and Little Shelford had:

> 'Intended on their pay-day (Friday 3 December) to demand of their respective farmers an increase in wages – e.g. from 10 shillings to 12 shillings per week-day work … and in case of refusal to meet altogether (with other villages) … and proceed in a body to Cambridge.'

A body of special mounted constables was enrolled, word got round and the weekend passed off peacefully.[43]

South Cambridgeshire was badly affected by incendiarism: the burning of corn ricks and hay stacks. On passing through southern Cambridgeshire, Sir James Caird wrote:

'Buildings of wood and thatch were subject to incendiary fires almost nightly and farmers live in nervous excitement and great discouragement … a country in a semi-barbarous state … a man might as well expose his life to a risk of a shot from a Tipperary Assassin, as live like a Cambridgeshire farmer, in constant apprehension of incendiarism.'[44]

An interesting sidelight to the onset and increase in incendiarism is the invention of the friction match; the first invented in England in 1826 and the first safety match invented in Sweden in 1855; the same year Bryant and May acquired the British rights to the process.[45] The coincidence of an easy means of lighting fires, even out of doors, and the increase in rick and other fires of opposition is significant. A comment by the correspondent to the *Cambridge Chronicle* in a report on a fire at Great Shelford in 1854 bears this out: … that fruitful source of mischief, in unskilled hands, Lucifer matches, which some children, unknown to their parents, had taken into a lodge where there was some straw.[46]

Some fires were started by accident such as one on 14 June 1851 at Sawston when: 'A haystack was set on fire by boys not above the age of 5 years with Lucifer matches'.[47] But many fires were started maliciously and deliberately: in Cambridgeshire there were 36 fires over the period 1830–1879, with one fire in 1790. Twelve fires were started by one man, a Mr Stallon of Great Shelford who was paid 6s 6d a time as an ancillary on the fire engine. He was caught and hanged.[48]

Thirty-six fires over a period of nearly 50 years can hardly be called a rash of fires, yet the newspapers made much of the criminality of the perpetrators and always mentioned if the landowners were insured. Many of the fires were outside this area of study and it is possible there were others that went unreported, yet the landowners and vicars particularly were often the newspaper correspondents and would not leave any opportunity to portray in print the sins of the poor. The introduction and popularity of local newspapers meant that news from further afield, which would normally take weeks to reach another part of the country, could now be read within a week of the incident occurring. Reports from other parts of the country under the influence of the mythical Captain Swing gave cause for concern to the owners of straw stacks and oat ricks although nearly all farmers were insured. On the other hand, the newspaper report of the second Pampisford fire, in 1842, and a fire at Stapleford in 1843 made much of the fact that the labouring poor turned out in numbers to put the fire out: 'The great exertion of the inhabitants was deserving of the highest praise.'[49] Resentment against the introduction of threshing machines must have simmered for many years; an early example of incendiarism happened when William Hurrell of Newton attempted to introduce a threshing machine in 1808 but lost several barns full of corn to fire.[50] The fire of December 1830 at Pampisford described a boy caught lighting matches at an oat stack and another boy lurking nearby. When discovered both boys ran away leaving their matches behind.[51] This date coincides with the rash of Swing Riots in the Home Counties.

It must be emphasised that the Swing Riots, which occurred mainly during the winter of 1830–31, were not primarily against enclosure and there is no evidence that the south Cambridgeshire rick fires were against enclosure either.[52] Incendiarism was usually the work of one or two individuals, and burning ricks was an easy way to vent one's wrath against a landowner for an act of perceived harshness. Although not all fires occurred at night, very few of the perpetrators were caught, with the exception of Mr Stallon (see above). A riot, on the other hand, involves many people but needs a spark to start it; usually one man who feels strongly enough to speak out in public against his perceived wrongs. He must be articulate enough to rouse those listening into follow him. No amount of muttering in ale houses will start a riot if there is no one to take the first step outside.

It is noteworthy that the only evidence we have for well-organised working class opposition to enclosure comes from a parish, Fowlmere, in which certain common rights were, unusually, extended to the entire population. Even here, however, much of the opposition was actually to the possible loss of the area set aside for spade husbandry on the common, rather than to the loss of common rights *per se*. Fowlmere, which was enclosed in 1845, was the last complete parish in south Cambridgeshire to be enclosed. Their neighbouring parish, Thriplow, enclosed five years before, had been left with only 2 acres (0.81 ha) of recreation land and Fowlmere who had the use of over 200 acres (80.9 ha) of common and some land devoted to spade husbandry, obviously feared a similar loss of land. The Great Moor and North Moor at Fowlmere covered 200 acres of marshy land fed by many springs and, until enclosure, all parishioners had the right to pasture cattle, cut sedge and dig clay on the moors.[53] The moors also provided sport for many visitors from Cambridge who shot duck, teal and other waterfowl there; they harboured the edible frog and provided sedge and reeds for thatching.[54] By 1841 the population of Fowlmere was 601 but how many used the Moors is not known and therefore the precise value to the poor of these 200 acres cannot be quantified.

Several of the Fowlmere labourers were concerned that they would not be compensated for the loss of these rights. They were fortunate in finding a leader who could write and who was determined to appeal against such a loss; William Dean, the landlord of the *Black Horse* Inn, took it upon himself to write to a solicitor recommended by a friend to ask him to help; the solicitor to whom they appealed was Samuel Wells of Lincoln's Inn in London. He was the solicitor of the Middle Level Drainage Commission and had an office in Ely[55] (Appendix 5).

The following documents tell the story of their endeavours to remedy this perceived wrong. William Dean wrote to Samuel Wells on January 15 1845 explaining that:

> 'There is upwards of 200 acres of wastes and commons exclusive of balks of which we have the privilege of mowing the fodder and gathering dry manure for fuel and of turning cows on if we can purchase them. These privileges we have had from generation to generation. From your humble and obedient servants – the Labourers of the Parish of Fowlmire.'

He goes on to say that the parish officers pay the rent for this land so that the poor can use it: 'The rent is demanded by the Parish Constable but late years has been paid by the Overseer. The rate is paid from the Parish Rate which thing we do not understand'. [56]

It would seem that the rate was paid by the parish to the landowners who were Mr Mitchell, the Lord of the Manor and the Rev Mr Metcalf, the Rector. This was a Fee Farm Rent dating back to feudal times and really not relevant to the spade husbandry agreement.[57] In another letter dated 8 February, William Dean also complained that a certain piece of land consisting of nine and half acres called Town Land brought an income of £22:

'Is of late years applied to the repairs of the church and incidental expenses but formerly was distributed among the poor of the parish and some other things which we think not right'.[58]

It is obvious from these letters that these men had seen money once used to help the poor being diverted to other purposes. But this land was charity land and nothing really to do with the commons or spade husbandry land that the petitioners were fearful of losing. It is obvious that they were confused as to what were common rights and what were other forms of charitable income. The letter goes on to say:

'Four years since this time they inclosed Thriplow the adjoining parish to us and they have left not a single foot of the extensive commons for the use of the poor with the exception of the recreation ground'.

The men from Fowlmere were determined that the same would not happen to them; the letter continues:

'We have about or near 20 acres of common land under spade husbandry for the poor to occupy let from 1¼d to 2d per pole broke up, under 1st and 2nd of William IV, an act to inclose part of the common for the use of the poor'.[59]

Here they were referring to a scheme set up under an Act of 1832 to enclose common land for the use of the poor by providing them with allotments to grow potatoes and other crops. The land was to be controlled by the overseers of the poor; a small rent was charged and the cultivation was to be by spade husbandry only. As the land was rented it was not a common right. The conditions are of great interest and very specific as shown in Figure 4.1. Legal representation was expensive and Wm Dean on behalf of his fellow poor writes:

'Sir, you are aware as Labourers chiefly we have not much money but we could collect a small sum for advice and if we can get any land it would seem poor land if it would not pay other expenses by a rent upon it and if you answer us we will pay by post the expenses for enquiring by directing to Mr Wm Dean, Black Horse Inn, Foulmire, Cambs.'[60]

He explains that because they are opposing the farmers, they cannot borrow money from them. Mr Well's reply to Wm Dean is both friendly and encouraging:

Are those allotments enclosed woe meadow.

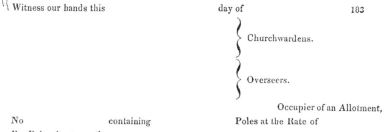

Allotments of Land,
PARISH OF
FOULMIRE.

Every occupier of an Allotment of Land, is to observe that it is held under an Act of Parliament, passed in the 1st. and 2nd. year of King William the 4th. chapter 42, and under the following conditions.   (1832)

1. He is to cultivate the Land by spade husbandry alone, and with his best skill and diligence.

2. Not to plant Potatoes unless the ground be first properly manured.

3. Half the land only to be cultivated with Potatoes, in any one year, and no crop to occupy more than one half of the Allotment.

4. If the Land be given up, the occupier to be paid for digging or planting, unless it be given up under the 9th. rule.

5. The holders of these Allotments agree to prevent depredations on each others property and to do their utmost to detect and assist in convicting all persons who destroy or injure the embankment or Fences upon the allotments, or the Crops of every description.

6. Every sort of encroachment is to be strictly avoided: and every occupier agrees to keep up the Banks and Fences, apportioned to his allotment, in constant repair.

7. No allotment or any part of an allotment shall be under-let.

8. The Rent to be paid to the Assistant Overseer, or such person as shall be appointed to receive it, within one week after the 29th. of September in every year. And if the Rent be not then paid, the Churchwardens and Overseers of the Poor (if directed by the committee) shall immediately distrain for such Rent, and proceed under the authority of the 59 Geo. 3. chapter 12. to remove such Tenant so in arrear from his allotment.

9. If any occupier of an Allotment be found Guilty of Theft, or other misdemeanour, he will be subject to an immediate ejectment, without the slightest remuneration for labour or planting.

10. That as a Stimulant to good cultivation, Annual Prizes will be awarded by the Committee, to such occupiers as shall keep their Land in the best and cleanest order, and produce the largest crops.

11. That the equitable construction of these Rules and Conditions be vested in the committee.

12. That the Occupiers of the Allotments may expect to be continued in possession of them so long as they fulfil the foregoing Rules and Conditions.

Witness our hands this   day of   183

} Churchwardens.

} Overseers.

Occupier of an Allotment,

No   containing   Poles at the Rate of
Per Pole, situate on the

FIGURE 4.1. Spade Husbandry Agreement, Fowlmere.

'I beg you and the poor labourers of the Parish will be assured that I feel both my Duty as well as natural inclination at all times and upon all occasions to stand up and support to the utmost of my power the rights and interests of the labouring poor for whose depressed condition I have always done my utmost for years to prevent. If therefore I can in regards to the Inclosure of Foulmire prevent any wrong done I will cheerfully do it. Nothing can be done until the Bills presented to the House of Commons and read a first time when we shall see what it contains. In the mean time I earnestly advise you and your poor neighbours not on any account to sign any paper whatever or give any assent, to any application respecting the Inclosure and you may rely upon me as soon as I obtain a copy of the Bill I will either come down or send for some of you up here to obtain all proper information as the proprietors may not intend to do any injustice and as it is my rule not to prejudice process. You may rely upon my Assistance and that it shall take place. Your friend Saml Wells.'[61]

By April they still had not collected all the money needed but could afford £20. Mr Wells replies: 'Mr Dean, twenty pounds will be quite sufficient at present. I don't know that more will be wanted but cannot fully say exactly'.[62] He requests a list of those who have got together to oppose the loss of the commons and a list of over 40 names is sent including five of the oldest inhabitants: Wm Ware aged 76, James Runham 72, Edward Harrop 70, Thomas Smith 65 and James Pearce 65. Only one of these men can sign his name; but a letter written by Wm Ware shows that *he* can write, Figure 4.2:

'Sir, I am sorry to say that I cannot attend threw infirmity but am ready to take my oath that the Rights of Commons have bene ingread by all the pore of the parrish & unmolested all my years and I have never heard to the Contrary from my Father or Grandfather or any one else
Witness my hand this day 5 April 1845

Wm Ware
Aged 76 years'

FIGURE 4.2. Letter from William Ware.

The petition was presented to the Committee at the House of Commons and was successful in that 28 acres (11.33 ha) were allotted for the use of the poor for spade husbandry, the rental from which was to be used for their benefit. A few years after the Award was granted, the income from this land was £18 10s and by 1988 the income was £1200 which was distributed among 90 people.

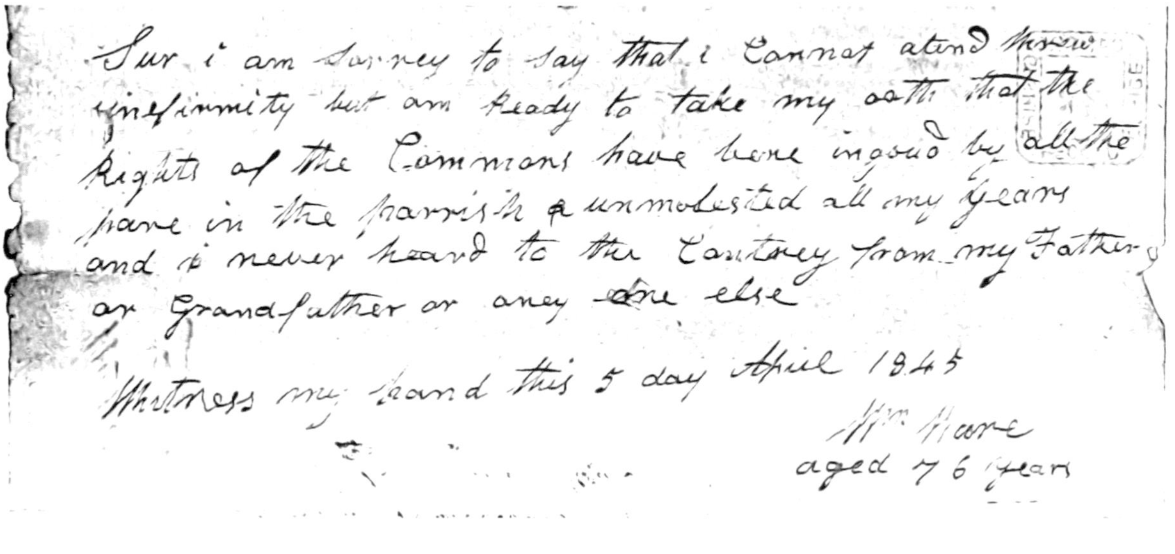

The trouble that William Dean went to on behalf of the labourers of Fowlmere was well worthwhile. Fowlmere had obviously learned a lesson from their failed riot in 1830 and Thriplow's plight and decided on a more legal fight and were lucky in finding a champion for their cause.

This petition seems to be unique in the history of enclosure in south Cambridgeshire and the question arises, why should 40 labourers go to the expense and trouble of hiring a solicitor to present a petition to Parliament when other parishes had not felt it worthwhile? Their incentive was obviously seeing their neighbouring parish lose its common land. Thriplow's other neighbours were already enclosed; it was too late for them; only Fowlmere was unenclosed and in a position to appeal. Although the petitioners were originally rather confused as to which were their rights and which were not, the most telling motivation for their petitioning Parliament was their fear of losing their Spade Husbandry allotments. This was something concrete that they could point to; 20 acres (8.92 ha) of land on which they were encouraged to cultivate, grow potatoes on and so supplement their families' diets. 'Common Rights' could be rather a nebulous concept, especially if the poor could not afford livestock or the land was in poor heart. J. D. Chambers describes the commons as a 'Thin and squalid curtain' hanging between the poor and even greater poverty.[63] If common land was over-grazed by those who had stock, those that could not afford animals but who might use the land to gather fuel or food, could be left with nothing.[64] At a time when the calorific intake of the poor was often not enough to enable a man to give a good day's work, a specific piece of land to cultivate and provide food was a more concrete and practical custom and worth fighting for.

Hobsbawn and Rudé have shown that in Suffolk there is some connection between literacy and unrest.[65] In Fowlmere, there were eight schools some of which educated the poor before 1846 when the National School was started.[66] This meant that many inhabitants could read and write: even the elderly William Ware could pen a letter. The labourers of Fowlmere were not rustic 'Hodges',[67] unable to string a sentence or thought-process together, but were able to discuss their problem and decide on a strategy. By 1818, there were two Sunday schools and three dame schools and one non-conformist academy in Fowlmere and in 1846 a National School was set up. Harston, on the other hand, enclosed in 1798, suffered quite considerably from incendiarism and also suffered a riot, but had no schools until the nineteenth century. It must be remembered that 47 years separated the enclosure of these two villages, yet it would seem that some education enabled labourers to assemble their thoughts in a more logical way and decide that a legal petition had more power than brute force.

As a piece of pure bathos, the last letter written by 'William Dean and the poor of the village of Fowlmere' in January 1846 complained that the land given them for a cricket pitch was not big enough:

'Sir, We are taking great liberty in writing to you before we discharge our debt but our Recreation Ground is set out so very inconvenient for cricketing as it is but 3 acres. It is 11½ chains long and 3 chains over which is of very little use for that purpose. We should feel grateful to you if you would let us know whether it could be altered to make it more convenient.'[68]

Here they were unsuccessful as 'The Butts' as it is known today is still only 3 acres (1.21 ha).

On balance, it seems that it was not enclosure *per se* that roused the opposition of the agricultural labourers and cottagers, but the losses of a tangible custom or privilege. To the labourers of Fowlmere, the loss of their spade husbandry, by which each family could augment their income, was perceived as a greater and more concrete loss than the more general loss of the use of the commons which were probably, to a significant extent, degraded environments, mainly exploited by the small and medium-sized farmers.

But perhaps the most important reason why there was so little organised opposition to enclosure is that the other social group usually seen as victims of the process – the small owners – seem on the whole to have been treated with a reasonable degree of fairness by the commissioners, at least if their claims to land could be substantiated: a matter to which I shall return in the next chapter. Meanwhile this chapter adds a small brick in a well researched wall of the study of the process of enclosure and reveals how the community used their environment to the best advantage they could.

Notes

1   Tate (1944), 56.
2   *Ibid.*, 75
3   Tate (1946), 270.
4   CUL Add and Doc papers in the Manuscript Department (See individual references and bibliography for further details).
5   Cambridgeshire Record Office (1812) 107 Bundle IV 117 Ickleton.
6   CUL Doc 652 Shelford October 1 1833.
7   CUL Doc 652.
8   Hammond and Hammond (1911), 61.
9   CRO P139/28/13, Letter to John Ingle September 1811.
10 Chapman (1993), 52.
11 Kain *et al.* (2004), 55.
12 CUL DOC 651 5, 5 February 1802.
13 *Ibid.*
14 CUL DOC 652, 21 November 1833.
15 CUL ADD 6065.
16 CUL DOC 651/106, 108.
17 *Cambridge Chronicle* 8 October 1796.
18 CUL ADD 6013, 28 and 29 August 1798.
19 *Cambridge Chronicle*, 9 September 1800.
20 CRO 107 uncataloged papers.
21 CRO 107 Bundle IV/117 Ickleton.

22   *Ibid.*

23   Vancouver (1794), 66.

24   Richardson (1993), 19.

25   CUL DOC 639/2, 1797.

26   CUL DOC 639/2.

27   Mingay (1997), 45.

28   Hammond and Hammond (1995), 49.

29   *Op cit.* in note 27, 29.

30   Richardson (1986), 19.

31   Postgate (1964).

32   Turner (1980).

33   *Op. cit.* in note 31, 296.

34   Cunningham (1909), 4.

35   Peterhouse documents, C7 1819 note both spellings of 'enclosure'.

36   Hobsbawm and Rudé (1965), 166.

37   Peacock (1964).

38   *Op. cit.,* in note 36, 51.

39   *Cambridge Chronicle*, 16 September 1797.

40   *Ibid.*

41   *Ibid.*

42   Hitch (1993), 41.

43   Hobsbawm and Rudé (1965), 166.

44   Caird (1852), 467.

45   Robinson (1983).

46   *Cambridge Chronicle* 29 April 1854, 4.

47   *Ibid.,* 14 June 1851, 5.

48   *Cambridge Chronicle* 27 January 1832, 2.

49   *Ibid.,* 29 October 1842, and 21 October 1843, 2.

50   *Ibid.,* 23 August 1808.

51   *Ibid.,* 10 December 1830.

52   Hobsbawm and Rudé (1965), 176.

53   CRO 292/02–36.

54   *VCH* 8, 155.

55   Hitch (1993), 172.

56   CRO 292/02.

57   *Op cit.* in note 55, 173 (a Fee farm was historically a grant of land for feudal services).

58   CRO 292/03, 1845.

59   CRO 292/03, 8 February 1845 (spade husbandry was created under an Act of 1832).

60   CRO 292/02.

61   CRO 292/02 16 February 1845.

62   CUL 292/06 2 April 1845.

63   Neeson (1993), 40; Chambers and Mingay (1966).

64   Vancouver (1794), 66.

65   Hobsbawm and Rudé (1965), 166.

66   *VCH* 8, 164.

67   'Hodge' was used by Richard Jeffries to denote an unlettered rustic labourer in *Hodge and his Masters,* (1880), the name has become synonymous with the overworked and undervalued labourer seen by his masters the farmers as boorish, inarticulate and rebellious.

68   CRO 292/034.

CHAPTER FIVE

Designing the New Landscape

Fence meeting fence, in owners little bounds
Of field and meadow, large as garden grounds,
In little parcels little minds to please,
With men and flocks imprisoned, ill at ease.
John Clare – *Shepherd's Calendar*

Enclosure commissioners were landscape designers on an enormous scale, 'one third of the whole of England was replanned by commissioners'.[1] Not since the introduction of the open fields in early medieval times had the character of large swathes of land changed so radically. The commissioners' legacy is the pretty patchwork of hedged fields that we like to think of as 'olde England,' forgetting that this type of landscape, in the eastern edge of the central province of England at least, is a mere 150–200 years old. The commissioners are not remembered as are the great garden designers such as Humphry Repton and Capability Brown, yet as Turner says:

> 'The action of the enclosure commissioners, their surveyors and road and hedge contractors, have left their indelible mark on the English countryside ... if for no other reason that that we constantly tread upon or traverse eighteenth and nineteenth century relief features'.[2]

The commissioners, together with the enclosure surveyors, had the difficult task of converting hundreds of open field strips, heaths and moors into compact individually-owned fields. They literally redesigned the countryside, from a 'landscape shaped by generations of labour into a place of short perspectives,' the result of which was the pattern of the land interrupted by hedges much as we know them today.[3] Mingay points out that the 'landscape before enclosure had a spacious appearance and that even after enclosure the number of houses built in the newly privatised fields were sparse'.[4] This was certainly true of south Cambridgeshire.

This operation was complicated by the fact that the tithe owners and manorial lords, be they vicars, rectors or lay owners, were entitled to extra land in lieu of the tithes or manorial rights they would lose. The owners of common rights were also entitled to extra land to compensate them for the loss of those rights. The fact that most enclosures in southern Cambridgeshire went through with a minimum of unrest is a tribute to the skill and dedication of these men.

Some time after their first meeting, the commissioners and surveyor and probably several landowners walked or rode the parish to be enclosed, measured out the area and decided on what changes were necessary:

> 'Harston – 5th–10th November 1798, Hoop Inn, Cambridge, Monday, received claims,
> Tues/Wed, Commissioners examined boundaries of Harston, Hauxton, Little Shelford and Newton.
> Thurs/Friday, Commissioners quantified the land of the said parishes.'[5]

This was three months after the first meeting of the commissioners. At Ickleton the commissioners were to perambulate the boundaries on 18 September 1810, two months after the first meeting, but this was postponed until the next day.[6] The commissioners for Sawston perambulated its boundaries on the 5 May 1803, eight months after their first meeting.

The cost and labour involved in fencing the newly allotted fields probably amounted to the greater part of the enclosure process. Specific instructions were given by the commissioners regarding the type and management of hedges, and a large part of the enclosure process was concerned with the business of fencing. The type of wood used for the fences and the spacing of the hedges provides useful evidence of the making of the field boundaries. For instance in Sawston:

> '12 days work on side of new drain in King's Farm and throwing the earth back to plant a Quick' and 'Ditching, Quicking and Battening with 2 rail fence & 7 thousand Quick', also '3 rails of Finland, ¼ Battens with 5ft Oakposts & 2 piles with 3ft ditch on each side properly banked up & 3 Quicks in each foot for 43s 6d.' Also 'public fencing 2 rows of good healthy Whitethorn Quick at the usual distance –Posts to be Oak, Piles also – Rails part foreign deal battens and part elm and ash – Gates and posts Oak – to be completed by end of March next.'[7]

'Quicking' is the process of planting quick or hawthorn (*Crataegus monogyna*), hedges although in the example it is called whitethorn, another name for the same plant. In Stapleford two people had anticipated enclosure as the Vicar wrote: 'A considerable number of young Hawthorns for Hedging growing on the premises of Messrs Atkinson and Headley.'[8]

Not everyone thought that hawthorn or 'quick' was the best plant to use. A letter from William Williamson, an absentee landowner from Buntingford holding land in Ickleton, to Christopher Pemberton stated that he: 'believed Quick would not grow upon that dry soil and would be a waste of money'. He would oppose any such measure.'[9] What he thought would grow instead he did not say.

To protect the young quick hedges, several villages put clauses into their Awards restricting sheep or cattle from going near them for seven years unless a fence was erected to protect the growing plants. The penalty for disregarding this instruction was a fine or if further ignored the offending cattle or sheep would be sold by the Commissioners to defray expenses.[10] The young plants also needed to be protected from weeds. The Churchwardens' Accounts for Sawston from 1805 have the following entries:

'November 5th 1805 – Howing the Quick – £1–6–9
May 10th 1806 – For Howing the Quick – 8s 11 p
November 7th 1806 – For Hoeing 53½ acres Quick – £1–6–9'[11]

Some fencing appears to have been organised directly by the commissioners, apparently acting as negotiators and notional bankers for the owners of adjoining allotments. In Stapleford they made numerous payments summarised in Table 5.1.

Judging by the type of people in each column, for instance the Dean and Chapter of Ely in the right column, it would seem that those in the left column were paying the commissioners' for organising their fencing. Those on the right had probably paid directly for the fencing and were being reimbursed by the commissioners. The commissioners had thus balanced the books.

When areas of former common were enclosed, the new owner would want to plough the land which he could not do unless any trees were felled and cleared away.[12] The cost of felling and selling the trees was often disputed by the old and new owners and in Great Shelford, where the poor were alleged to have planted the trees on the common, they would have wanted the value of these trees to be given to them. In a sparsely wooded county such as Cambridgeshire, trees were valuable; Great Shelford commissioners instructed the 'Proprietors to cut down trees within a month of allotting their old land,' and Fowlmere specified that 'All timber growing on common or waste land shall be paid to Lords or Ladies of the Manor.'[13] Between 1841 and 1844 a correspondence was conducted between St John's College, who owned Barrenton's Manor, Thriplow, and Alexander Watford, the surveyor to the enclosure commissioners for Thriplow, regarding the felling of trees. The argument centred on who was responsible for felling the trees and who should benefit from selling them:

		Received from			Paid to		
Date	Name	Amount			Name	Amount	
19.4. 1813	Rev Wm Atkinson	11	18	0	Edmund Baker		15	0
	Tregonnell Collier	61	4	6	John Bevis		18	0
	Mary Coxall	1	0	0	John Carter	2	6	6
	Robert Heffer	2	2	6	Wm Cocks		11	0
	John Johnson	9	0	0	Richard Collier	3	0	0
	Rev Chas Mulis	5	18	6	Henry Headley	3	0	0
	Wm Parkins	15	16	6	Thomas Keath	6	0	0
	Francis Smith	2	14	0	Lord Osborne	5	15	0
	Old fences made part of Vicars fencing as required by Parliament	24	0	0	Ch/Wardens of Stapleford	2	8	0
	Sum due from Alice Brand	1	3	0	Ann Townsend	3	0	0
		134	17	0	D & C Ely	106	14	6
						134	8	0
					Sum remaining due		9	0
						134	17	0

TABLE 5.1. Payment for Timber and Fencing, Stapleford. *Source*: CUL, ADD 6068c.

'Sir, The £21.13.3 was the sum you had to pay when the Timber on the three acres which you gave up to Mr Perkins was supposed to be taken by him, but he refused to take the Timber and I make no doubt the Bursar (of the college) ordered them to be cut down and sold on your account therefore you must be charged with it. Timber which you took – £54.7.8, Commission for measuring £1.16.3.'[14]

The low-lying commons often needed to be more effectively drained – a reminder, perhaps, that their pre-enclosure condition was far from perfect. In 1803 the commissioners for Sawston: 'Considered the drainage of low and wet lands and enlargement of drains to 10 feet [*c*.3 m] wide at top, 4 feet [*c*.1.2 m] wide at bottom and 4 feet deep.' Indeed, alterations to drainage and waterways are often described in the documents. In 1805, when Stapleford was thinking of enclosure, Sawston noted that 'Stapleford requested River between them and Sawston be straightened and 2 sluices built.'[15] The great jig-saw of allotting the land fairly that was the commissioner's responsibility had to take into account the building of roads and straightening of rivers and boundaries. The surveyor for Ickleton was requested to:

'Ascertain names of proprietors of land in Parish of Hinxton lying in parish of Ickleton and Mr Pemberton to write to them to agree an exchange of lands for purpose of shortening and straightening boundary between the two parishes.'[16]

The enclosure map of Thriplow shows the two rivers which formed the east and west boundaries of the parish with their new straightened routes. They were probably straightened to increase the drainage and to make the allocating of the land easier. Figure 5.1 shows the eastern edge of Thriplow and the river diverted by a straightened drain called in the enclosure award, the forth public drain.

Old roads were closed and new ones made, fencing and ditching set in motion, and the moors drained to enable the previously poor, water-logged land to be ploughed. Details of all these operations are often found in accounts and bills among the commissioners' papers, and provide useful information regarding this little studied part of the enclosure process. The Awards list all the roads and footpaths that were closed by the commissioners; Thriplow had 33 roads, footpaths and bridleways closed, leaving only three footpaths that exist to this day, while Great Shelford only lost five roads.[17] Turnpike roads were exempt from closure or alteration.

Whilst there were no complaints of land being allotted unfairly, there were complaints of compensation not being paid for loss of land owing to roads being made or for damage caused by gravel being extracted. At Ickleton:

'In consequence of a representation made by Mr Pytches respecting a Gravel Pit proposed to be set out in his allotment … Commissioners relieved Mr Pytches from having a gravel pit on his land provided he is willing to take the acre of land intended for the pit and pay the price fixed upon it.'[18]

Later the solicitors reported that: 'That they had taken possession of proportion of Mr Pytche's estate in consequence of his not paying his Rate'. Mr Pytche's solicitor said he should be able to produce the money due and prepared

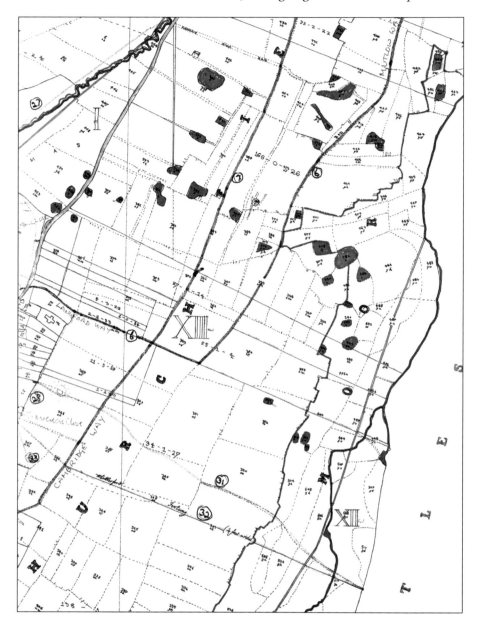

FIGURE 5.1. Map of
Thriplow showing steam
converted to drain.

the necessary deed.[19] There were a number of other disputes concerning the
construction of roads. A protracted argument arose between the commissioners
and Mr Martindale a mill owner of Sawston regarding the building of a bridle
road to the mill: the Commissioners felt Mr Martindale should pay for the
road and compensate the proprietors over whose land it would run, but Mr
Martindale felt it should be paid for by the commissioners:

> 'Mr Martindale claimed he could sustain serious injury unless he was permitted to
> have the use of the bridle road from his leased mill, Durnford, over old common
> to his mill called Burns Mill.'[20]

New roads were sometimes built over arable land, ditches dug and gravel extracted. If these cut into a farmer's land he could expect compensation for the damage. On the 26 August 1812, Samuel Hanchet of Ickleton complained that:

> 'Thomas Hopkins and his men were injuring his land by improperly digging gravel thereon and carting the same away. The Commissioners went to Ickleton to see but as the corn was still growing they were not able to ascertain the extent of the injury.'[21]

If the damage was really bad it would surely have been easy enough to follow the trail of the gravel takers. Was the damage exaggerated or were the commissioners not bothered to ascertain the extent of the damage? At Sawston Peter Nash was obviously smarting from a letter accusing him of not paying his rates; he replied that: 'He had given up an orchard to widen the road. The orchard made many shillings per year yet no compensation had been received from Commissioners.'[22] In Stapleford Mr Collier and Mr Cocks applied for compensation for the damage sustained by the drain cut across their old enclosure and allotments. Mr Collier also applied for an allowance for the waste of his land in consequence of gravel being dug for the making of roads.[23]

Susanna Wade-Martins suggested that farmers were not consulted as to where their new fields would be:[24] But there is a way of discovering whether farmers' requests for allocation of land was acceded to, by studying the commissioners' papers. By the time the commissioners and the surveyor walked over the land to be enclosed, the inhabitants would know what was happening. Judging by the amount of correspondence between the enclosing officers and landowners there was no shortage of opinions and requests being made between the two. As the surveyor and his men measured the land, they would be open to requests and opinions from the landowners. There was nothing secret about the allocation process. The following excerpt from the commissioners' minutes for Ickleton shows that claims were heard and the new allotments shown to the public in order for objections to be made:

> '24–7–1811 – Quantified land. Notice that requests for situations be received at next meeting
> 29–8–1811 – Claims heard and settled.
> 27–9–1811 – Notice for advert and affix to church door re next meeting which would show new allotments on plan.
> 14–10–1811 – Requests for allotments heard.
> 18–10–1811 – Commissioners produced Plan of allotments for proprietors to inspect.
> 21–11–1811 – Objections to allotments received. Only Mr Hanchett produced his objection in writing.'[25]

The three parishes in this study area whose written requests have survived are Ickleton, Great Shelford and Stapleford; these requests for allocation are mainly by small landowners showing that they took it into their own hands to ask for land where they wanted it. Other parishes must have done the same though the notes of requests have not survived. The Ickleton papers record 25 requests for land, mostly adjacent to land already owned; William Williamson wrote:

> 'I have 60 acres [24.3 ha] immediately adjoining the back gate of my Farm yard which opens upon the land I now request to have. Or if not as near as may be to the Windmill somewhere about Shortlands, Hill Field, Clay Pit corner and Rose Field, where I have at present a considerable quantity.'[26]

Joseph Ellis requested his allotment: 'to be at the Bottom of Bird Close or as near as my Homestall as possible. I request for Mr Christalls allotment to be set next to mine.'[27] Obviously Ellis and Christall worked together probably sharing tools and equipment. The nearness of a road is often mentioned when requesting land. John Haughton of Ickleton wanted his land: 'To be set out on West side of Turnpike Road opposite Clunch Pit;' Henry Clinton Fynes Esq wanted his land: 'Set out in South Field adjoining Littlebury Parish and Turnpike Road;' John Knott senior, Richard Nelson, Sam Pilgrim and Joseph and Robert Wakefield all wanted their allotments to be against the Turnpike Road.[28] Their desire to be near the Turnpike Road was presumably because it would be the best kept and repaired road in the vicinity and easiest for their carts and wagons to fetch and carry their produce to and from the markets. Arthur Young, in his travels for the Board of Agriculture in 1771, rated most of the turnpikes as 'good' to 'excellent', and both Telford and MacAdam designed improved road surfaces for the turnpike roads and by the first half of the nineteenth century the surfaces of these roads were greatly improved.[29]

In Great Shelford there are only two requests; William Dobson asked for his allotment to 'Be adjoining Turnpike Road from Trumpington to Great Shelford and as near the parish of Trumpington as conveniently be so.' And Dr Smith the Vicar of Wilbraham an absentee landowner wrote: 'As this land is usually occupied together with a small farm at Cherry Hinton, the Commissioners are requested to set out the allotment contiguous to the parish of Cherry Hinton.'[30]

An unusual request in the Stapleford Claims Book is from W. Atkinson who asks for an exchange of four small pieces of land for:

> 'A very small triangular bit of waste ground of not more than a few square yards and lying in a corner bounded by fences of Mrs Bran's yard, a close of Mr Heffers and the bye road leading from Turnpike Road past the front of my house, which is now an eye-sore to it, and was always covered with willow trees till I bought them and cut them down for the purpose of planting it with something more ornamental.'[31]

This desire of a man to make his view from his house more attractive reveals the human face, so often absent, behind the business-like activity of the enclosure process.

Mingay suggests that: 'Small landowners who requested their allotments to be near their houses usually received priority.'[32] An examination of existing sources can reveal whether this was so in south Cambridgeshire. By using the Ordnance Survey 25 inch first edition of 1886 together with maps from Railway

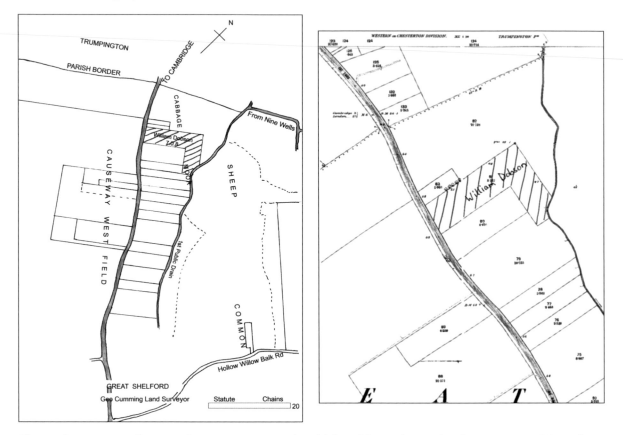

Plans of 1843, as well as enclosure maps, we should be able to locate land mentioned in the above mentioned requests. So were these requests granted? The commissioners' minutes give no clue, but from enclosure maps we should find each claimant's allotment of land. If the allotment was too small to write a name on, the amounts and names together with a number which corresponded with a number on the map would be placed in a box at the bottom of the enclosure map.

The Enclosure map for Great Shelford dated 1835 does show that William Dobson was given his requested piece of land near to the Trumpington border and on the Turnpike Road (see Figure 5.2) but the Rev Dr Smith, Vicar of Wilbraham, on the other hand, did not get his piece of land on the Cherry Hinton border but on the opposite side of the parish on the Little Shelford border! Perhaps, as an absentee landowner, his rather peremptory note was objected to.

Figure 5.3 shows the land requested by those owners in Ickleton (mentioned above), seven of the names are the same on both maps showing a continuity of occupation and land use over the intervening years. As to what became of the land, this is a more difficult question to answer. The first OS large scale map for the area under study was the 25 inches to the mile dated 1886, and though this is a wonderful historical source showing every building and even

FIGURE 5.2. Maps of Great Shelford showing William Dobson's allotment.

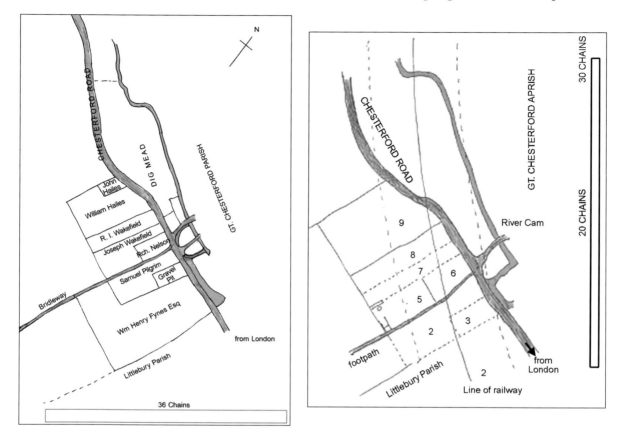

FIGURE 5.3. Map of Ickleton showing allotments requested.

every tree[33] it does not show ownership and it comes over 70 years after the enclosure of both Ickleton and Stapleford. It is unlikely that farmers involved in enclosure would still be alive in 1886. Great Shelford is the latest parish enclosed for which we have commissioners' records – 1835 – even this is 51 years before the first OS map made on a scale large enough to identify individual houses. The piece of land allocated to William Dobson is still shown as a piece of land by 1886 and had not been built on, though ownership is not shown on this map. There is a small anomaly between the amount shown in the 1835 Enclosure map, just over 7 acres (2.83 ha), and that shown on the 1885 map, just over 8 acres (3.24ha). His claim was for 6 acres 5 roods 20 perches [2.4 ha] of copyhold and 1 acre (*c.*0.4 ha) arable plus something for his right of common so 8 acres would seem nearer the correct amount. Consequent upon the *Tithe Commutation Act* of 1836, detailed parish maps were produced which showed how the land was used, it was divided into arable, pasture or woodland. Unfortunately if the parish was enclosed before 1836, the process of enclosure normally commuted the tithes to extra land for the tithe owner in lieu of his tithes and so no maps or schedule would be needed later on. Neither Ickleton (1810) nor Great Shelford (1835) has tithe maps. But maps can reveal clues as to how the land requested was used. Although the land at Ickleton east of the turnpike road shown on Figure 5.3 is wet the land on the west of the turnpike, the land that was requested, is slightly higher and based on a band of gravel as evidenced by the gravel pit shown on the map. By 1843, the railway map shows a windmill on plot 5, against the footpath or bridleway, and indeed those parts of the land that have not disappeared under the railway and two branches of the M11 motorway, are still (2010) being used to grow crops. As for Great Shelford, William Dobson's plot and indeed all that land bordering the turnpike, were built on with between-the-wars ribbon development houses.

It would thus seem that commissioners were indeed influenced by the requests of small owners; the large owners had so much land that requests were superfluous, although they did exchange land with other owners by mutual agreement.[34] This may well be a major reason for the fact that there appears to have been little opposition to the enclosure process on the part of the small proprietors and cottagers of south Cambridgeshire. If they managed to establish their claims to common rights, what they actually received in compensation for the loss of those rights may have been as valuable as anything they had lost, given the fact that they could choose where their allotment was located. As Lord Ernle put it:

> 'There can be no question that, from an agricultural point of view, five acres of pasture, added in individual occupation to the arable holding of a small occupier, and placed near the rest of his land, would have been a greater boon than pasture rights over 250 acres [101ha] of common.'[35]

The commissioners not only needed to redesign an entire landscape, they also needed to manage the transition, in practical terms, from the old landscape to the new. Beckett, Turner and Cowell have suggested that 'Historians, in concentrating on the economic aspects of enclosure, and on some of the more politically significant social effects, have neglected the interests of the farmer and the practice of farming'.[36] The period between the Act and Award from Parliament varied from parish to parish, but however long or short it was, the land still had to be farmed, the fields ploughed, the seeds sown and the harvest gathered. The period was a hiatus, a vacuum as old ownerships were cancelled and new ownerships established but farming life had to continue. During this time it was the commissioners who were responsible for the day-to-day running of the agricultural business. Together with the surveyor and solicitor, they made sure that parity of crops sown and crops harvested was ensured for the people concerned. Susanna Wade Martins has suggested that farmers must have had a sense of disorientation immediately after the new lands were allocated as they would not know where their new lands would be.[37] But Beckett, Turner and Cowell state, 'Much of the work of the commissioners was concerned with ensuring a smooth transition from a pre to a post-enclosure village.'[38]

Becket *et al.* noted that the length of time between Act and Award was on average one year, though this could be much longer if there were a large number of claimants. They also noted that later enclosures could take considerably longer.[39] This is borne out by the figures for south Cambridgeshire, as we have seen; only Great Shelford was enclosed from Act to Award in one year, the average length of time being six years.

The commissioners would set a date for the closure of the moors, heaths and wastes and the termination of all common rights. Great Shelford completed the allotments and extinguished all Common Rights at a meeting between 28 November and 3 December 1834, only five months after the first meeting with the commissioners.[40] Ickleton extinguished all Rights of Common on 2 November 1811, 17 months after the first meeting with the commissioners.[41] So it would seem that not much more than a year's farming had to be organized by the commissioners. Indeed, in some cases they carried out farming operations themselves, although the reasons are unclear. The chequebook stubs for Great Shelford have at least 14 people paid under 'Tillage Account', with sums varying from under £1 to over £80. Some seem to be landowners, for instance, Elizabeth Clarke was paid £83: she would be paying men to plough for her and presenting the composite bill. Others seem to be men ploughing perhaps at the request of the commissioners and being paid directly out of the rates, such as Thomas Betts (£3 5s 7d) and William Dean (14s). [42] All those listed seem to have had property bordered on at least one side by a public road, but this may be coincidental.

The attitude of the farmers themselves to the upheavals to the farming routine caused by enclosure is difficult to gauge as very little has survived of their opinions and hopes: Beckett, Turner and Cowell were of the opinion that farmers, although grudgingly ploughing land that would be used by another, recognised that a certain amount of concurrence was necessary if they were to receive the land they wanted. [43] Those that ploughed and sowed seed during the early stages of the process were not necessarily those that harvested that crop at its end. Most of the parishes that have commissioners' papers have lists of people both paying for and being paid for ploughing. The Stapleford Minute book entry for February 1812 runs: '15–2–1812 – Crown Inn, Great Chesterford – Settled the price to be paid for ploughing and folding and ordered the surveyor to make the account'. [44]

Some records include the instructions given by the commissioners regarding the continuance of the agricultural year. The commissioners for Ickleton posted a notice a month after being appointed giving authority to previous occupiers to benefit from their husbandry even after the land had been allocated to a new owner:

'Also all proprietors who shall sow their land with turnipseed must feed off the turnips arising therefrom notwithstanding the lands on which the same shall be growing may happen to other proprietors.'[45]

And a little later a notice of 4 November 1811 specified that: 'Those who have sown any of their land with Turnip seed will be allowed until March 25 1812 to fold them off.'[46] It must have placated the sowers of the seed to know that they could profit from their work. The Sawston commissioners instructed the incoming owner to pay the sower for the crops he was harvesting as a letter from John Guiver shows:

'I understand the person who had the crop as it stands when the Inclosure took place were to pay for it. Mr Gosling took the crop and I have not had anything for it – as such I beg you will make the deduction for it, as I stand all the Town charges that come against me.'[47]

The transformation of the landscape wrought by the commissioners involved a vast amount of work and by no means was all of this undertaken by local proprietors or their workers. Indeed, just as the commissioner's papers can throw dramatic light on the manoeuvring behind the scenes to choose a commissioner, so too it can provide vital information about precisely who profited from the employment possibilities presented by enclosure. While much has been written of the losses incurred by cottagers at enclosure, rarely mentioned in the enclosure debate was the number who profited from the enclosure process. As Beckett, Turner and Cowell suggest, the 'subject has slipped through the historical net'.[48] Of course the officers, commissioners, surveyors and solicitors made a good living from so many enclosures during the first half of the nineteenth century, and the tithe owners benefited enormously by not only receiving extra land to recompense them for losing their tithes but also from having their fences and hedges paid for by the other parishioners. But other classes of people, often overlooked, also profited; these fall into two categories; the contractors, the people who dug the ditches, planted the hedges, built the drains and bridges, and made the roads, and those who had plowed land that would soon be someone else's, receiving compensation for the loss of their crops. Mingay quotes Arthur Young; 'Consider the great numbers of men that … are constantly employed in hedging and ditching;'[49] each of the above-mentioned categories will be examined in this section.

The local builders, road makers and carpenters must have looked upon the ensuing enclosure as a great opportunity. They would know, from neighbouring parishes already enclosed, the conditions governing the planting of hedges, the draining of the moors to enable the new landowners to plough the once sodden ground, the vast lengths of fencing to be erected and the new straight roads to be built, straighter and wider than any since Roman times. The *Enclosure Act* of 1781 specified that roads built by commissioners should be 40 feet (*c.*12m) wide; the same act also laid down details of fencing.[50] The villages of south Cambridgeshire tended to follow these guidelines; the Thriplow enclosure map shows Turnpike roads as 60 feet (18.3 m) wide, other roads as 30 feet (*c.*9 m) wide and footpaths as 4 feet (1.2 m) wide.[51] Sawston and Harston both specify that turnpike roads must be 60 feet wide and other public roads to be 40 feet wide.[52]

The competition to obtain these lucrative contracts must have been fierce and often several men were employed to undertake parts of the work. Table 5.2 shows a close analysis of the bills presented by the various contractors for payment reveals not only how much they were paid but that some men became contractors to more than one village.

John Morgan worked in two parishes but did not earn as much as the others; John Love worked only in one parish but made a good amount purely on fencing and hedging. Thomas Gell also made a good sum; his figures come

Name	Parish	Fencing	Ditching	Roads	Total
John Love	Sawston	✓			£1200 4s 9½d
John Morgan	Ickleton	✓			£98 6s 3d
John Morgan	Stapleford		✓	✓	£100 1s 0d
				Total	£198 7s 3d
Thos Hopkins	Sawston	✓	✓	✓	£1144 6s 0d
Thos Hopkins	Ickleton	✓	✓	✓	£1486 6s 5½d
Thos Hopkins	Stapleford	✓		✓	£1088 6s 0d
				Total	£3718 18s 5½d
Thomas Gell	Harston	✓			£786 18s 0d
Thomas Gell	Harston		✓		£154 1s 10d
				Total	£940 19s 10d

TABLE 5.2. Contractors earning over £500 or working in more than one parish.

from an insert in the Enclosure Award but little else can be found regarding him. Thos Hopkins worked in three parishes, Sawston, Ickleton and Stapleford, and earned £3718 18s 5½d (perhaps £85,000 by today's standards)[53] a princely sum considering the commissioners earned between £300 and £400 (£6900–£9200) each per parish for being responsible for the whole organisation of the enclosure. Obviously Hopkins had to employ men to do the work and his bill for their wages and beer would be quite considerable, and he presumably had to purchase the hedge plants and timber for the fences; the timber is difficult to cost but the hedge plants can be; Quickthorn plants rose from 5s per thousand in 1777 to 8s per thousand in 1833.[54] The Sawston accounts mention the total of '7000 quicks' which at a cost of 8s shillings per thousand would come to £2 16s and they were to be planted '3 quicks to each foot.'[55] Costs could be cut by growing the plants oneself as seen above but nevertheless Hopkins probably made a substantial sum for himself.

This work did not always go smoothly or meet with approval. At Sawston where there seems to have been much acrimony, the following entry in the commissioners' minute book:

'6–7–1807, The Eagle and Child, Cambridge. – Messrs Jones and Cooper complaint that as drains had not been laid at West Common their land had flooded. Proprietors of small allotments in West Fen Common complained their roads were in bad state of repair. Several small proprietors had carried away the banks from the sides of the Drains to the injury of other lands. Mr Thorpe ordered to find out who they were. Two men were later apprehended and ordered to pay the costs of repairing the banks.'[56]

Enclosure, however long it took, incurred many costs; 'The finance of this outlay on enclosure is one of the least explored features of agricultural and financial history'.[57] Without the accounts found among the commissioners' papers it would be difficult to reveal the true costs of enclosure and how these costs were paid: of particular importance are the solicitor's chequebooks which have survived among the bundles of papers for Great Shelford and Ickleton. The banker for Great Shelford was John Mortlock of Cambridge and the chequebook covers the period 1834–1836, Ickleton's bankers were Searle and Son of Saffron Walden and the stubs list all the payments made throughout the period of enclosure from 1810–1814. They cover the building of roads, drains, fencing, and compensation due to loss of land as a result of road building and damage to property, tillage, printing, surveys and fees.[58] The papers for other parishes are also very detailed, individual items of expenditure include the cost of the Award Book for Ickleton (£13 4s: it needed 35 skins and was bound in London in Russia (a type of leather)); and the payments for the solicitor's 'Chaise hire going and returning having many papers to carry and being also too ill to travel on horseback – drivers and tolls'.[59]

An early nineteenth century estimate of enclosure costs suggested about £1 per acre,[60] Turner quotes Tate's figures as 25s per acre but counters this with figures worked out by Martin estimating the costs for Warwickshire as approximately 11s per acre before 1760 but well over 62s by the nineteenth century. These figures were further refined by Holderness, who worked them out as 10s 5d per acre before 1760, rising to 42s 8d between 1800 and 1815 and 67s 3d thereafter. Michael Turner's own work on Buckinghamshire suggested that the average costs per acre were rising from nearly 17s in the 1760s to 40s in the 1790s and nearly 82s (£4 2s) by 1815.[61]

How do these figures compare with those for south Cambridgeshire? The commissioners' fees for Great Shelford (1834) came to £407 5s 8d each; those of the Surveyor about £650 and of the solicitor £644. The whole cost of enclosing Great Shelford came to £3430, a cost of 28s per acre of the area enclosed. Ickleton, however, cost £5986 9s 0d. Table 5.3 shows the various enclosure officers' fees and Table 5.4 shows the total cost of enclosure and the cost per acre for the three parishes for which records are available.

It should be noted that Gt Shelford was enclosed in only one year, which probably reduced the cost considerably.

These figures include the cost of fencing for the tithe owner and incumbent who had part of their fences paid for out of the enclosure rates, but excludes the cost of fencing which was the responsibility of the proprietor. It also includes parliamentary fees, cost of making the maps and awards and farming costs.

To raise these sums a rate was raised within the parish: sometimes two or three rates had to be raised as costs escalated and prices rose. These lists of ratepayers and how much they paid are also included in the account books of three parishes and whether the rates were paid or not. The following Table 5.5 shows the highest and lowest rate paid by individuals for the three parishes that have available records. Sawston and Stapleford had to raise two rates.

It cannot be assumed that because an owner appears as a 'small owner' in a certain parish he is necessarily a small scale owner overall; in a number of cases he may own a small plot of land in one parish but be a large proprietor, farming land in several parishes.[62] This is certainly the case with Sarah Allix; she was a very small landowner in Sawston but in Stapleford she was the lessee of the Dean and Chapter of Ely Cathedral and the proprietor of Stapleford Bury and the Rectory with its Great Tithes; she owned 310 acres (125.4 ha) of arable land and 275 acres (111.3 ha) of Heath. She received £290 5s 0d 'due to her for

Parish	Commissioners' fees	Solicitors' Fees	Surveyors' fees
Harston/Hauxton 1798	£512 8s 0d	£887	£643 19s 0d
Sawston 1802	–	£195	–
Ickleton 1810	£374	£975	£629
Stapleford 1813	£331 16s 6d	£441	£411
Gt Shelford 1834	£408	£644	£650

TABLE 5.3. Commissioners', solicitor's and surveyor's fees.

Parish	Total cost of enclosure	Cost per acre
Ickleton	£5986	£2 (40s)
Stapleford	£3479	£2 (40s)
Great Shelford	£3430	£1 8s (28s)

TABLE 5.4. Total cost of enclosure per acre.

	Owner or proprietor	Amount – £.s.d		
Sawston				
1803 – highest	Ferdinand Huddlestone	2048	15	7
1803 – lowest	John Allix		3	9
1811 – highest	Richard Huddlestone (crossed out)	390	13	2
1811 – lowest	Sarah Allix		1	6
Ickleton				
Highest	Wm Parker Hammond Esq	1077	6	6
Lowest	Thomas Livermore		10	0
Stapleford				
1812 – highest	Sarah Allix	1039	14	0
1812 – lowest	Richard Foster		3	6
1814 – highest	Sarah Allix	39	0	0
1814 – lowest	Daniel Rydon, Rich Foster not mentioned		2	0

TABLE 5.5. Greatest and least enclosure rates paid by individuals.

fencing in lieu of Glebe and Tithes.' This would have considerably lowered her final costs.[63]

Sometimes a landowner refused to pay these rates and a letter would be sent requesting payment. For example, the clerk to the Ickleton commissioners was ordered to write to those in arrears; written in pencil in the margin notes is: 'Wrote 12 letters 31–8–1812.'[64]

Mingay suggests that the outlay for drainage could also be a major expense and certainly ditching and draining were significant items of expenditure in most south Cambridgeshire villages.[65] It can be difficult to separate the process of digging ditches needed for planting hedges from those for draining wet land so that it can be ploughed and cultivated. Costs for ditching and hedging are often combined but, as far as can be ascertained, the costs of draining the commons and moors can be found in four of the five parishes with commissioners' papers. Some of the costs, of necessity a conservative costing, can be shown – Great Shelford: £350, Ickleton: £199 and Sawston: £680. Stapleford shows no amounts but in 1812 the minutes recount: 'Proceeded to Stapleford to determine the best plan of draining the common and gave instructions to John Morgan to begin cutting the drain'. And further instructions were given to Morgan a year later. [66]

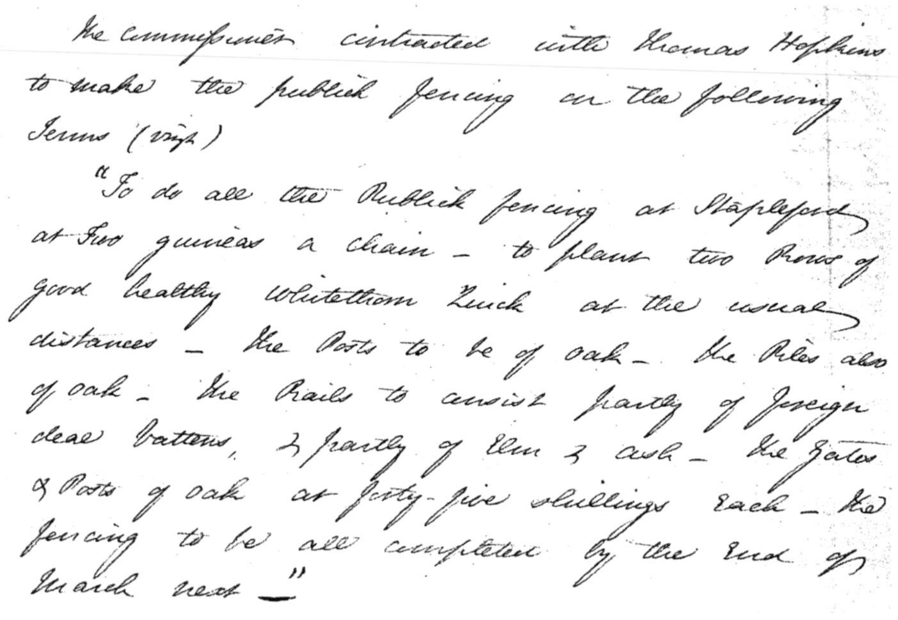

The commissioners contracted with Thomas Hopkins to make the publick fencing on the following terms (viz)

"To do all the Publick fencing at Stapleford at Two guineas a chain — to plant two Rows of good healthy Whitethorn Quick at the usual distances — the Posts to be of oak — the Piles also of oak — the Rails to consist partly of foreign deal battens, & partly of elm & ash — the gates & Posts of oak at forty-five shillings each — the fencing to be all completed by the End of March next —"

FIGURE 5.4. Instructions to John Hopkins.

The costs of fencing for individual owners, and how these varied between holdings of different sizes, is of particular importance because the cost of fencing rises relative to the value of the land enclosed as plot size increases; this was one of the ways in which smaller proprietors lost out at enclosure. We cannot know how each owner divided his land internally, but we can perhaps calculate the costs of fencing the perimeter. In Stapleford, the commissioners paid Thomas Hopkins two guineas a chain for the public fencing[67] (Figure 5.4). This seems a very large sum at a time when labourers were earning just 1–2s a day but, as mentioned above, Hopkins presumably had to pay for the hedging plants, the timber for the fences as well as for labour and beer (Table 5.6).

A small owner may have done his own fencing, thus decreasing the cost, but for the sake of this experiment we must assume that all costs are equal, and can use this figure to compare the likely costs of fencing the largest, and the smallest, allotments.[68]

Adding these costs to the enclosure rates paid by the individuals in question, and dividing by the acreage of the allotments (and ignoring, of course, such things as the costs of internal fencing, subdividing the holdings) gives the costs of enclosure per acre paid by these two men.

The difference between the two men is staggering; William Parkin's final amount of £4.49s per acre is comparable with Ferdinand Huddlestone's of Sawston and Turner's figure of £4 but John Johnson's final amount of £24 is way above this and proves beyond surmise that the small landowner paid appreciably more than the large; it is no wonder the small landowners were apprehensive of enclosure and feared that the costs would be way beyond their means.

But one important factor is missing here. Most allotments of land shared one or more boundaries with other allottees; therefore they also shared the

TABLE 5.6. Cost of ring fencing land, Stapleford, at 2 guineas per chain.

Name	Length in chains	Total cost
William Parkins	175	£367.50
John Johnson	15	£31.50

TABLE 5.7. Total costs of enclosure by acre, Stapleford.

Name	Costs-rates + fencing	Acreage	Cost per acre
William Parkins	£113 + £368 = £481	107	£ 4.49
John Johnson	£4 + £32 = £36	1.5	£ 24

TABLE 5.8. Corrected total costs of enclosure by acre, Stapleford.

Name	Costs-rates + ½ fencing	Acreage	Cost per acre
William Parkins	£113 + £183.7 = £296.7	107	£2.77
John Johnson	£4.4 + £15.75 = £20.15	1.5	£13.43

TABLE 5.9. Enclosure rates per acre for Stapleford, 1814.

Name	Costs	Acres	Cost per acre
Tregonnell Collier	1st Rate: £334 2nd Rate: £13 Total: £347	167	£2.07
Robert Heffer	1st Rate: £298 2nd Rate: £11 Total: £309	163	£1.9
Frances Smith widow of James	1st Rate: 238 2nd Rate: £9 Total: £247	128	£1.9
William Parkins	1st Rate: £106 2nd Rate: £7 Total: £113	107	£1.0
Rev. Chas Mullis, vicar	No rate paid	42	–
John Johnson	1st Rate: £4 14s 6d 2nd Rate: 3s 6d Total approx: £4 18s 0d (£4.40)	1.5	£3.3

costs of perimeter fencing. In the Stapleford Enclosure Award, the land of Mary Johnson wife of John Johnson (she must have actually owned the land) contained this phrase:

> 'The Hedges, Ditches, Mounds and Fences of which said allotment on the **North** side thereof shall be made and forever maintained and kept in repair by and at the expense of the said Mary Johnson and the owner of the same.'[69]

All the other allotments described have a similar clause, showing that the allotee was only responsible for half his boundary, as is usually the case at present. Therefore the amount calculated for fencing is approximately half that shown in Table 5.7, making the correct total enclosure costs as follows in Table 5.8.

This still makes William Parkin's costs comparable with Mr Huddlestone and Mike Turner, but again leaves John Johnson having to pay a much greater amount per acre than the large landowners. Even taking into account the fact that larger plots might have required more subdividing fences, which would even the differences a little, the difference is still marked.

Table 5.9 shows the cost per acre paid by the largest and smallest landowners in the parish:[70]

While smaller proprietors may have paid more per acre for their allotments than the larger landowners, the latter obviously paid more in absolute terms, and some clearly got into financial difficulties. The commissioners for the Ickleton enclosure ordered Mr Pemberton to write to Mr Hammond of Ickleton or his agent: 'to inquire whether he intended to sell part of his estate to offset cost of Inclosure.'[71] Mr Hammond leased Ickleton Priory, one of the manors of Ickleton, from the Dean and Chapter of Windsor: it included 360 acres (145.7 ha) in the open fields and 40 acres (16.2 ha) of pasture, now old enclosure. As Lord of a Manor, he was considered to be the owner in enclosure matters;[72] as his rate for Inclosure was a staggering £1077 6s 6d it is understandable that he might have been obliged to sell some of his property.[73] Mr Hammond did indeed sell some land, as a receipt from John Hill for 'purchase of old enclosure by Mr Hammond' is in the account book.[74] An interesting side-light on Mr Hammond is a note saying that the 'Sale of the Old Enclosure can go ahead when Mr Hammond comes of Age.'[75] An anomaly arises here; how could he have sold land that he rented from the Dean and Chapter of Westminster? We can only assume that Mr Hammond must have had some land that he owned himself. This was probably so as the entry for 10–14 May 1813 notes:

'Commissioners sold by auction the following allotments of land **belonging** to Mr Hammond for the purpose of raising the proportion of the expenses of obtaining and executing the act. Lot 1 – 9 acres 3 rods in South Field – to Mr Gosling for £820, Lot 2 – 2a 3r 3p an Old Enclosure called ? Buchinglers to Mr John Hill £240, Lot 3 – 5a or 0p in Dig mead to Mr John Gosling for £270.'[76]

Turner has emphasised that 'Most arrears arose from distress rather than from opposition to enclosure, or obstinacy.'[77] Some landowners were, however, not so much unable as unwilling to pay their allotted rate. Mr Pytches of Ickleton, as we have seen, is one notable example. The commissioners reported that they 'had taken possession of proportion of Mr Pytches estate in consequence of his not paying his rate.'[78] Conversely, some of the smaller proprietors were occasionally given help with their enclosure costs in the form of a mortgage. The commissioners for the Stapleford enclosure thus 'executed a mortgage of the allotments set out to James Smith and Frances his wife to John Heath of Stapleford, Higler, for the sum of £247 8s 6d being the proportion of the Just Rate charges upon the said allotment.'[79]

The enclosure commissioners' papers provide an unparalleled view of the practical character of the enclosure process; of the great range of activities, and the complex management, involved in transforming the old open landscape into the new, enclosed one. They are well worth seeking out by historians.[80]

The next question we must address is that of how far the revolution in the landscape was matched by a revolution in the social and agricultural character of local communities.

Notes

1 Chapman (1993), 51.
2 Turner (1980).
3 Paxman (1999), 17.
4 Mingay (1989), 23.
5 CUL ADD 6013.
6 CRO 107.
7 CUL DOC 651, 163, 155, 211, (1802).
8 CUL ADD 6069; 6068 (1812).
9 CUL DOC/5 (1810).
10 CRO Q/RDc 70, Fowlmere Enclosure Award.
11 CRO P136/5/1 Sawston.
12 CUL DOC 652 Great Shelford.
13 CRO Q/RDc 50 Q/RDc 70.
14 St John's College Archives D99, Letter dated 8 March 1844.
15 CUL ADD 6065, Sawston.
16 CRO 107, 12 November 1810, Commissioner's Minute Book.
17 CRO 124/P78 Q/RDc 50.
18 CRO 107, 29 October 1812, Ickleton Minute Book.
19 CRO 107, 10 January 1834.
20 CUL DOC 6065, same date.
21 CRO 107, Ickleton, Commissioner's Minute Book.
22 CUL DOC 651/177.
23 CUL ADD 6068. 2 August 1813.
24 Wade-Martins (1999), 125.
25 CRO 107, unindexed (1811) Ickleton.
26 CUL DOC 640/81.
27 CUL DOC 640/70.
28 CUL DOC 640/74, 75, 77, 78, 79 and 80.
29 Wright (1992), 21.
30 CUL DOC 652/81, 104.
31 CUL ADD 6069, 11 June 1812.
32 Mingay (1997), 84.
33 The 1886 25 inch map for Thriplow shows a tree in the school grounds which was remembered by the author and felled within living memory.
34 CRO 107 unindexed, Ickleton Minutes 1810.
35 Ernle (1912), 159.
36 Beckett *et al.* (1998), 141.
37 Wade-Martins (1999), 125.
38 *Op. cit.* in note 36, 153.
39 *Ibid.,* 142.
40 CRO R72/54.
41 CRO 107.
42 CUL DOC 652/21.
43 *Op. cit.* in note 36 153.
44 CUL DOC 651/223 Sawston nd; CUL ADD 6068 Stapleford Tillage Account 1813/14.
45 CRO 107 Ickleton Minute Book, 31 August 1810.
46 *Ibid.,* 4 November 1811.

47   *Ibid.*; CUL DOC 651/192 Sawston.
48   Beckett *et al.* (1998), 141.
49   Mingay (1997), 145.
50   *Ibid.*, 49.
51   Thriplow Enclosure Map 1840.
52   CUL ADD 6065; CUL ADD 6031.
53   Multiplied by 23 as suggested in Munby (1996), 38.
54   Harvey (1972), 146.
55   CUL DOC 651 155, 1802.
56   CUL ADD 6065.
57   Presnell (1956), 349, quoted in Turner (1981), 236.
58   CUL DOC 652; CRO 107/137 Ickleton bundle IV.
59   CRO 107/137 Ickleton bundle IV.
60   Board of Agriculture (1808) *General Report of Enclosures*, as quoted in Turner (1981), 238.
61   Turner (1981) references quoted include Tate (1952); Martin (1967), 138; Holderness (1971); Turner (1973), 286–7.
62   Mingay (1997), 116.
63   CUL ADD 6068 Stapleford.
64   CRO 107/26 August 1812.
65   Mingay (1997), 109.
66   CUL ADD 6067 Gt Shelford; CRO 107 Ickleton; CUL DOC 651 Sawston; CUL ADD 6068 Stapleford.
67   CUL ADD 6068 Stapleford 7 December 1812.
68   CRO R60/24/64 1812.
69   CRO Q/RDz7 84–128, 1814.
70   CUL ADD 6068 6069.
71   CUL DOC 640/32.
72   Allen (1992), 72.
73   CUL DOC 640/32.
74   *Ibid.*, no date.
75   *Ibid.*, 11 November 1813.
76   CRO 107, Ickleton 10–14 May 1813.
77   Turner (1981), 240.
78   CRO 10, 10 January 1814.
79   CUL ADD 6068, 28 February1814.
80   Wittering (2004), 104.

CHAPTER SIX

Post-enclosure Agriculture

'Whoever could make two ears of corn, or two blades of grass to grow on a spot of ground where only one grew before, would deserve better of mankind, and do more essential service to his country than the whole race of politicians put together.'
Jonathan Swift, *Gulliver's Travels*, 1726

As discussed in Chapter 3, some innovative farmers put much 'industry and effort' into their farms before enclosure and were often successful in growing the new crops of turnips and trefoils. Their abilities in this respect must, of necessity, have relied on the agreement and co-operation of their neighbours; the full integration of turnips, in particular, into field rotations was difficult as long as the traditional three-course rotation was in place. In addition, contemporaries, and later commentators, have highlighted the many other ways in which open field agriculture held back productivity; stinting rules often restricted the number of animals farmers might keep, and the regulation of open field management restricted individual choice. The small size and the scattered nature of the multiple strips reduced the efficiency with which labour could be deployed on holdings, and this in turn reduced the intensity with which crops could be weeded, ground prepared, and the soil improved through applications of manure or fertiliser. Robert Shiel in describing husbandry experiments undertaken at Rothamsted found that by the mid-nineteenth century much of the old arable land in Britain appears to have lost two-thirds of the soil nitrogen which was present before farming began.[1]

One of the reasons given in the preamble to most enclosure Acts was the benefits which the revolution in landholding would bring in terms of increased crop yields through the use of the four-course rotation. This involved, as already described, the regular integration of courses of roots and grasses within arable rotations, that is – year One: Clover; year two: Wheat; year three: turnips; and year four: Barley.

Both the clover and turnip tops were grazed by sheep or other livestock, so that manure was also added to the soil, rotations such as this enabled the farmer to achieve continuous use of the soil without recourse to fallowing. Yields were rather low by modern standards, but at the same time the agricultural inputs were small and were derived almost entirely from local sources of energy and nutrients.[2]

Before assessing the extent to which enclosure in south Cambridgeshire did indeed lead to a major change in farming methods, and the consequences which this may have had for agricultural productivity, it is important to emphasise certain aspects of the 'new husbandry' which are not, perhaps, always given sufficient prominence in agricultural literature. Most historians emphasise the benefits that the new crops brought to arable farming:

> 'Turnips and clover, when integrated into arable rotations, have an impact on output per acre. Turnips can smother weeds, and when sown in rows can easily be hoed, they provide fodder, leave organic residues when ploughed in, can improve the soil structure because they are deeper rooted than grain crops, and provide a break between grain crops to help prevent the carry-on of disease. Much the same is true of clover except it is not hoed. By far the most important property of clover, however, is its ability to fix nitrogen from the air.'[3]

But many contemporaries were equally aware of the more immediate benefits which the new crops brought; simply in terms of the additional livestock which could be kept and hence the increased amounts of money that could be made from sales of meat or wool. Pusey describes the four course rotation as 'Wheat providing the bread, barley the beer, and clover and turnips the beef and mutton.'[4] South Cambridgeshire may have been a predominantly arable area, even more so after the ploughing of the heaths and the moors, but stock always comprised a significant part of the farming business, and enclosure by removing fold courses, allowed more farmers to become involved in sheep production. Havinden came to the same conclusion in his study of the open fields of Oxfordshire, he points out that that the use of the new crops enabled more stock to be kept and therefore improved the fertility of the fields.[5] Overton points to one other advantage of the new crops:

> 'This new system of farming was remarkable because it was sustainable; the output of food was increased dramatically, without endangering the long-term viability of English agriculture. But just as a sustainable agriculture had been achieved, the development of chemical fertilisers and other external input undermined this sustainability. An essentially organic agriculture was gradually replaced by a farming system that depended on energy-intensive inputs dependant on the exploitation of fossil fuels.'[6]

The second point to emphasise is that the importance of the 'four-course rotation' can be easily exaggerated: it was rarely practised in its pure form.[7] The great south Cambridgeshire 'improver', Samuel Jonas, describes his own practice as: 'First year, fallow for turnips, rape or mangold-wurzel, second year, Barley, third year, seeds, tares or peas and the fourth year, wheat or oats.'[8] It is also important to emphasise that the benefit of the root crops were related to the method of cultivation, and that they only functioned as a 'cleaning' crop if well hoed and weeded. Jonas noted that in Mr Gooch's time (1811) the turnip seed had been:

> 'Generally sown broadcast, in a few instances only, were drilled and that the weeding not being known by the inhabitants, the work was done by persons who travel the country for that purpose, and who make great earnings.'[9]

He rightly pointed out that turnips only thrive if they are sown with a drill and hoed either by hand or with a horse hoe. Not only does this benefit the turnips but it also renders the land free of weeds for the next crop.[10] From the farmers' point of view one drawback was that: 'the new crops [turnips and clover] required finer seed beds, improved weed control, liming and drainage before they would grow',[11] which would certainly require more labour. It is with these qualifications in mind that we need to address the question of how soon and how far the new husbandry was adopted in south Cambridgeshire after enclosure, and with what benefits.

The first question is easily answered. The following agreements reveal that a version of the four course rotation was implemented as soon as possible once the enclosure process had started. A lease of 457 acres (185 ha), including 167 acres (67.6 ha) of heath, from the Lord of the Manor of the Bury, Thriplow, to Joseph Ellis in 1841 gives explicit instructions as to the way he must cultivate his fields:

> 'Joseph Ellis is to farm, manage and crop all the arable lands belonging, according to the four course shift in manner following, that is to say, One fourth part Wheat, one fourth part Barley or Oats, one fourth part either Clover layer, Trefoil Cinquefoil or other Vegetable crops save and except that one half part thereof may be Cinquefoil or Clover Layer trefoil or other green or vegetable crops. And the other half part thereof Peas and Beans and the remaining quarter part thereof to be Clean Summers Fallow save and except that one third part thereof may be Turnips or one half part thereof maybe Tares. Provided that such Turnips and Tares are folded and fed off by Sheep or other stock.'[12]

This is a complicated course of cropping which, while clearly deviating from the normal four course, preserves all of its essential features, except for allowing some degree of regular fallowing. The lease was drawn in 1841, only one year into the enclosure process, and reveals how keen some landowners were to introduce the new cropping systems. Another lease, also from Thriplow but for Manor Farm, owned by St John's College, directs the lessee to introduce a four course rotation and in a similar manner to the other lease instructs the tenant that this should involve:

> 'One-forth [*sic*] part to be Fallow or Turnips, Mangle, Coleseed or Tares, to be fed on the land or consumed on the premises by sheep or cattle (the Tares not to be allowed to stand for seed, and no Tares to be sown on the fallow shift in the last year). One-fourth to be Barley or other Corn; one-fourth part to be clover or artificial grass seeds, or pulse crop, but only a moiety thereof to be a pulse crop, and the same to be twice hoed and kept clean. One fourth-part to be Wheat or other corn, and so leave the said Arable land at the expiration of the term.'[13]

The fact that in both cases it is assumed that some land will continue to be fallow is noteworthy: turnips never completely replaced bare fallows, which would be useful as a method of weed control.

The second question – that of the extent to which the new crops raised productivity – is less easy to answer, because of a paucity of relevant sources of information relating to crop yields in the period both before, and just after, enclosure. The 1801 crop returns have been used in chapter three but there are few of them and they were discontinued in 1802 following a good harvest, and there was no further national collection of agricultural statistics until 1867 when a continuous series of surveys began. Even these give crop acreages and livestock numbers only; crop yields per acre were not recorded until 1885, some 40 years after the last enclosure date in our area.

The best records for agricultural output are individual farm records, though Turner points out that only large estates kept records in any detail and Cambridgeshire was not known for its large estates. Occasionally farm records of working farmers do survive and these records are of great importance. An exhaustive search of the current records has not, unfortunately, revealed any farm record books that record yields per acre in south Cambridgeshire.

The sources are thus limited but it is possible to say something, albeit tentatively, about the character of crop yields across the enclosure period. Although most parishes in the district commuted their tithes at enclosure, a few did not, and for these, tithe files and tithe awards survive, documents which can be used, with caution, to gain some picture of what local people considered were normal yields. Following the *Tithe Commutation Act* of 1836, commissioners were sent out to each parish to record details and make maps. These sources fall into two categories, the Tithe map and attached schedules record owners and the type of land owned, usually divided into arable, wood, grass and occasionally orchards. It also shows the number of bushels of wheat, barley and oats for the whole parish. The second record is the Tithe file, which note the type of soil and farming for a given parish, the amount of tithes paid and often but not always the acreages of crops grown. Thus we can divide the bushels into the acreages and get the yield per acre as shown in Table 6.1. We need to be careful, however, for the figures often appear similar and rounded: Turner reminds us that these returns were often 'Nominal figures when the assistant commissioner made estimates rather than ascertaining the true quantities and only relate to the tithable portion of the produce.'[14]

In Table 6.1 two local parishes have tithe records made some time after enclosure – Foxton and Shepreth – but the Foxton tithe file unfortunately fails to include crop acreages. In addition, three parishes have tithe records compiled during the process of enclosure – Melbourn, Newton and Thriplow. [15] Table 6.2 shows crops per acre for those parishes where the figures are usable; for two parishes, these calculated yield figures can be compared with those given by Vancouver in the 1790s.

Such as they are, these figures suggest that there was no great revolution in yields across the enclosure period. This is especially so when it is remembered that the land, in terms of cereals, was then less intensively cropped for two years in four, rather than two in three. These figures are, moreover, broadly in line with those presented by Mr Thurnall, a Duxford farmer, to the select committee of 1836: of 25 bushels of wheat and 25 bushels of barley per acre.[16] These figures can

TABLE 6.1. Crop yield per acre from Tithe records.

	Melbourn	Thriplow	Newton	Shepreth
Wheat				
Acreage	565	400	257	240
Yield (bushels)	1088	736	326	375
Yield per acre	19	18	13	16
Barley				
acreage	565	600	257	240
Yields (bushels	1929	1305	579	665
Yield per acre	34	22	23	28
Oats				
Acreage	565	100	257	240
Yields (bushels)	2777	1879	833	957
Yield per acre	49	19	32	39

TABLE 6.2. Comparison of yields (bushels) per acre between Vancouver (1794) and tithe records 1838/1840.

Parish	Wheat		Barley		Oats	
	Vancouver	Tithe	Vancouver	Tithe	Vancouver	Tithe
Shepreth	22	16	26	28	22	39
Thriplow	24	18	24	22	24	19

TABLE 6.3. Comparison of acreage per crop pre and post-enclosure. *Source*: 1838–47 Tithe files; NA MAF 68 (1867).

Parish	Wheat		Barley		Oats	
	1838–47	1867	1838–47	1867	1838–47	1867
Melbourn	565	975	565	1123	565	107
Thriplow	400	452	600	390	100	101
Newton	257	173	257	258	257	44
Shepreth	240	228	240	269	240	48

be compared with Duxford's figures recorded by Vancouver in 1794; of wheat as 18 and barley as 24 bushels per acre (wheat has thus risen by 38% but, as the acreage cropped each year under the new system was 25% rather than 33%, the real increase would have been around 4%). It is perhaps worth noting that Thurnall, in his evidence to the 1836 Select Committee, claimed to have made no profit for four years, the failure of turnips resulting in sheep being kept at a loss, less wheat grown as the price was so low and that less manure was made during the summer. He went on to state that two Duxford farmers were in jail as a result of debt, and that 'We are paying fifty per cent more for labour than we ought to do, as a sort of premium of insurance, to prevent our farms being burnt down.'[17]

Yields may not have increased dramatically as a result of enclosure, perhaps because, as we have seen, elements of the 'new' husbandry had already been adopted in the open fields; and possibly also because the enclosure and cultivation of the local heaths had brought into use land of poorer quality, thus depressing average yields per acre. However, both contemporary and recent historians have also argued that the production of cereals was increased by this same expansion of cultivation as more land was now being cropped. Table 6.3 compares the acreage per crop of wheat, barley and oats before or at enclosure and 30 years after, in 1867, using the tithe files and the Government crop returns.

Wheat, barley and oats represent the amount of grain grown and by adding and contrasting them, one can see that one parish (Melbourn) decreased but

Parish	Acreage under crops	Wheat	Barley	Oats	Beans	Peas
Duxford	2813	860 (31)	780 (28)	95 (3)	101 (4)	47 (2)
Fowlmere	2007	352 (18)	466 (23)	190 (9)	6 (0.3)	40 (2)
Foxton	1459	288 (20)	361 (25)	10 (1)	88 (6)	43 (3)
Harston	1574	347 (22)	351 (22)	66 (4)	87 (6)	34 (2)
Hauxton	570	117 (21)	106 (19)	19 (3)	6 (1)	7 (1)
Hinxton	1501	302 (20)	355 (24)	13 (1)	7 (1)	5 (0.3)
Ickleton	2457	550 (22)	514 (21)	96 (4)	65 (3)	26 (1)
Melbourn	3885	975 (25)	1123 (29)	107 (3)	10 (0.2)	63 (1)
Meldreth	1961	408 (21)	416 (21)	82 (4)	161 (8)	37 (2)
Newton	958	173 (18)	258 (27)	44 (4)	3 (0.4)	0
Pampisford	1212	280 (23)	323 (27)	47 (4)	20 (2)	64 (5)
Sawston	1581	235 (15)	301 (19)	83 (5)	35 (2)	40 (3)
Shelford Gt	1725	455 (26)	417 (24)	118 (7)	4 (0.2)	21 (1)
Shelford Lt	678	135 (20)	147 22)	17 (3)	10 (1)	14 (2)
Shepreth	1147	228 (20)	269 (23)	48 (4)	36 (3)	11 (1)
Stapleford	1463	261 (18)	329 (22)	86 (6)	0	17 (1)
Thriplow	2120	452 (21)	390 (18)	101 (4)	7 (1)	58 (3)
Whittlesford	1191	280 (24)	305 (26)	86 (7)	16 (1)	16 (1)

TABLE 6.4. Crop Returns 1867: corn crops, acreage/(% of total). Source: NA MAF 68 (1867).

three parishes increased their acreage of grain.

A more detailed examination of the 1867 figures shows why. Crops are divided into three categories: 'Corn Crops', which were crops harvested and dried; 'Green Crops', which were probably harvested and eaten fresh, and 'fallow or uncropped arable land, clover and artificial grasses under rotation, and permanent meadow, pasture and grass not broken up'. This last category specifically excludes Heath or Mountain Land, in other words any surviving areas of rough grazing (of which there can have been very little in the district by 1867): Table 6.4 shows the 'Corn' crops.

The first impression on looking at Table 6.4 is how little the corn crops have changed since the crop returns of 1801. The only significant change is the dramatic fall in the acreage devoted to rye, with only Stapleford growing as much as 22 acres (8.9 ha; 1.5%) in 1867. The second impression is the similarity of the relative percentages of the other cereal crops; only Fowlmere stands out in devoting nearly 10% of its acreage to oats:

Table 6.5 shows the acreage for 'Green Crops'. The majority of the 'green crops' cultivated in 1867 were for animal feed, rather than human consumption. The figures show much variation in the precise balance of crops, and particularly in the relative proportions of turnips/swedes. Evidently, local farmers frequently substituted Lucerne or rape/cabbage for the root course in rotations: indeed the tithe commissioner for Shepreth commented in 1836 that 'Cole seed is frequently grown instead of turnips, occasionally this is suffered to come to maturity for seed'.[18] Twenty years after the last enclosure, the 1867 crop returns show potatoes as a commercial crop, although the Vicar of Stapleford mentions them being grown in the open fields in 1811, Vancouver mentions potatoes being grown in gardens in 1789 and reports that the practice in Cambridgeshire was to mix potato flour with wheat to make bread. Potatoes were scarcely known

Parish	Potatoes	Turnips/ swedes	Mangolds	Carrots	Cole/rape/ cabbage	Lucerne exc. clover/ grass
Duxford	2 (0.1)	186 (7)	17 (1)	0	58 (2)	9 (0.3)
Fowlmere	13 (1)	249 (12)	52 (1)	2	52 (3)	60 (3)
Foxton	13 (1)	116 (8)	22 (1.5)	1	38 (3)	90 (6)
Harston	10 (1)	95 (6)	43 (3)	4	46 (3)	59 (4)
Hauxton	3 (0.5)	20 (4)	22 (4)	1	28 (5)	5 (1)
Hinxton	1 (0.1)	160 (11)	74 (5)	0	115 (8)	18 (1)
Ickleton	5 (0.2)	218 (9)	89 (4)	0	91 (4)	85 (3)
Melbourn	13 (0.3)	489 (13)	79 (2)	6	113 (3)	241 (6)
Meldreth	15 (1)	136 (7)	31 (2)	1	99 (5)	111 (6)
Newton	3 (0.3)	160 (17)	11 (1)	3	10 (1)	27 (3)
Pampisford	2 (0.2)	121 (10)	32 (3)	0	74 (6)	3 (0.2)
Sawston	6 (0.4)	109 (7)	63 (4)	0	30 (2)	146 (9)
Shelford Gt	4 (0.2)	26 (2)	62 (4)	3	180 (10)	51 (3)
Shelford Lt	2 (0.3)	95 (14)	25 (4)	1	0	5 (1)
Shepreth	2 (0.1)	156 (14)	26 (2)	3	10 (1)	27 (2)
Stapleford	6 (0.4)	137 (9)	23 (2)	0	75 (5)	51 (3)
Thriplow	13 (0.1)	170 (8)	220 (10)	11	42 (2)	90 (4)
Whittlesford	5 (0.4)	59 (5)	37 (3)	1	84 (7)	8 (1)

TABLE 6.5. Crop returns 1867, Green Crops, acreage/(% of total). *Source*: NA MAF 68 (1867).

Parish	Bare fallow or uncropped	Clover/sown grass	Permanent pasture exc. heath	Total area under crops
Duxford	103 (3)	330 (11)	224 (8)	2813
Foulmire	19 (1)	434 (22)	71 (4)	2007
Foxton	46 (3)	495 (34)	148 (10)	1459
Harston	140 (9)	111 (7)	180 (11)	1574
Hauxton	8 (1)	41 (7)	169 (30)	570
Hinxton	30 (2)	249 (17)	170 (11)	1501
Ickleton	243 (10)	327 (13)	148 (6)	2457
Melbourn	34 (1)	442 (11)	177 (5)	3884
Meldreth	84 (4)	160 (8)	217 (11)	1961
Newton	7 (1)	175 (18)	82 (9)	957
Pampisford	2 (0.2)	198 (16)	93 (8)	1211
Sawston	78 (5)	133 (8)	307 (19)	1581
Shelford Gt	55 (3)	212 (12)	115 (7)	1725
Shelford Lt	4 (1)	129 (19)	96 (14)	678
Shepreth	9 (0.7)	173 (15)	151 (13)	1147
Stapleford	197 (13)	170 (12)	88 (6)	1463
Thriplow	110 (5)	331 (16)	123 (6)	2120
Whittlesford	37 (3)	162 (14)	92 (8)	1190

TABLE 6.6. Crop returns 1867, Clover and Grass, acreage/(% of total). Source: NA MAF 68 (1867).

before 1767,[19] and were originally used to feed cattle. 'They were important addition to the diet as they contain Vitamin C and their nutritional value per acre is greater than that of cereal crops.'[20] In Northumberland, it was said that: 'In the vicinity of great towns, potatoes are the chief fallow crop.'[21] Even as late as 1867 there are very few carrots and potatoes grown and even the Fenland parishes devoted no more than 2% of their area to carrots, in sharp contrast to the present when carrots form a large proportion of the crops grown there. In south Cambridgeshire, as elsewhere in England, field vegetables were essentially grown for livestock. As for pasture crops these are shown in Table 6.6.

The figures in Table 6.6 show that only a small proportion of land was fallowed (an average of around 3.6%). Substantial areas were sown with clover and other grasses – around 14.5%. In all, over a third of the cultivated acreage was thus now devoted to good quality livestock feed.

Although turnips, clover and the rest had been cultivated by local farmers before enclosure, they were now being grown on a much larger scale. Whereas in the pre-enclosure period most livestock had been fed on heather, poor fallow weeds, and the indifferent herbage of the overgrazed commons, they were now fattened on turnips and other green fodder. Rather than seeing changes in rotations simply in terms of cereal production, it is perhaps more useful to think of them in terms of the advantages they brought to livestock husbandry; and to consider more generally the development of the latter in this predominantly arable district.

In the late eighteenth and throughout the nineteenth century great interest was taken by farmers and landowners in the work of men such as Coke of Holkham. One such was Jonas Webb who rented land in Babraham (just outside the area studied here) from 1822. He reared Southdown sheep:

> 'I had the conviction that the Southdown breed would produce more mutton and wool of the best quality per acre than any other breed … on the arable land of this county, where sheep are regularly folded, especially where the land is poor and the animals have far to walk to fold.'[22]

Webb's reference to the importance of meat and wool, but not to the dung provided by the animals, is noteworthy in this context. In 1843 he initiated sheep lettings, where he let his rams to local farmers for as much as £200, and his fame spread far and wide. He sold his flock in 1861 when special trains were run to Cambridge for a sale of his Southdowns. Between 1000 and 1400 people sat down to lunch in one of his barns and he could count four dukes, two earls, a count and two barons among his guests. He sold 968 sheep for £10,830.[23] But his lasting legacy was the breeding of the 'Suffolk' sheep. His father kept Norfolk Horns and he crossed those with Southdowns to improve the wool and meat, this produced the most ubiquitous breed of Great Britain, the Suffolk:[24]

Originally renowned as a producer of mutton, the breed has developed over the years to match consumer demands. Suffolks are now found throughout the world's sheep producing countries. They are the flag-ship breed in the British Isles and recognised as the leading terminal sire on a variety of ewes to produce top quality prime lamb. [25]

Webb was an extreme case but his interest in livestock is a useful reminder that, even in this area, farmers kept large numbers of stock. Indeed, they presumably kept far more stock than before, as the removal of fold courses permitted anybody to keep sheep on their own land. For the new rotations not only allowed stock to be better fed, they also permitted the development of new breeds designed to put on weight quickly, rather than to endure the daily trek from grazing ground to fold and pick meagre feed from the heaths and rough grazings. The improved breeds of sheep with their better meat producing

Parish	Sheep pre-enclosure	Sheep 1867
Duxford	1,200	2315
Fowlmere	550	1891
Foxton	600	1060
Fulbourn	2,800	4568
Hinxton	450	1592
Harston	400 (1806 Gooch)	1072
Newton	480	845
Ickleton	1,400	1899
Pampisford	400	1106
Sawston	460	1480
Great Shelford	1,000 (CUL. Doc 652)	1768
Little Shelford	300 (CUL. Add 6012)	492
Shepreth	300	613
Stapleford	600	1704
Thriplow	1,160	1067
Whittlesford	840	1125

TABLE 6.7. Comparison of number of sheep pre- and post- enclosure. Source: Pre-enclosure sheep numbers from Vancouver (1794), unless stated. Those after, from NA MAF 68 (1867).

capability and their relative immobility, together with the improved winter feed, evidently enabled more sheep to be kept in the same area and this, perhaps, is how we should read the real benefits of the 'new rotations'. They allowed the farmers in an essentially arable area to cash in on the expanding market for meat provided by an increasingly affluent urban population.

It is possible to compare the numbers of sheep kept in south Cambridgeshire parishes before and after enclosure (Table 6.7). The numbers for pre-enclosure sheep in some cases refer to the late eighteenth century but nevertheless provide a good indication of densities a few decades later, on the eve of enclosure.

The numbers of sheep appear on first sight to have risen by a staggering amount, in every parish except Thriplow. But it is probable that we are not, in fact comparing like with like. Vancouver, and the other pre-enclosure sources, were almost certainly recording only the numbers of breeding ewes: lambs did not count as they were soon to be sold and slaughtered (and the numbers would anyway have varied widely across the year). The 1867 returns place sheep in two columns: those 'one year or more' and those 'one year and under one year' under one top heading of 'Number of sheep and lambs'. If we consider only the numbers in the first category, the results are more believable: Table 6.8 shows that 12 parishes have still increased their numbers of sheep and only four have decreased.

The overall average increase is still significant averaging around 20% across the district, with a commensurate increase in the number of young lambs these sheep would have produced. The 1867 returns show that other stock were of less importance in the farming economy of this light, chalkland district (Table 6.9): we have no figures for the pre-enclosure period which allow comparisons to be made.

One of the more unexpected effects of enclosure was the increasing emphasis on meat production in this largely arable district: the observed rise in sheep numbers and the comparatively small rise in grain output can only be a

Parish	Before enclosure	After enclosure	Increase or decrease
Duxford	1200	1432	↑
Fowlmere	550	1267	↑
Foxton	600	809	↑
Fulbourn	2800	2804	↑
Hinxton	450	937	↑
Harston	400	505	↑
Ickleton	1400	1277	↓
Newton	480	595	↑
Pampisford	400	1089	↑
Sawston	460	970	↑
Great Shelford	1000	978	↓
Little Shelford	300	324	↑
Shepreth	300	436	↑
Stapleford	600	1037	↑
Thriplow	1160	403	↓
Whittlesford	840	758	↓

TABLE 6.8. Number of adult sheep pre- and post-enclosure over one year old.

Parish	cows in milk or calf	cattle 2 yrs or more	cattle below 2 yrs	pigs
Abington Gt	20	4	53	162
Abington Lt	12	9	23	124
Duxford	50	46	38	219
Foulmire	23	3	7	243
Foxton	18	23	26	241
Fulbourn	74	61	91	456
Harston	29	6	42	233
Hauxton	8	27	33	36
Hinxton	9	142	1	244
Ickleton	28	20	48	167
Melbourn	66	4	44	613
Meldreth	68	31	65	419
Newton	8	5	66	98
Pampisford	35	77	26	147
Sawston	42	43	28	438
Shelford Gt	33	50	21	249
Shelford Lt	18	10	28	104
Shepreth	33	1	44	321
Stapleford	26	15	22	160
Triplow	25	71	46	226
Whittlesford	20	22	31	123

TABLE 6.9. Livestock returns, 1867. Source: NA MAF 68 (1867).

result of farmers reacting to the demand for more meat from the increasingly industrialised towns. The coming of the railways in the 1840s enabled meat and livestock to be transported further afield than had previously been the case.

The next chapter will study what effect enclosure had on the social and community life of the villages of south Cambridgeshire. Whether the privatisation of the land had an effect on the attitudes of the village elite towards the poor and whether the very idea of personal privacy changed to match the idea of private property inherent in the enclosure of the common fields.

Notes

1   Shiel (1991), 62.
2   Bayliss-Smith (1982), 6.
3   *Ibid.*, 294.
4   Coletta (1944), 88.
5   Havinden (1961), 83.
6   Overton (1996), 3.
7   *Op. cit.* in note 5, 312.
8   Jonas (1847), 7, 40.
9   *Ibid.*, 44
10   *Ibid.*, 45.
11   *Ibid.*, 53.
12   CRO 413/T27 (1841).
13   St John's College Archives D99-20 (1857) Lease of Manor Farm, Thriplow.
14   Turner *et al.* (1996), 24. An English bushel was equivalent in dry weight to 8 imperial gallons or 36.37 litres.
15   NA IR 18/13593 Ickleton (1810) and Stapleford (1801).
16   BPP 8 Vol. 2.
17   *Ibid.*
18   NA IR18/13628.
19   Beckett (1991a), 82
20   Mills (1978), 399.
21   Bailey and Culley (1800), quoted in *Farmers Magazine* I, 423.
22   *Cambridge Independent Press* 6 July 1861. Cambridgeshire Collection.
23   *Ibid.*
24   Wade-Martins (1993), 309.
25   Suffolk Sheep Society web site www.suffolksheep.org.

CHAPTER SEVEN

The Post-enclosure Community

'Ere mockd improvements plans enclosed the moor
And farmers built a workhouse for the poor.'
John Clare, *The Parish.*

So far the consequences of enclosure have been discussed almost entirely in economic and agrarian terms. Many historians, however, have emphasised the deleterious effects of the process on the local poor, now denied their right to exploit the resources offered by the commons and the common fields. We must now look at the post-enclosure impact on the lives of those working in the countryside. Once the land had been privatised what was the effect on population, housing and occupations?

In common with the rest of the country the population of south Cambridgeshire grew in the first half of the nineteenth century. This was exactly the period when most of the south Cambridgeshire enclosures took place. Samuel Jonas, the Ickleton farmer who wrote a prize report for the Royal Agricultural Society in 1847, stated that the population of Cambridgeshire increased from 89,364 in 1801 to 164,459 in 1841: an increase of 75,113 (84%) in a period of only 40 years.[1] The increase in the villages of south Cambridgeshire across the same period was rather less, at around 55%, but significant nevertheless.

It is a common belief that the loss of commons resulted in the emigration of labourers to the industrial towns to find work, and even to the colonies to make a new life for themselves and their families. Those that were left were obliged to become wage slaves to masters who stood them off when times were hard, leaving them at the mercy of the parish officers, who paid them little more than subsistence level or sent them to the workhouse. In the words of George Bourne:

> 'Changes have obliterated the country crafts and cults, breaking down the old neighbourly feelings, turning what was an interesting economy into an anxious calculation of shillings and pence, and reducing the whole village of people from independence to a position bordering on servility.'[2]

But the increase in population of 55% makes it clear that there was no great exodus of the rural population consequent upon enclosure but whether the conditions of the poor deteriorated in its aftermath is a different question. Many contemporaries (and not a few modern historians such as J. D. Chambers[3]) have argued that enclosure, and the more intensive methods of husbandry that

	1831 census	*1851 census*
Gt Shelford (1834–5)		
Population	812	1038
Houses	155	196
Families	171	233
Families in agriculture	83	94
Proportion of agricultural families to total pop.	10%	9%
Thriplow (1840–6)		
Population	417	521
Houses	87	103
Families	88	109
Families in agriculture	62	80
Proportion of agricultural families to total pop.	15%	15%
Fowlmere (1845–50)		
Population	610	597
Houses	124	128
Families	127	129
Families in agriculture	77	80
Proportion of agricultural families to total pop.	13%	13%

TABLE 7.1. Proportion of labouring families to total population after 1830, the figures in brackets are the enclosure dates.

came in its wake, actually increased levels of employment in the countryside. Samuel Jonas in 1847 for example argued that:

> 'This county is purely an agricultural one … how the breaking up and converting the waste into productive land, by thorough-draining the clay district, draining and claying the fens, and the improved system on the light land district, has created such a demand for labour, as to have absorbed the amazing increase of our population since 1801 … This increase has found employment in agricultural pursuits or as tradesmen, mechanics, and artisans, in supplying the wants of those engaged in agriculture.'[4]

The last sentence is probably the most significant in the whole paragraph but first let us study those people still engaged in agriculture. Nationally, the total number employed in agriculture during the first 50 years of the nineteenth century was expanding, albeit at a slower rate than for those in industrial employment.[5] Yet by 1850 only 22% of the British workforce was in agriculture.[6] The amount of employment on the farms such as hedging, ditching, stock keeping and growing the new labour-intensive crops, may have increased during and after enclosure in south Cambridgeshire as elsewhere. It is noteworthy that Little Shelford, when answering question 4 of the Royal Commission on Poor Laws in 1834, stated that there were too many labourers and therefore under-employment:[7] and to some extent the expansion in the demand for agricultural labour is borne out by the census figures, which indicate that the numbers actually employed in agriculture remained fairly stable across the enclosure period. After 1841 the criteria required for the census changed and the figures for families in agriculture were no longer included as a separate category: but the number of these families can still be extrapolated by manually counting the individual families from each census (although the chances of inaccuracies occurring may increase). Table 7.1 shows the proportion of agricultural families to the total population of the three villages enclosed after 1830 using the 1831 and 1851 censuses.

Although the overall population in Fowlmere dropped, the number of 'families in Agriculture' rose. The census enumerator noted on the 1841 returns for Thriplow: 'The Inclosure of the Parish being in Progress has caused this influx of Labourers at this time. No Vagrants.'[8] The other two parishes show no change in the proportion of agricultural families.

The picture of mass unemployment brought about by enclosure seems, therefore, to be inaccurate but it remains true that the number of poor claiming relief (now under the terms of the New Poor Law) rose across the enclosure period. This may indicate that, prior to enclosure, some cottagers working as labourers had been able to exploit common rights to avoid claiming relief during the slack periods of the agricultural year. But the increase was, in fact, relatively small in comparison with the overall rise in the population, and it is hard to see it as other than the consequence of rapid population growth within rural communities which could provide few opportunities for work. It is also noteworthy that the numbers of individuals dwelling in each house in the area did not appear to have increased significantly compared with pre-enclosure figures. Appendix 9 shows the average number of people per house for 21 parishes in south Cambridgeshire from 1851 to 1871. The results are extremely close with the number per house over the three decades all being within the range 4.3–5.2, compared with 5.9–6.5 before enclosure, (see Chapter 2). In part, there may have been some expansion of the village 'envelope' following enclosure, onto the former open fields or onto the lost commons: but on the whole the evidence from manor court rolls and tithe schedules suggests that a growing population was housed through the subdivision of existing dwellings.

A good example is a house in Church Street, Thriplow; in 1700 it was described as 'a messuage', (a moderately large house) and continued to be so until 1826 when it was described as 'two cottages formerly one messuage'; in 1855 'all that cottages mentioned as before and also all that other cottage lately erected and built upon part of the said premises'. In 1865 it was described as 'All those three cottages lately two tenements and formerly one messuage with garden, orchard and close adjoining.' Also 'all that cottage lately erected on said premises'. So what had been one dwelling with its orchard and close was now four dwellings, three of them made by dividing the original house.[9] The small flint and slate cottage built in the grounds has since been demolished and two houses built in its place (2005) (Figures 7.1 and 7.2). The original dwelling, divided into three, was pulled down and rebuilt as one house in the 1970s. So what had originally been one dwelling, then four, is now three dwellings.

The census is not very helpful in differentiating between houses divided and new dwellings, although a mark on the form was meant to denote a separate building, the enumerator did not always bother to make one. The census also shows that some people lived in makeshift accommodation; in 1851 a footnote mentions that Fowlmere had two people in barns, Sawston noted as not

FIGURE 7.1. Flint and Slate cottage, Thriplow.

FIGURE 7.2. Two houses that replaced cottage, Thriplow.

enumerated '3 males, 2 in barns or sheds, 1 in tent,' and Sawston also had a sweep in the 'open field' in 1841.

But in most cases, temporary accommodation was associated with temporary events. The census for Little Shelford had 27 temporary buildings owing to Shelford Park being built; three villages mentioned 'The formation of the

Village	1841			1851		
	No. Single persons	No. houses	% single occupancy	No. single persons	No. houses	% single occupancy
Fowlmere	4	124	3.2	7	128	5.5
Harston	7	151	4.6	5	153	3.3
Ickleton	2	140	1.4	4	140	2.9
Hauxton	1	140	0.7	2	165	1.2
Lt Shelford	4	106	3.8	7	117	6.0
Gt Shelford	0	169	0	5	196	2.6
Pampisford	2	71	2.8	2	70	2.8
Sawston	7	204	3.4	5	225	2.2
Stapleford	1	93	1.1	3	103	2.9
Thriplow	0	92	0	0	103	0

TABLE 7.2. Percentage of single occupancy households.

Shepreth and Cambridge branch of the Eastern Counties Railway causes an influx of many navvies with wives and children.'[10] In Sawston there were six temporary residents, 'males being Scotch Engineers, who are residing here to construct a paper factory.'[11] In Thriplow in 1841 it was noted that:

'The Inclosure of the Parish being in Progress has caused this influx of Labourers at this time':[12] this concurs with Keith Snell's statement that 'Farmers reduced their enclosure expenses … by employing mobile piece workers who followed the awards, taking work wherever enclosure was occurring'.[13]

The census does not, unfortunately, inform us about the relationships between people living in each household before 1851. Table 7.2 compares the number of single occupancy houses and the percentage of the total number of houses in single occupancy in ten villages between 1841 and 1851.

It might be argued that this rise also reflects, in some sense, a growing desire for privacy. Indeed, what is really striking is the fact that in contrast to the present time when so many people live on their own, there were few houses with only one occupant.[14] It is possible that the single poor were moved to the Union Workhouse if they had no-one to care for them, but this argument does not apply to those single people who could afford to live in their own house and yet still chose to have either a lodger, servant or guest living within their house. In part this must reflect pressure on housing, rising rents and the need to provide for members of the family even when grown up but it also shows a different mindset to that of the early twenty-first century.

But social factors may be important too: in the nineteenth century people just could not imagine living on their own in a building; widows, even if they were paupers, had at least one other pauper living with them. In addition, as Richard Wall has pointed out:

'Poor relief was only a contribution to the standard of living. If able the poor were expected to work and could seek assistance from relatives or charity. In addition the policy of the Overseer was often to board one poor person with another. This was one (cheap) way of providing care (the more able of the less able). It offered also some companionship to the poor. And of course it reduced the burden on the poor rates.'[15]

Householder	Lodgers	Servants	Apprentices	Paupers	Other
Farmer		3 house, 1 farm	1		
Farmer	1 Ag lab				
Ag lab	1 Ag lab				
1				1 widow	
1	1 Ag lab				
Publican	1 carpenter				
Farmer		1 house			
Vicar		2 house			
Publican	1				
Farmer		2 house			
1		1 house, 1 general			
1	1 Ag lab				
Ag lab					sick nurse
1				Ag lab's widow	
Farmer		1 house, 1 farm			
1	1 Ag lab				
Clergyman's widow		1 house			
General servant				Mother/ag lab's widow	
Ag lab				Mother-in- law/ carpenter's widow	
Widow		1 house			
Ag lab	Shepherd				
Widow		1 cook 1 groom			
1 Pauper wid Ag lab	1 Ag lab				
Ag lab	1 Ag lab				
1				Mother/widow/ pauper	
Miller			2		
Ag lab				Pauper/ carpenter	
Pauper/ag lab		1 house-keeper		Bricklayer's widow	Housekeeper's granddaughter
Ag lab	Ag lab				

TABLE 7.3. Relationships within houses, Thriplow 1851. Servants are either house servants or farm servants.

The wealthier members of the community, of course, still had living-in servants (Table 7.3), but the number of farm servants 'living-in' was declining rapidly across the enclosure period. Keith Snell, in his seminal study, quotes a witness to a Government Select Committee in 1826/7 who, when asked 'Are farming servants less frequently lodged in farmers' houses than before?' stated, 'They have been less generally so than used to be twenty years ago, within the last few years.'[16] But just as south Cambridgeshire was late in adopting enclosure, some farmers still had servants in husbandry living under their roofs long after the period normally considered the end of such practices – that is, the early 1830s, as Nigel Goose shows.[17] Although the hiring of labourers was abolished by the year 1834, and generally this put an end to servants living in with their masters, the practice did continue in some districts. In Thriplow Joseph Ellis had farm servants living under his roof in 1838.[18] Even in 1851 two large landholders in the parish seem to have had farm servants living under their roof as shown in Table 7.3. We may have hints here that enclosure may have brought about less tangible, but nevertheless valid, changes in the attitudes to personal space and privacy, of the kind discussed by Snell.[19]

After enclosure, the countryside had been changed dramatically; once the last fence post was in place and the last hedge sapling planted, the inhabitants of each parish could stand back and view their new surroundings. Apart from the rather raw newness of the scene, with the mounded soil and newly dug ditches which bordered the fences, another fundamental change had taken place; instead of huge open fields covered in growing crops or ploughed strips, with the furlongs divided by green balks, unimpeded by obstructions except for the odd boundary post or tree, there were large square fields surrounded by fences and young hedges. Where the small landowners had been allotted their land, a virtual forest of fences and young hedges met the eye. But the greatest effect must have been emotional; the land now enclosed was completely private, belonging solely to its new owner, barred to all others. More importantly, the men of the village could no longer walk the many footpaths through the fields from one parish to another, as John Wesley had walked from Stapleford to Thriplow in 1759.[20] Since 33 footpaths, bridle ways and carriage ways were closed in Thriplow at enclosure only a few public footpaths remained and these, together with the roads, were the only routes to work in the fields, adding perhaps several miles to the daily journey. On the other hand the new fields were more compactly placed saving much time and effort. As John Barrell neatly puts it:

> 'For those inhabitants who rarely went beyond the parish boundary the parish itself was so to speak in the centre of the landscape, and every place outside a point on the circumference of the parish, or beyond, the horizon. The roads, as we saw earlier, were for them primarily an internal network, to connect different places within the parish. For those inhabitants accustomed to moving outside, however, and for those travellers who passed through it, the parish was simply one of many in a district defined not by some circular system of geography but by a linear one, as part of a complex of roads and directions which 'intersected' each other.'[21]

Trades and occupations

Wrigley has shown that, in rural counties, employment in the trades of blacksmith, bricklayer, butcher, carpenter, mason, publican, shoemaker, shopkeeper and tailor increased from 134,189 to 164,418 in England and Wales in the 20 years before 1851.[22] It is difficult to provide similar figures for the area under consideration here because the local *Directories* do not cover the smaller villages until the 1840s: moreover, some of the trades used by Wrigley in his study are not mentioned in the *Directories* and, in Table 7.4, a certain amount of

Occupation	Fowlmere 1847	Fowlmere 1864	Foxton 1847	Foxton 1864	Gt Shelford 1847	Gt Shelford 1864	Thriplow 1847	Thriplow 1864	Whittlesford 1847	Whittlesford 1864
Baker	0	3	0	0	2	2	2	2	0	1
Blacksmith	1	1	1	1	2	2	1	2	1	1
Bricklayer	1	2	1	1	2	2	1	2	1	1
Butcher	2	2	0	0	2	1	0	0	2	2
Carpenter	1	2	1	1	2	2	2	2	1	3
Farmer	3	5	6	9	9	6	5	7	9	8
Miller	1	0	0	0	1	1	1	0	1	1
Publican	5	5	3	3	8	10	4	5	3	5
Shoemaker	1	2	0	1	5	3	0	1	2	2
Shopkeeper	1	2	2	3	2	4	2	1	2	5
Tailor	0	2	0	0	0	0	0	0	1	1

TABLE 7.4. Village Industries by parish, 1847 and 1864.

compression and amalgamation has been necessary. 'Mason' has been replaced by 'bricklayer and plumber', and 'glazier and builder' has been included in the same category; 'publican' includes beer retailer, and 'shopkeeper' includes grocer and draper. A comparison can be made of five parishes with relevant enclosure dates, using Kelly's *Directories* of 1847 and 1864.[23]

Wrigley only mentions nine occupations while the Cambridgeshire *Directories* mention many more, including wheelwright, cooper, carrier, brewer/maltster and miller as well as dressmaker and milliner. By 1864, with the coming of the railways, further occupations included railway workers, station masters, inspectors and superintendents. As the country became more industrialised, the number of occupations increased, so that even in purely agricultural parishes, purely agricultural pursuits became diluted by occupations associated with this increasingly industrial world. As the number and variety of manufactured goods increased, even the less well off became consumers. For instance, George Sturt writing of his own village of Bourne in Surrey was of the opinion that:

'The once self-supporting Cottager turned into a spender of money at the bakers, coal-merchants, provision dealer and to spend money he had to acquire it, this meant working for a wage; instead of selling their surplus they sold their labour. Unemployment, hitherto not much worse than a regrettable inconvenience, became a calamity.'[24]

Such changes, far more than enclosure, must have impacted on the lives of the people living in south Cambridgeshire in the middle and later decades of the nineteenth century, and may, to some extent, have ameliorated the problems caused by enclosure and demographic growth. As Samuel Jonas put it in his prize essay, despite the increased population 'This increase has found employment in agricultural pursuits or as tradesmen, mechanics and artisans, in supplying the wants of those engaged in agriculture.'[25]

So the changes in the environment caused by enclosure resulted in a loosening of social commitments as well as a change in attitudes to work and private property. The villages of south Cambridgeshire were moving one step nearer to our modern world.

Notes

1   Jonas (1847).
2   Bourne (1912), 129.
3   Chambers and Mingay (1966).
4   *Op. cit.* in note 1, 35.
5   Mingay (1997).
6   Overton (1996), 8.
7   BPP 30 (1834), question 4 Little Shelford.
8   CRO Census Enumerator's Returns Thriplow 1841.
9   CRO 1700–1865 Manor Court Rolls of Bacon's Manor Thriplow.
10 CRO Census for 1851 Great Shelford.
11 CRO Census for 1851 Sawston.
12 CRO Census for 1841 Thriplow.
13 Snell (1985), 182.
14 Cambridgeshire County Council, personal communication.
15 R. Wall, Cambridge Group for the Study of Population and Social Structure personal correspondence November 2007.
16 *Op. cit.* in note 13, 69.
17 *ibid.*, 71; Goose (2004), 77; (2006), 274.
18 Wittering (1999), appendix A.
19 *Op. cit.* in note 13, 69.
20 Curnock (1909), 17 July 1759.
21 Barrell (1972), 95.
22 Wrigley (1986), 300l.
23 Kelly's *Directories* 1847 and 1864.
24 Bourne (Sturt) (1912).
25 *Op. cit.*, in footnote 1, 35.

CHAPTER EIGHT

The Environmental Consequences
of Enclosure

'... and idle thistles reared
Their bristling heads; the crops began to die,
A prickly growth of lady's bedstraw sprang
And caltrop, and amid the shining corn
Unfruitful darnel and wild oats held sway.'[1]

Remarkably little attention has been focused on the environmental history of enclosure compared with the interest shown in its social, economic and agrarian consequences, in spite of the urgings of historians like Malcolm Chase[2] and John Sheail:

> 'All too many historical studies ... still give the impression that the farmer's crops and livestock were the only living things on the holding. By continuing to overlook the incidence and significance of weeds in the past, such historians may be portraying an unreal world, very different from the one perceived by the farmer and his family.'[3]

Sheail's words, written in the second half of the twentieth century, are equally applicable to historical research in the early twenty-first. This chapter attempts to remedy this gap by examining the history of habitats and biodiversity in south Cambridgeshire both before and after enclosure in the early and middle decades of the nineteenth century.

Academic neglect of the environmental impact of enclosure is remarkable given the extent that interest in nature and the natural world has expanded steadily among the educated elite of Britain over the last three centuries or so. Such an interest, and the emotional and ideological attitudes with which it is associated, was, of course, not universal. In Thomas's words, 'The explicit acceptance of the view that the world does not exist for man and man alone can be fairly regarded as one of the great revolutions in modern western thought',[4] one which developed gradually in Britain from the late seventeenth century. For most of history, God's exhortation in the Bible to 'Replenish the Earth and subdue it',[5] was taken literally: an Act of Parliament of 1566 typically ordered all churchwardens to catch and destroy foxes, polecats, weasels, stoats, otters, hedgehogs, rats, mice, moles, hawks, buzzards, ospreys, jays, ravens and even kingfishers.[6] Churchwardens' accounts reveal many payments for the killing of various birds and animals such as moles, sparrows and hedgehogs which, today, are not seen as a threat, indeed some are considered worthy of protection.[7] By the end of the seventeenth and the beginning of the eighteenth centuries attitudes to nature were gradually changing

from that of man's superiority and dominion over the rest of the living world to
an appreciation of the value and beauty of the natural world in which man was
an integral part. In the course of the eighteenth and nineteenth centuries, poets
such as Wordsworth wrote lyrically about the wild places of the Lake District,
and artists such as Turner painted the mountains of Wales and the Highlands of
Scotland. Queen Victoria visited Scotland for her holidays and what had been
thought of as wild and savage became picturesque and fashionable. 'The rural
landscape began to be experienced as an object of consumption, rather than as a
means of production.'[8] In addition, a feeling of revulsion against the degradation
of both man and animals caused by the industrial revolution, resulted in writers
and artists using their skills to bring such conditions to the notice of people of
influence.

A reaction was even setting in against the regularity and uniformity of the
enclosed fields: some asserted that the countryside was 'Too much chequered
with enclosures for picturesqeness'.[9] Wordsworth bemoaned the fact that:

'Whereso'er the traveller turns his steps,
He sees the barren wilderness erased,
Or disappearing.'[10]

While in 1848 John Stuart Mill similarly complained:

'Is there much satisfaction in contemplating the world with nothing left to the
spontaneous activity of nature; with every foot of land brought into cultivation,
which is capable of growing food for human beings; every flowery waste or natural
pasture ploughed up, all quadrupeds or birds which are not domesticated for man's
use exterminated as his rivals for food, every hedgerow or superfluous tree rooted
out, and scarcely a place left where a wild shrub or flower could grow without being
eradicated as a weed in the name of improved agriculture.'[11]

But the change was a gradual one. As early as 1660 John Ray described his
conversion to the fascination of plants:

'When I was forced, following an illness that affected me both physically and
mentally, to rest from more serious studies, and to spend my time riding and
walking, I had leisure in the course of my journeys to contemplate the varied beauty
of plants and the cunning craftsmanship of nature that was constantly before my
eyes, and had so often been thoughtlessly trodden underfoot. Once I had become
more aware of these wonders, I ceased to pass them by and treat them as matters
unworthy of my attention.'[12]

But such ideas only really spread among an elite not directly connected with
food production: among farmers, understandably, perceptions of the natural
world might be very different. In 1803 William Forsyth argued that it would
be 'of great service to get acquainted as much as possible with the economy
and natural history of all these insects, as we might thereby be enabled to find
out the most certain method of destroying them'.[13] Farmers trying to wrest a
living from weed-infested and insect-ridden soil did not have the time to stop
and contemplate the beauty of their surroundings; it is only now in the early
twenty-first century, after years of using modern and all enveloping methods of

pest and weed control, that farmers are beginning to appreciate that beauty and practicality can go hand in hand to create a healthy, pleasant and productive place to live in. As Landry has emphasised:

> 'Pastoral fantasies have always had a particular appeal for audiences removed from agrarian realities. It takes a knowledgeable eye to recognize the difference between sweet pasture and a sour one, sheep cropped old turf and rye-grass monoculture, healthy fields and too great a presence of yellow buttercups or ragwort – pretty but not indicative of good husbandry.'[14]

'Environmental history' now exists as a growing sub-discipline; and historical ecologists have long attempted to understand the character of habitats and plant communities in terms of past developments and processes. Yet it remains true that the detailed environmental history of the period before the twentieth century has received scant attention from historians, and is certainly seldom integrated into wider histories of agriculture and rural communities.

It is fortunate for us that enclosure in south Cambridgeshire coincided with the increasing enthusiasm for natural history shown by members of Cambridge University. In the words of S. M. Walters, 'The first half of the nineteenth century, in Cambridge as in Britain generally, saw the rise of the professional natural science which is familiar to us at universities, museums and scientific institutions at the present day.'[15] The proximity of the villages of south Cambridgeshire to the University City thus provides a number of important sources of information for the study of environmental change. During the late eighteenth and the nineteenth centuries members of the Cambridge colleges interested in botany made regular excursions to the surrounding villages to explore the landscape and record a variety of natural phenomena. The list of illustrious botanists goes back to John Ray, who wrote the first Cambridge Flora in 1660, it continues through Thomas Martyn (1735–1825), Professor of Botany at the University and a fellow of the Royal Society from 1786; to men like Charles Babington, who was Professor of Botany to the University from 1861 and who kept a detailed journal of his findings, which includes references to 11 of the villages in the area studied here. The Rev J. S. Henslow was Babington's predecessor (1825) and founded the Cambridge Botanic Garden: both men wrote Floras. Henslow's son George (1835–1925) was Professor of Botany at the Royal Horticultural Society (1880) and Lecturer in Botany at the university; he wrote Floral Rambles in Highway and Byeways, in which he divided the plants into habitats such as chalkland, bog, sheepwalks (grasslands) and cornfields. Darwin was the pupil of the first Henslow and accompanied him on many of his journeys in search of plants. Other local naturalists of note include George Nathan Maynard, a keen amateur naturalist living in Whittlesford (1829–1904), whose notebooks span 12 volumes; and Alfred Kingston (1890), both historian and naturalist, who lived at Royston, just over the border in Hertfordshire.

The comments and descriptions supplied by such men can throw a great deal of light on changes in habitats, and especially in the fate of a particular species of plant, for their notebooks and collections can be used to construct a database, first by collector within each habitat, then by parish also within each habitat. As these databases are large and rather unwieldy (Appendix 6), the tables in this chapter only present the most frequently mentioned *or* the rarest plants within each parish. All this information can then be compared with a modern list of plants, compiled by G. G. Compton and updated by Millar and Leslie.[16] Such comparisons are not, of course, without their problems. One is that the names used for certain species of plant have changed over the years (in the databases, constructed here both the old and new names of plants have been included by using Stace's *New Flora of the British Isles* and Perring *et al. A Flora of Cambridgeshire*)[17] Another is that while the printed 'Floras' were designed for general use and included all the plants to be found, many of the early botanists were searching for rarities in the manner described by Thomas Martyn:

> 'The chief part of Cambridgeshire, indeed if we except the Fen country, consists of open Fields, which it is well known are not very productive of the more rare plants: yet there is sufficient Difference of Soil, and enough uncultivated land to reward the Search of a curious Botanist.'[18]

The various sources, in other words, are not always strictly comparable. Nevertheless, to a significant extent it is possible to compare the kinds of plants observed before enclosure with those observed after, within each parish. In addition, it is possible to compare likely losses by looking at the range of species found in what are restricted environments now, but which, before enclosure, covered extensive areas of ground. The effects of enclosure on the fauna of the area are rather less easy to quantify, as less detailed records were kept in the period under consideration, but a variety of references can provide some indication of the likely pattern of change. Of particular importance are the exhaustive notes made by the Rev Leonard Jenyns in 1826 which are kept in the University of Cambridge Department of Zoology. It is worth pointing out here that the ubiquitous grey squirrel was not introduced to England until 1876 after the period of this book.

A more serious difficulty, however, is that enclosure was not the only influence on wildlife in the early and middle years of the nineteenth century. Other aspects of agricultural change, and the activities of sportsmen, gamekeepers and collectors also took their toll, and many of the early records of bird species relate to specimens that were shot. The Cambridge University School of Botany has over one million dried specimens of plants within their Herbarium of which 250,000 are British, all picked by enthusiastic collectors.[19] Charles Babington was one of the first to complain about habitat destruction, but ironically he was also aware of the impact of collectors, of which he was one, describing how in 1840 he went to Linton and:

> 'Walked in the usual hills open places to which Henslow's classes have been accustomed to go, but found that the two open places on which the most interesting plants were found, had been ploughed up. Turning down to the station for *Ophrys aranifera* (early spider orchid), but found that someone had been before us and dug up all the plants.'[20]

Fauna as well as flora were collected on some scale. There are 86 large glass cases of stuffed birds and animals collected by the Hon Richard Neville, eldest son of the third Lord Braybrooke, at Audley End just over the border in Essex: 80% of the specimens are British and were collected around 1840.[21] The Maynards of Whittlesford produced 12 volumes of notebooks, at least three of which had dried specimens mounted within them, and there were probably many other collections made which have now been lost or destroyed.[22] While such things as the ploughing up of heaths and moors probably accounted for the majority of losses of plants that grew there in the nineteenth century, the depredations of Victorian sportsmen and collectors must also be taken into account when analyzing the disappearance of species once common in the area.

This chapter will analyse the effect of enclosure on the five types of habitat within the study area; trees and hedges, moors, heaths, grassland and arable. Within each habitat both flora divided into trees and flowers and fauna into animals and birds will be studied.

Habitats and enclosure

Trees and hedges

Before enclosure the landscape of south Cambridgeshire had been largely bare and open with few hedges or trees: Oliver Rackham has noted that open field agriculture is strongest where there is little or no woodland,[23] and it is certainly true that in historic times before enclosure south Cambridgeshire seems to have been remarkably deficient in woodland. By the time of enclosure some limited areas of woodland had been established in the village 'envelopes' of south Cambridgeshire, mainly in the form of relatively small plantations which will be discussed in more detail later, but for the most part the landscape was, in Cobbett's phrase, 'Bare and treeless'.[24]

Table 8.1 shows a percentage of the total acreage of woodland for various parishes shown on those tithe award maps and schedules still available.

All the parishes were sparsely wooded but Melbourn seems exceptionally so: indeed, the Royal Commission of 1834 stated that Melbourn had no woodland at all.[25] It was, though, noted for its orchards. Most of these woodlands in the parishes of south Cambridgeshire were plantations, often long and narrow running along property boundaries within the village envelope but sometimes planted along field boundaries: Cambridgeshire could be said to be not well wooded but well treed.

TABLE 8.1. Percentage of woodland in five south Cambridgeshire parishes from Tithe Maps and schedules.

Parish	Total acreage	Acreage of woods	%
Duxford	3130	104	3
Melbourn	4567	4	0.08
Newton	987	10	1
Shepreth	1318	30	2
Thriplow	2350	22	1
Whittlesford	1969	100	5

It is, perhaps, worth noting in this context that while historians and historical ecologists have generally emphasised that the nineteenth century was a period in which the quantity of hedgerows was increasing, in certain parts of the country, in old-enclosed districts, this was a period in which there was much loss of this kind of habitat. A government report in 1792 described how 'The grubbing up of hedgerows is become common, and the growth of timber in them thereby totally destroyed.'[26] One contributor to the *Farmers' Magazine* in 1800 observed that:

'Hedges are often allowed to run wild in enclosed parishes, and are sometime 18–20 feet wide. There is a loss of half an acre or five acres in every one hundred acres. They give shelter to immense numbers of small birds and other vermin which destroy the crops, they are full of gaps which allow the cattle to pass through.'[27]

Pusey had similar opinions: 'By removing fences and trees, in many districts, Landlords may add one-tenth to the size of their farms … In Devonshire the roots of Elms meet sometimes in the middle of the field, eating up altogether the food of the turnips'.[28] Hedges, he argued, encouraged mildew in wheat, harboured weeds, provided a home for birds and other creatures that would consume the crops, occasioned serious loss of time to the ploughman in turning at the land's end, and make it almost impossible to use larger implements such as a drill drawn by five horses.[29] Nevertheless, while the disadvantages of hedges were widely accepted by many writers by the start of the nineteenth century, they were planted as a matter of course around newly-enclosed parcels in south Cambridgeshire, and hedges were invariably used by private landowners when they came to subdivide their allotments. The planting width of the former, and the ways in which they should be protected in the initial stages of growth, was set down by the Commissioners as described in Chapter 5, but subsequent management was left to the individual proprietor.

An interesting aspect of this management was the influence of hunting on the height of the hedges. After several years of growth hedges would become too high for hunters to jump, so, to encourage farmers to cut their hedges, hunts often introduced hedge laying competitions. This would result in hedges approximately 4 ft [1.22 m] high, suitable for hunters to jump.[30] Although fox hunting was not common in south Cambridgeshire, hunting the hare was very popular and stories of the amazing stamina of hares were often printed in local newspapers.[31]

One farmer described in 1845 the character of the local hedges:

'In some parts of Cambridgeshire ditches are not used even in raising a fence, a double row of quick being planted upon a raised bank of about 18 inches in height, and guarded on each side with posts and triple rails. The bank is entirely composed of surface soil, which causes the hedge to grow most luxuriantly.'[32]

The dry, porous character of the chalk soils meant that hedges did not need to be accompanied by drainage ditches, unlike those created in clayland districts. As for the planting species used for the new hedges, as Rackham points out, 'The large scale and commercial character of the operation (enclosure) encouraged simplicity';[33] Rackham estimates that around 200,000 miles (321,800 km) of

FIGURE 8.1. Blackthorn growing in a Hawthorn hedge at Newton, Cambridgeshire, April 2005.

hedges were planted during the great enclosure movement between 1750 and 1850.[34] The overwhelming majority of the hedges planted around the villages of south Cambridgeshire, as elsewhere in England at the time, were thus of 'Quick' or Hawthorn, *Crataegus monogyna*. Indeed, these were the only plants specified in the Commissioners' minutes and other enclosure documents. As time went by other plants gradually colonised these hedges, either from seeds dropped by birds or windblown; blackthorn, rose and ash were found to be the commonest species in a survey of Huntingdon and Peterborough enclosure hedges and generally for the midland and eastern counties of England.[35] Some blackthorn *Prunus spinosa* might have been planted with the hawthorn in south Cambridgeshire hedges, but it was never as favoured by enclosers as it tends to spread into the fields (see Figure 8.1).

Some enclosure hedges in southern Cambridgeshire are now composed mainly of elm, probably originating as trees planted for timber. Since the introduction of Dutch Elm disease in the 1960s, these plants grow no higher than hedge height before they suffer again. Once felled, the plant suckers freely from the stump and has gradually taken the place of the original hawthorn over long lengths of hedge. Privet is another species which, in certain circumstances, can gradually take over significant lengths of hedge. As a result of colonisation, and of suckering from timber trees, the hedges in the area today contain a wider range of species than when they were first planted.

A survey undertaken in Thriplow in the summer of 2000 found that while the most frequent hedgerow species was still hawthorn, elder, *Rosa* sp., privet and sycamore were all well represented.[36] Many hedges in the area also contain walnut trees; these were already abundant in hedges by the nineteenth century, but whether planted, or adventitious, remains unclear.[37]

By the later nineteenth century many of the hedgerows in south Cambridgeshire contained timber trees, presumably planted at or soon after enclosure. The planting of such trees was not, of course, stipulated by the terms of the various awards, and many contemporaries doubted whether hedges were a good place to plant timber trees, suggesting instead that they should be grouped into plantations. Some, like the contributor to the *Farmer Magazine* in 1840, worried about the impact of trees on the hedge itself:

> White-thorn will not grow if overshadowed, and a perfect fence cannot be made when the line is broken by hedgerow timber … their roots extend on all sides, extracting the nourishment from the soil, and robbing both the fence and the corn.[38]

Another contributor, in 1800, similarly insisted that 'Hedgerow trees are often seen in a very unthriving state … they are disagreeable objects, and if they thrive … they prove the destruction of the hedge'. He also, noted other problems:

> 'Trees are injurious to the growing of corn. In spring they prevent the land from drying out and in winter they allow the snow to drift. In summer the corn is liable to mildew and large flocks of small birds eat the crops. In pasture the grass under tall trees is poor.'[39]

It is not surprising, then, that as in other late-enclosed landscapes, the hedges of the south Cambridgeshire chalklands today carry relatively few trees. Nor is this entirely a consequence of relatively recent changes. The first edition of the Ordnance Survey (OS) 6 in and 25 in maps of 1886 attempted to record every non-woodland tree, although the size of the symbols on the maps sometimes prevented trees that were less than 30 ft (9.1 m) apart from being shown. A count of the number of farmland trees in the parish of Thriplow, away from the village 'envelope', from the 1886 25 in OS map, excluding those in gardens and closes, comes to 259: this divided by the total acreage of 2353 acres gives 0.11 trees per acre, or 4.05 per hectare, a fairly low figure. For comparison, a Forestry Commission survey taken in 1951 estimated that there was an average of 2.3 trees per acre of farmland in England;[40] while Rackham has estimated that in eastern England in 1951 there were approximately 1.5 hedgerow and field trees per acre and only 0.6 even in 1980.[41]

Where hedgerow trees did occur in the district in the 1880s, they were often spaced quite closely along the hedge length. In the three parishes of Melbourn (enclosed in 1836), Newton (1841) and Thriplow (1840), for example, there are typically 4–6 to the inch on the 25 inch map – that is, they were between 35 ft (10.6 m) and 52 ft (15.8 m) apart.

Trees along roads appear to be closer together than those along field boundaries, perhaps because here they only shaded the crop along one side or possibly to provide shade to the road, and possibly as a display of the landowner's status (tree-planting and ownership had long been intimately associated). Proximity to roads may also have made it easier to extract timber when it was ready for felling. Due to lack of subsequent replanting, the landscape is now much more open than in the late nineteenth century. To judge from surviving examples, some oak and ash were planted, and as already noted, the large quantities of elm suckers now spreading through the hedges suggest that a very high proportion of enclosure-period trees must originally have been of this species. Several hedgerow trees are walnut – a naturalised tree originally introduced by the Romans – probably planted as they grow at regular intervals and there was a good market for walnuts and walnut timber (Figure 8.2).

Figures 8.3 and 8.4 show an example of a large field, once divided by hedges along which telegraph poles were placed; the hedges have now gone and only the telegraph poles are left to show where they were. The landscape is beginning to revert to the large open fields of the pre-enclosure landscape.

FIGURE 8.2. Walnut trees in hedge along the Whittlesford footpath.

FIGURE 8.3. Telegraph poles crossing a field in Thriplow.

FIGURE 8.4. The same scene featured on the 1886 OS map.

Trees within the village

While enclosure unquestionably added to the numbers of hedgerow trees in the wider countryside, the fate of existing trees, largely concentrated within the village envelopes in this period, is less clear. There was, at the time of enclosure, a significant contrast between the sparsely-timbered fields around the village, and the village 'envelope' itself – the area of closes, gardens and greens making up the settlement area. As the Tithe Commissioner remarked in 1842, 'There are many trees in and immediately about the village of Thriplow which is pretty, but the parish generally has a very bare and bleak appearance'.[42] Although, as we have seen, some trees were established in the wider landscape following enclosure, this contrast remained. The First Edition OS maps of 1886 record a density of 0.6 free-standing trees per acre in the village envelope, compared with only 0.11 in the surrounding fields, and in addition there were numerous smaller areas of enclosed wood and plantation here. The tithe maps certainly show that most areas specified as 'wood' were in plantations running along edges of roads and property boundaries: the exceptions being in parks of manors and large houses such as Thriplow Bury, though some, such as Pampisford Hall were not planted until well after enclosure[43] (Appendix 7).

Traditionally, there were three main ways of managing trees. They could be grown in woods, in which a proportion were allowed to mature into full timber trees but most were coppiced – cut back to near ground level on a regular rotation in order to supply a crop of 'poles' suitable for firewood, fencing and other domestic uses ('coppice with standards'). They could be grown in hedges, pastures, and meadows, either as standards or as pollards – in effect, aerial coppices, cropped out of reach of browsing stock. Or they could be grown in plantations, largely or entirely composed of standard trees, which were first thinned in stages and then felled or – in some cases – left to become an aesthetic feature of the landscape. In an area where wood was scarce, many of the free-standing trees within the village envelopes were pollarded. The wood and timber advertised for sale at Melbourn in February 1819, for example, included 56 'fine Elm trees', and ten ash of 15–21 in (381–533 mm) girth, but no less than 150 ash and elm pollards. Pollards began to lose their usefulness during the nineteenth century with the introduction of cheaper coal and metal implements instead of wooden ones, and can now be seen to have become so top heavy through lack of cutting that some species, especially willow, eventually collapse (Figure 8.5). Examples of oak, sycamore, and willow pollards still survive in south Cambridgeshire villages; pollarded elms also existed before the onset of Dutch Elm Disease in the late 1960s.

The character of the various small areas of woodland shown growing within the area of villages is unclear. Tithe maps for the area do not distinguish plantations from coppiced woods[44] (Figure 8.6).

The survival of such old trees makes it clear that the 1886 OS maps, accurate as they were, did not show every free-standing tree within village envelopes. The example shown in Figure 8.7 and 8.8, for example, must certainly have existed in the 1880s, for it is at least 200 years old. It was presumably omitted because of limited space and a cluster of other cartographic symbols. [45]

One tree that was marked on the 1886 OS 25 inch map is still standing; the fact that it was pollarded may have contributed to its longevity (Figure 8.9).

A number of sale particulars, auctioneers notebooks and sale advertisements, however, throw some light on this issue, especially the notebooks of Crocket and Nash of Royston, which cover the period 1822–1883, when the majority of enclosures occurred in south Cambridgeshire. These indicate the kinds of species growing in woodland, and hint at their density. Tables 8.2–8.5 show the number of timber trees sold in three villages in the area between 1821 and 1883:[46]

In Thriplow a total of 2383 timber trees were felled in the 62 years covered by the sale books, all from just one estate, the Bury, (Crocket and Nash, it should be emphasised, were not the only local auctioneers to sell timber during the nineteenth century). Larch is the most numerous species in these lists, followed by elm, ash and poplar.

Larch was often grown as a nurse species to the more slow-growing broadleaved species, and would be removed once the main trees had reached a good height: the dominance of this species probably suggests that most of these trees were from plantations which were of no great antiquity, perhaps planted in the middle or later decades of the eighteenth century, in turn suggesting that the various areas of woodland shown on the tithe award maps were of this character, rather than being older coppices. Large numbers of 'poles' were sold from Cambridgeshire villages throughout the nineteenth century, again mainly thinnings from plantations. The virtual absence of oak from advertisements and sale particulars is interesting; but it does not necessarily mean that there were no oaks, only that very few were sold; it is possible that trees of this species were retained by the Cambridge colleges for use in their own building maintenance programmes.

It must be emphasised that not all the timber felled and sold came from plantations, to judge from the wording of newspaper advertisements. The *Cambridge Chronicle* for February 1818, for example, advertised:

'Thriplow, 6 February 1818–99 Large Elms, 27 fine Sycamores, 13 Ash, 2 Oaks and 24 Pollards in Messrs Faircloth and Francis's farms..
Also, In the Avenue (of the Bury), 30 fine Elms, 26 large
Sycamore, 4 Ash and 10 Pollards.
By the Moat, 1 Ash and 1 Sycamore
In New Close 4 Elms, in Capon's Close 9 Elm and 1 Ash.
In Townsend Close and Spinney, 30 Elm, 4 Ash and 14 Pollards.
In Upper and Lower Gentleman's, 9 Elm.
Also a considerable quantity of Logwood and Brush'.

At Fowlmere in 1821, similarly, many of the trees advertised for sale stood in pasture closes and hedgerows:

'Neat Grove – 14 Oak Trees
Off Field Grove – 1 oak, 4 elms. 1 ash,
Flaxlane Farm yard – 5 elms, 2 ash,

FIGURE 8.5. An old unused pollarded willow in a collapsed state.

FIGURE 8.6. Pollarding still being practised in Fowlmere Bird Reserve.

FIGURE 8.7. Goward's Oak, Thriplow, Autumn 1997.

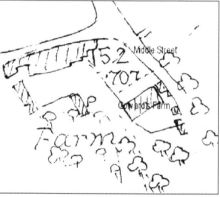

FIGURE 8.8. Goward's Farm, Thriplow, traced from 1886, 25 inch OS Map.

FIGURE 8.9 Old Pollard Sycamore marking the corner of a field in Thriplow.

Species	No.
Larch	2460
Poplar	410
Spruce	230
Ash	211
Elm	93
Black poplar	81
Abele*	29
Beech	16
Scotch	8
Willow	3
Sycamore	2
Walnut	2
Total	3545

TABLE 8.2. Number and species of trees sold by Crocket and Nash in Fowlmere, 1821–1883. *species now considered rare.

Species	No.
Larch	883
Elm	590
Spruce	220
Scotch	178
Ash	166
Poplar	156
Wych elm	85
Beech	37
Oak	14
Birch	14
Maple	10
Sycamore	10
Willow	6
Acacia	4
Chestnut	4
Apple	3
Abele*	2
Lime	1
Total	2383

TABLE 8.4. Number and species of trees sold by Crocket and Nash in Shepreth, 1821–1883.*species now considered rare.

Species	No.
Ash	603
Fir	500
Elm	331
Black poplar	63
Oak	31
Poplar	14
Sycamore	9
Abele*	6
Willow	1
Total	1558

TABLE 8.3. Number and species of trees sold by Crocket and Nash in Thriplow, 1821–1883. *species now considered rare. Source: CRO 296/B/870-968.

Village	Date	No. poles etc	Total timber sold
Fowlmere	1815	944	
Fowlmere	1862	800	1,744
Melbourn	1819	150	150
Meldreth	1808	406	
Meldreth	1810	50	456
Whittlesford	1818	406	
Whittlesford	1819	129	535
Shepreth	1845	2940	
Shepreth	1862	500	
Shepreth	1873	300	
Shepreth	1878	10	3750
Thriplow	1821	74	
Thriplow	1858	200	
Thriplow	1862	830	
Thriplow	1868	300	
Thriplow	1872	500	
Thriplow	1873	600	
Thriplow	1874	300	
Thriplow	1877	1000	
Thriplow	1878	500	
Thriplow	1880	300	4604

TABLE 8.5. Fencing, from sale particulars by village and date.

Date	Thriplow	Fowlmere	Shepreth
1821	157	92	27
1822		84	
1833			2000
1844		60	
1845		800	481
1858	200		
1860	503		
1862	113		
1863	99		
1864	564		
1865			230
1867	103		
1868	144		69
1869	306		
1870			541
1872	631		40
1873	611		270
1874	748		
1875	507		
1876		125	
1877	501		
1878	316		80
1880	541		
1883	117		74

TABLE 8.6. Number of trees sold in three parishes between 1821 and 1883.

Hog Yard Grove – 11 elms,
Calves Pightle – 1 ash, 1 oak, 3 elms,
Great Pasture Close – 6 elms,
Orchard – 3 elms.'

Overall, however, the largest source appears to have been small groves and plantations, and some of the trees felled were evidently of an ornamental or semi-ornamental character. In 1849 an advertisement for the sale of a house and land in Thriplow refers to 300 Italian Black Poplars (*Populus serotina,* a hybrid of Black Poplar and the American Eastern Cotton- wood).[47]

It is possible that the costs of enclosure prompted large scale fellings: enclosure would also have led to increased local demand for 'poles' and small timber to provide fencing to protect young hedges. Indeed, even rumours of impending enclosure could apparently stimulate sales. In September 1819, over 20 years before Thriplow's enclosure actually began the *Cambridge Chronicle* carried the following advertisement:

'THRIPLOW INCLOSURE
Notice is hereby given, that application will be made to the Honourable the Commons of the United Kingdom of Great Britain and Ireland in the ensuing Sessions of Parliament, for leave to bring in a Bill to divide, allot, inclose and discharge from Tithes, all open and common fields, meadows, commons, waste and other lands and grounds within the Parish of Thriplow in the County of Cambridge.'[48]

The same year an advertisement for a timber sale in the same parish included, besides full-grown trees, 'One hundred and twenty five lots of large ARMS (branches) useful *for posts and piles for inclosing* and good Firewood arising from 300 large Timber Trees'; going on to emphasise how *'application has been made to Parliament for Inclosing the Parish of Triplow.'*[49] Thriplow was not actually enclosed until 1840, 21 years later.

Table 8.6 shows the number of trees sold in the three parishes of Thriplow, Fowlmere and Shepreth between 1821 and 1883.

When the pattern of timber sales by Crocket and Nash is plotted, some relationship with the dates of enclosure is certainly evident. A peak in sales at Fowlmere in 1845 coincides exactly with the date of enclosure in that parish, as does the peak for Shepreth in 1833. Unfortunately the number of trees sold in Thriplow is missing from the sale books during the time of enclosure so no comparison can be made though we have seen that many trees were sold in anticipation of enclosure.

It is thus likely that enclosure had an indirect but, nevertheless, significant impact on the management of existing woods and plantations: few, if any, actually disappeared, but large scale fellings could have had a localised, if temporary, impact on wildlife. Maynard thus described the loss of Crossbills from Whittlesford: 'Since this parish has been by the woodman's axe so largely divested of its Firtrees the visits of this bird into the parish has been like that of Angels.'[50]

Tables 8.7 and 8.8 shows woodland plants affected by enclosure (by parish).

Latin name	English name	Before	After	Dates
Nine Wells				
Galium odoratum* *(Asperula oderata)*	Sweet woodruff	√	√	1835, 1915, 1990
Daphne laureola	Spurge laurel	√	√	1835, 1915
Epipactis helleborine	Helleborine	√		1835
Lysimachia nemorum	Yellow pimpernel	√		1835
Shelford				
Astragalus glycyphyllos	Wild licorice	√	√	1802, 1991
Sedum telephium	Orphine	√		1763, 1802
Stachys officinalis *(Betonica offinialis)*	Wood betony	√	√	1835, 1915
Whittlesford				
Allium ursinum	Ramsons		√	1835. 1915, 1939, 1991
Aristolochia clematis*	Birthwort	√		1763, 1802. 2001
Narcissus pseudo-narcissus	Daffodil	√	√	1763, 1802, 1835, 1915, 1939, 1978
Ranunculus auricomus	Goldilocks		√	1835, 1836
Sanicula europaea	Sanicle		√	1835, 1915
Hauxton				
Lysimachia vulgaris	Yellow loosestrife		√	1835, 1939, 1993
Mercuralis perennis	Dog's mercury		√	1835, 1915
Thriplow				
Iris foetidissima	Stinking iris		√	1847, 1939
Listera ovata	Twayblade	√	√	1835, 1915
Lonicera caprifolium*	Perfoliate honeysuckle	√	√	1835, 1847, 1915, 1962
Scrophularia aquatica	Figwort		√	1915

TABLE 8.7. Plants affected by enclosure (by parish): Woodland. Current names according to Stace (1997), the old names are in brackets. *species now considered rare.

Parish	No. before	No. before and after	No. after
Ninewells	5	2	18
Shelford	7	1	4
Whittlesford	7	1	24
Thriplow	8	2	8
Hauxton	0	0	4

TABLE 8.8. Number of plants mentioned before and after enclosure.

On the whole there are more plants mentioned after enclosure. While it is possible that more woodland plants were recorded after enclosure, showing that some plantations or groups of trees were cleared letting in more light to allow the flowering plants to thrive, it must be borne in mind that these lists are not foolproof, they are the result of collectors' searches and perhaps more assiduous searches were made in woodland after enclosure.

Heathland

Heaths were the most important environment of south Cambridgeshire to be affected by enclosure. Heaths are not, of course, truly natural habitats. With some exceptions, they occupied areas which were originally tree-covered but, lying on easily-worked sandy soils, they were attractive to early farmers. Once cleared of trees – deliberately for cultivation, by felling for wood and timber, or through the depredations of sheep and other stock – their soils deteriorated. This, coupled with sustained grazing, favoured the development of a characteristic vegetation, dominated by various combinations of heather or ling (*Calluna vulgaris*), bell heather (*Erica cinerea*), gorse or furze (*Ulex europaeus*) and broom (*Sarothamnus scoparius*). Certain grasses also thrive on such poor soils, including sheep's fescue (*Festuca ovina*), wavy hair grass (*Deschampsia flexuosa*), and common bent (*Agrostis tenuis*), while some areas become dominated by bracken (*Pteridium aquilinum*). Not all English heaths are the same, however. In some places, as Rackham has emphasised, heaths can form in an extremely thin layer of sand overlying chalk.[51] This affects their flora to a significant extent; for instance, the deeper rooted plants such as heathers and gorse do not flourish as well on bare chalk soils as on sand as they need an acid soil. It was heaths of this specialised type, different from the acid sandy heaths of the Breckland and Dorset, which existed in south Cambridgeshire before enclosure, and in vast quantities – as already described, they formed a continuous band extending all the way from Royston in north Hertfordshire to Newmarket in Suffolk (Figure 8.10). More easily reclaimed than heaths of more 'normal' type, such heaths were everywhere rapidly destroyed through ploughing after enclosure.[52] Indeed, the tithe map for Thriplow, made the year after enclosure (1842) shows '280 acres of Heath under plough.'[53]

How long the local heathlands had existed is not certain, but the former presence of large numbers of Bronze Age round barrows in the area – mostly, like the heathland vegetation, destroyed following enclosure – suggests that the area was already open at this time, for otherwise the visibility of the mounds would have been limited. Certainly, the essential openness of this landscape was what struck most eighteenth and nineteenth century visitors. Conybeare thus described the heaths on either side of the Icknield Way simply as bleak,

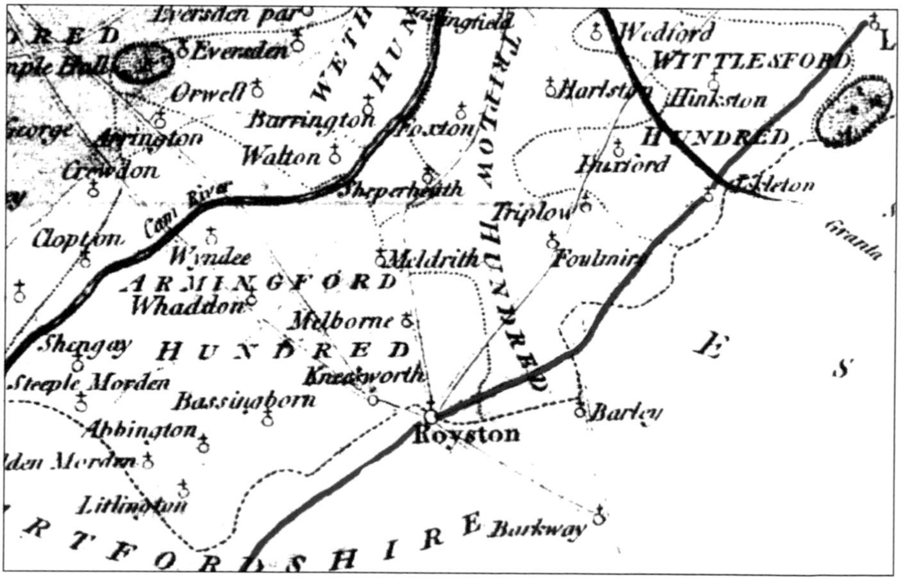

FIGURE 8.10. Map showing the Icknield Way (after Vancouver 1794).

Parish	Sheep	Heath (acres)	Sheep per acre
Fowlmere	550	222	2.5
Ickleton	1480	1210	1.2
Sawston	460	120	3.8
Stapleford	600	500	1.2
Thriplow	1160	339	3.4
Whittlesford	840	411	2.0
Total	5090	2802	ave. 1.8

TABLE 8.9. Number of sheep per acre on heathland. Figures taken from *VCH* (Vol. 8) and Vancouver (1794).

treeless, un-enclosed turf-land: most agricultural improvers regarded such land as symbolic of unimproved husbandry.[54] Fortunately, the Cambridge botanists thought differently, and recorded many of the plants found there. Even more fortunately, some substantial fragments of these great heaths managed to survive enclosure, where they lay close to (and were used in common by the inhabitants of) two large towns – Newmarket and Royston. The amount of heath in the villages bordering the Icknield Way varied from 120 acres (*c.*48.6 ha; 8%) to 411 acres (*c.*166.3 ha; 20%) with 13% of the total acreage.

It is evident that the presence of innumerable sheep would have kept the heathland grasses and other vegetation very short, so that the heaths would, for the most part, have perhaps resembled the chalk downland found in areas like Sussex. The actual intensity of grazing is hard to calculate from surviving records of sheep numbers, for the pre-enclosure flocks also grazed over the arable fields at certain times of the year, but they do provide some indication of the situation (Table 8.9).

The average number of sheep per acre at present on similar habitats is one. Even allowing for the additional grazing supplied by the arable and the fact that pre-enclosure sheep breeds were smaller than those of today, it is evident that these areas were being grazed with some intensity.[55]

Chalk heaths support a unique and special collection of plants, including *Anemone pulsitilla,* the Pasque flower, once common in the area but now only to be seen on the protected areas of Royston, Therfield and the Devil's Dyke. Charles Babington saw them in plenty at Fulbourn in 1840.[56] Alfred Kingston writing in 1890 of the different plants he found on Royston Heath mentions 34 different species,[57] and H. Godwin found 25 different species in 1938.[58] Royston Heath, however, is strictly speaking pure chalk grassland, rather than a true heath. Some writers have assumed that it was thus different from the heaths lost at enclosure, Godwin for example noting that:

> 'The flora of the lower-lying south Cambridgeshire 'heaths' was more like Newmarket Heath than it was Therfield, because Newmarket Heath is thinly covered by glacial debris (striped ground), while Therfield (at least the remaining undisturbed chalk slopes) is a true chalk grassland, with a subtly different flora.'[59]

It is, however, likely (to judge from the soils and geology maps of the area) that both types of environment were represented in the south Cambridgeshire villages before enclosure, even if chalk heath was dominant. A comparison of

Plants on Newmarket Heath 1660–1915	Plants at Royston (Kingston 1890)	Other parishes (dates mentioned)
Pulsatilla vulgaris	√	√ 1840, 1848, 1939
Antennaria dioica	√	√ 1825, 1835, 1860
*Asperula cynanchuca**		√ 1915,
*Campanula glomerata**		√ 1763,
Carlina vulgaris	√	√ 1939,
Cerastium arvense		√ 1940
Geranium sangiuneum		√ 1911
*Gymnadenia conopsea**	√	√ 1915
*Hippocrepis comosa**	√	√ 1840
Ophrys insectifera		√ 1830, 1890,
Rumex acetosella		√ 1835
Trifolium glomeratum		√ 1860
Ulex europaeus		√ 1915
Veronica officinalis	√	
Veronica spicata		

TABLE 8.10. Plants found on Newmarket Heath, compared with Royston and other parishes. *species now considered rare.

the flora of Newmarket and Royston heaths throws up the following comparable plants as shown in Table 8.10: those marked with a star are strong Indicator species, that is plants that are regarded as typical of a particular habitat.[60]

'Other parishes' include Meldreth, Sawston, Shepreth, Thriplow, Whittlesford, Ickleton, Shelford, Fowlmere and Pampisford. The table shows the plants mentioned most frequently by early botanists visiting the parishes named with their dates.

The south Cambridgeshire heaths were thus important and diverse environments, and not only in botanical terms. Their destruction was total in the parishes studied, in spite of the fact that some contemporaries, including William Marshall, were uncertain whether they would repay cultivation:

'Heath sheep walk – This land appears to be chiefly appropriated to the original design of nature, the surface or skin, forming a tender and wholesome food for the sheep, which is generally depastured thereon. The staple of the land is so very dry and thin, that once broken, it will be ages before it can acquire an equally valuable turf or covering with that it now produces. The less this land is disturbed the better.'[61]

When Babington in 1897 recorded their recent destruction, he was also aware of the destruction wrought on the area's archaeological heritage:

'Chalk Country – Until recently (within 60 years) most of the chalk district was open and covered with a beautiful coating of turf, profusely decorated with *Anemone pulsatila*, *Astragalus hypoglottis* and other interesting plants. It is now converted into arable land, and its peculiar plants mostly confined to small waste spots by road-sides, pits and a very few banks that are too steep for the plough. Thus many species which were formerly abundant have become rare; so rare as to have caused an unjust suspicion of their not being really natives in the minds of some modern botanists. Even the tumuli, entrenchments and other interesting works of the ancient inhabitants have seldom escaped the rapacity of the modern agriculturalist, who too frequently looks upon the native plants of the country as weeds, and its antiquities as deformities.'[62]

Latin name	English name	Before	After	Dates mentioned
Shelford (enclosed 1834)				
Astragalis glycphyllos	Wild licorice	√	√	1763, 1820, 1835, 1991
Inula conyza	Plowman's spikenard	√		1802
Crepis foetida*	Stinking hawkbeard	√	√	1802, 1976
Antennaria dioicam	Cat's foot	√		1802
Gnaphalium luteoalbum	Jersey Cud weed		√	1802
Thriplow (1840)				
Ajuga chamaepitys*	Ground pine	√		1660, 1763, 1802
Minuartia hybrida*	Fine leaved sandwort	√		1660
Pulsatilla vulgaris* *(Anemone pulsatilla)**	Pasque flower	√		1660, 1842, 1860
Thesium humifuseum*	Bastard toad-flax	√	√	1763, 1860
Filipendula vulgaris	Dropwort	√	√	1835, 1960

TABLE 8.11. Plants affected by enclosure (by parish): heath. Names in brackets are current names. *species now considered rare.

Table 8.11 shows the scale of the destruction from the records of Cambridge botanists.

As can be seen, in these parishes few of the heathland plants found before enclosure were also to be found afterwards: only where chalk heath (or, in the case of Royston, chalk grassland) survived unploughed, did these valued species continue to be recorded. The loss of the Pasque Flower (*Anemone pulsatilla*), now *Pulsatilla vulgaris*, was particularly mourned, and not only by botanists (Figure 8.11):

> 'This plant formerly grew on the Heathy land near Ninewells (between Whittlesford and Thriplow) … and in 1842 my Father gathered it there … but since that time it has been through breaking up the ancient turf eradicated so that no vestige of it is left on the spot where it once abounded.'[63]

The ploughing-up of this specialised habitat also had a profound effect on local fauna, and especially on bird populations. Birds of the open heaths are often ground-nesting, and reluctant flyers, preferring the tall grasses and heather to hide them; their chicks are capable of running and feeding soon after they are hatched. Not only destruction of food sources, but also of nesting ground, affected them. Jenyns, in 1826, records the Stone Curlew, the quintessential bird of the heaths, in terms which suggest that it was common. It subsequently disappeared from the area, although there are currently attempts to re-introduce it.[64] But not all disappearances were solely the consequence of land use change. Jenyns, in his catalogue of local wildlife, states that the Great Bustard (*Otis tarda*) was 'formerly not uncommon in open and unenclosed lands especially Newmarket and Royston Heaths; now extremely rare'[65] (Figure 8.12) It would seem that the last Great Bustard was killed in Great Shelford around 1832, though solitary birds were seen until 1856. A. H. Evans tells the story of a Bustard being shot: 'By a man of the name of Davy of Hinxton, his gun being loaded with a black-lead pencil. The bird was wounded, but flew to Shelford, where I suppose it was taken.'[66]

In the Norfolk Breckland, where the bird was also once common, the introduction of the horse-hoe for weeding purposes and the sowing of corn in

FIGURE 8.11 *(left)*. The Pasque flower.

FIGURE 8.12 *(centre)*. Great Bustard.

FIGURE 8.13 *(right)*. The Dotterill.

drills, rather than broadcast, was a major factor in the bird's extinction, together with the disappearance of open heathland and the fact that the landscape was increasingly subdivided by plantations and hedges.[67] Similar changes doubtless contributed to the bird's disappearance from south Cambridgeshire. Other heathland birds, once plentiful in south Cambridgeshire and now rare or extinct, include the Corncrake (*Crex crex*) and the Dotterel (*Charadrius morinellus*) (Figure 8.13). Jenyns described both as summer visitors and commented in 1849 that the Dotterel was less common than hitherto. In fact, the Dotterel breeds in the far north of Britain pausing in East Anglia on its way: it is of a confiding nature and therefore popular to hunt.[68] James I made a detour on his way to the racing at Newmarket to watch the vicar of Whittlesford who was said to 'charm' the Dotterels into his hands.[69] Unfortunately his method was not described. A post-enclosure farm on what was Thriplow Heath is called *Dotterels*; the bird was last seen in 1962.

The destruction of the heaths by ploughing after enclosure may have been the major reason why these birds declined rapidly in numbers in the course of the nineteenth century, but other factors, including mechanised cultivation on the new and existing arable land, and the activities of sportsmen, evidently also contributed to their demise.

Moorland

We must now turn to the other main area of non-arable land-use in the district, the low-lying 'moors'. Vancouver, writing in a local context, used the words 'common' and 'moor' interchangeably, as when writing about Pampisford – 'The moor or common contains 150 acres. [60.7 ha].'[70] In this district all moors, as we have seen, were common (although of course not all commons were moors); they were mainly used for digging peat and grazing animals (Appendix 4). For the most part, their vegetation appears to have corresponded to the community catalogued by Rodwell as M24 – Fen-meadow, its most indicative plants being *Molinia Caerulea–Cirsum dissectum*. (Purple Moor Grass–Meadow Thistle)[71] They were associated with 'hummocky ground' affected by periglacial action, characterised in particular by ice hollows filled with peat and debris from the Ice

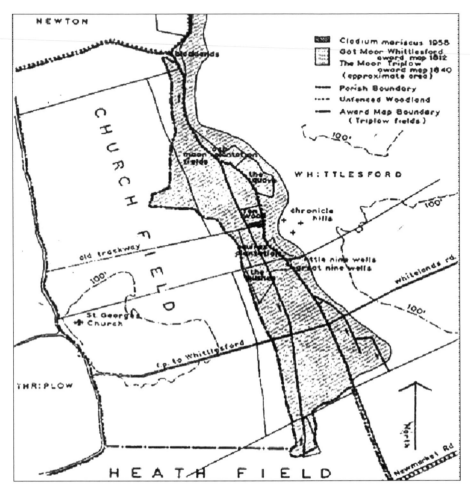

FIGURE 8.14. Map showing Moor between Thriplow and Whittlesford.

Ages, which were eventually colonised by carr and woodland before clearance by grazing and cutting. Although reduced, they remain wetlands to the present day. Often small brooks or streams ran through the area, making drainage difficult. Figure 8.14 shows the moor between Thriplow and Whittlesford.

Vancouver's references to moors in south Cambridgeshire are frequent; every parish had a moor which he describes as wet, unwholesome and of little value. The moor at Pampisford for example was 'extremely obnoxious to the rot in cows'; the cows of Sawston 'have lately been carried off by the absolute rot, which is communicated by the foulness of the herbage, it also produced the rot in sheep'; while at Fowlmere 'the soil is cold, wet and hungry, bounding upon a moor, and which seems greatly to require the helping hand of skill and industry.'[72] Some, probably most, of these areas were used in part as meadows, producing rough fen hay. At Thriplow, for example, sheep were kept on the moor from December to February, but the area was mown in summer for hay. General opinion among nineteenth-century agriculturalists was that such land was of little economic value unless it could be reclaimed and drained. Marshall, for example, described in 1815 the 'half-yearly meadow land:

Parish (date of enclosure)	Total acreage	Moors	%
Fowlmere (1845)	2212	200	9
Hauxton (1798)	568	20	4
Ickleton (1810)	2672	70	3
Melbourn (1836)	4692	400	9
Pampisford (1799)	1250	150	12
Sawston (1802)	1856	300	16
Shepreth (1811)	1240	100	8
Stapleford (1812)	1780	140	8
Thriplow (1840)	2353	180	8
Total	18,623	1,560	8

TABLE 8.12. Moors as percentage of total acreage, 1834. Source: BPP (1834), Section B Answers to Rural Questions, County of Cambridge.

'These lands lie dispersed through the hollows of the open fields and receiving the richest juices of the surrounding lands, even in their present neglected state, are rented on an average, at 12 shillings 6 pence per acre only; but would by proper draining, and being put into severalty, readily be improved to thirty shillings per annum, as the crop which is now only mown twice in three years, would then be annually secured.'[73]

Many of these damp commons were removed by enclosure, but by no means all. Speaking from a naturalist's point of view Maynard remarked in 1849, a few years after Thriplow's enclosure:

'This plant (Greater Bladderwort *Utricularia vulgaris*) grew on Triplow Common where my father N. Maynard, gathered it ... will only flourish in stagnant waters, and before the parish was subjected to that operation called enclosure, which means a thorough rooting up of everything in the way of plants uncommon or rare, it grew abundantly in the boggy and peaty holes that abounded on the moor towards the parish of Triplow where my father used to gather it. The last specimen in his herbarium has the date 1835 'From near Ninewells''.[74]

In 1834 the report of the Royal Commission into the Poor Laws included a calculation of the extent of unimproved wetlands in the area (Table 8.12).

The percentage of moors to total acreage in south Cambridgeshire parishes averaged at this stage around 8%, quite a sizeable amount of land. What is interesting is that even those parishes that had been enclosed before 1834, such as Pampisford, Ickleton, Hauxton, Shepreth and Stapleford, still had extensive areas of moor, largely because it was not so easy to drain land that was watered from underground streams or springs.

The distinctive flora of such areas was much appreciated, and recorded, by botany students from Cambridge who undertook excursions to the surrounding villages to collect plants for their 'herbariums'. Of particular importance were the 'peat holes' especially those at Thriplow, which in Babington's time were famous for their rare fen species. In July 1860 he described how he 'Went with Dr Cookson to Triplow: examined the turf-holes, and went to a good piece of boggy land at the Great and Little Nine Wells. Found there plenty of *Epipactis palustris* (Marsh helliborine).'

In a footnote in his *Flora,* he mentions that he had also seen this plant at Sawston Moor and Fowlmere Moor.[75] The wildfowl that thronged the extensive

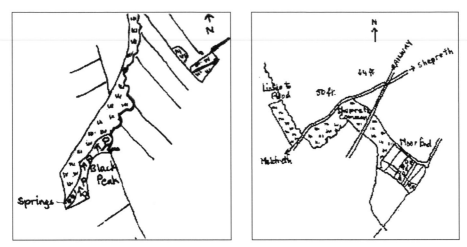

Fowlmere Moor   Shepreth L Moor

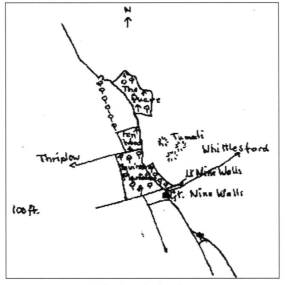

Whittlesford and Thriplow Moor

FIGURE 8.15 Wet areas now SSSIs, copied from 1886, 6 inch OS map.

Fowl Mere attracted the young men from Cambridge who would come out for a day's shooting. The area was also noted for its edible frogs, known as Cambridge Nightingales; judging by the number of 'Frog Ends' in the district, these creatures may have been a common item of diet.

Figure 8.15 shows the three Sites of Special Scientific Interest (SSSI). Fragments of such land still survive around the site of the Fowlmere watercress beds, now the Royal Society for the Protection of Birds, Fowlmere Bird Reserve, and at Great and Little Nine Wells and the Quave (Whittlesford and Thriplow respectively), now nature reserves managed by Cambridgeshire County Council; while the wet meadows in Thriplow are managed by English Nature, and support 'the largest surviving population of marsh orchids *(Dactylorhiza praetermissa* and *D. incarnata)* in East Anglia', numbering around 1000 plants in some years (Figure 8.16).

The area of Nine Wells was divided between the parishes of Thriplow and Whittlesford: more of its area was reclaimed on the Thriplow side of the parish boundary, and the effects of this and subsequent land improvement, on the local flora were recorded by Nathan Maynard, whose notebooks are filled with beautiful watercolours of plants, local customs and butterflies, such as the common Butterwort:

> 'Common Butterwort – This lovely flower grew in abundance in this parish, but since the drainage and enclosure of the commons the plant has become extinct. My father used to gather it near the beautiful stream of water on what is Thriplow Common or Nine Wells in 1849. I have looked for it repeatedly since that time but never found it. It still grows on Sawston Moor. 1862.'[76]

FIGURE 8.16 Marsh Orchid in Thriplow meadows.

He describes how he and his brother would bathe in the cool waters of the 'pellucid' stream when helping their father at harvest time, and how many and beautiful were the flowers. Nevertheless, although the area of 'moor' contracted markedly in some parishes, overall this kind of habitat survived enclosure remarkably well, and in some parishes, such as Shepreth, very little reclamation has taken place.

In his notebook Maynard describes the scene in Whittlesford where he spent his boyhood:

> 'This spot and neighbourhood furnish a rich harvest to the botanist, and it has been near here that I and my father have gathered some of our choicest specimens for our herbariums, especially before the parish of Triplow was enclosed upon the open wild uncultivated common that lies between this spring of water in the foreground of this view, and the Church.'[77]

Moors were thus more resistant to change than heaths, and it is thus perhaps unsurprising that fewer losses of flora over the nineteenth century are suggested by botanical records, although precise calculations are rendered difficult by the fact that some wetland areas (most notably Nine Wells) crossed parish boundaries, and by the failure of many early botanists to distinguish areas of 'moor' and 'heath', sometimes using the terms interchangeably.[78] Nevertheless, as Table 8.13 indicates, in most parishes there were few losses of characteristic species across the nineteenth and twentieth century's, in marked contrast to the pattern already described with heathland plants.

Meadow

As well as having low-lying 'moors', the pre-enclosure south Cambridgeshire parishes also contained some better-quality meadow land, usually in closes beside the village, although in most cases such land was in very limited supply. Expressions such as 'There is a great deficiency of hay lands; this is poorly supplied by pea straw and trefoil straw'; 'The meadows are small of middling

Latin name	English name	Before	After	Dates
Fowlmere				
*Drosera rotundifolia**	Round-leaved sundew	√	√	1802, 1849, 1860
*Parnassia palustris**	Grass of Parnassus	√	√	1835, 1939
Melbourn				
*Cladium mariscus**	Mother sedge	√	√	1835, 1939
Conium maculatum	Hemlock	√	√	1835, 1886, 1913
Drosera anglica	Great sundew	√		1835
Thriplow				
Achilla ptarmica	Sneezewort		√	1835, 1939,
Butomus umbellatis	Flowering rush		√	1835, 1867
*Epilobium palustre**	Marsh willow herb	√	√	1835, 1939
Eriophorum angustifolium	Common cotton grass		√	1842, 1860
Nymphae alba	White water lily	√	√	1763, 1802, 1991
Oenanthe crocata	Hemlock-leaved dropwort		√	1868, 1915
Oenanthe fistulosa	Water dropwort	√	√	1835, 1939
Pinguicula vulgaris	Common Butterwort		√	1849, 1860
Utricularia vulgaris	Bladderwort	√	√	1802, 1939, 1991
Shelford				
*Anagalis tenella**	Bog pimpernel	√	√	1835, 1860
Circaea lutetiana	Enchanter's nightshade		√	1835, 1868, 1939
*Eriophorum angustifolium**	Cotton grass	√		1802
*Juncus bulbosus**	Bulbous rush	√		1802, 1820
*Parnassia palustris**	Grass of Parnassus	√	√	1802, 1839
Sawston				
*Drosera intermedia** (*Drosera longifolia*)	Long-leaved sundew	√	√	1802, 1835, 1939
*Drosera rotundifolia**	Round-leaved sundew		√	1835, 1939
*Parnassia palustris**	Grass of Parnassus	√	√	1802, 1849
*Pedicularis palustris**	Marsh lousewort		√	1835, 1939
*Pinguicula vulgaris**	Butterwort	√	√	1802, 1862, 1849
*Schoenus nigricans**	Black bog rush	√	√	1802, 1939
Selinum carvifolia	Cambridge milk Parsley		√	1990
Whittlesford				
*Blysmus compressus** (*Schoenus compressus*)	Compressed bog rush	√		1763, 1802
Nine Wells (Thriplow/Whittlesford)				
Cephalanthera damasonium (*Epipactis grandiflora*)	White helleborine	√	√	1835, 1867
*Epipactis palustris**	Marsh helleborine	√	√	1835, 1867
Eupatarium cannabinum (*Eupatorium bonum*)	Hemp agrimony	√	√	1835, 1868
Gallium palustre	Marsh bedstraw	√	√	1835, 1915
*Liparis loeselii**	Fen orchid	√	√	1835, 1915
Lychnis flos-cuculi	Ragged robin	√	√	1835, 1868
*Dactylorchis incarnarta**	Early marsh orchid	√	√	1835, 1870, 1915, 1993
Orchid sphegodes (*Orchid moria*)*	Green-winged orchid	√	√	1835, 1870

quality and pretty generally fed off'; or 'The small quantity of Inclosure Meadow or Pasture land is generally mown for hay yielding about a ton per acre,' are common.[79]

Land use is not immutable and as we have seen the heaths were ploughed and became arable: land that was once moors could be drained, ploughed and used for growing crops. The enclosure awards do not clearly distinguish the area

TABLE 8.13. Plants affected by enclosure (by parish): moorland. Names in brackets are current names. *species now considered rare.

Latin name	English name	Before	After	Dates
Shelford				
Alisma gramineum *	Water plantain	√		1802
Polygonum bistorta	Common bistort	√		1763, 1820
Pulicaria dysenterica	Fleabane		√	1835
Sanguisorba officinalis *	Great burnet	√		1763, 1820
Thriplow				
Achille ptarmica	Sneezewort yarrow	√		1820, 1975
Menyanthes trifoliata *	Buckbean	√		1820, 1848
Gymnadenia conopsea (Orchis conopsea)	Sweet scented orchis	√		1802
Filipendula vulgaris	Dropwort	√	√	1820, 1960

TABLE 8.14. Meadow plants affected by enclosure (by parish). Plants mentioned either before or after the date of enclosure. Names in brackets are current names. *species now considered rare.

of 'meadow' from other grazing, for example in the Fowlmere Tithe schedule a field entitled the 'five acre meadow' is classed as 'pasture'.[80] The schedules often lump together 'open and common fields, meadows, pastures, commonable lands, commons and waste ground'.[81] Specific mentions of meadow shows that around 6% of the farmed area was mown for hay at the time of enclosure

Interestingly, the available evidence suggests a rather greater loss of meadow plants than of those characteristic of the 'moors' in the course of the nineteenth century (Table 8.14). As most of the meadow land recorded before enclosure was mainly held in severalty in closes or along low-lying land beside river banks and remained relatively unchanged, this must be the consequence of changes in farming practice, rather than of enclosure *per se*, perhaps including re-seeding and improvements to drainage; both practices much advocated by contemporary agriculturalists. Old flowering meadows are now rare; most meadows are regularly ploughed and re-sown with grass, reducing the number of well established plants to a few areas now protected as nature reserves.

Arable

After enclosure the old open fields were divided up and enclosed by hedges and fences: they were universally arable, cultivated by a version of 'improved' rotation featuring artificial grasses and root crops. The planting of hedges which followed enclosure obviously provided some cover and additional food sources, especially for birds. Nevertheless in 1934, according to David Lack, the area was: 'Rather deficient in birds – Almost the whole area is under the plough, the fields are large and the hedgerows tend to be small, conditions are not suited to abundant bird life'.[82]

It has, however, been suggested that the introduction of clover, tares and turnips as winter crops resulted in a population explosion of the wood pigeon and, from being a fairly scarce bird, it became, by the late nineteenth century, a major pest, preferring to nest and roost in woodland edges and the narrow plantations so common in south Cambridgeshire. Sparrows also probably 'increased in numbers in the countryside with the spread of mixed farming'.[83] Cambridge's treatise on hedges complains that tall hedges give shelter to birds such as sparrows that eat the grain,[84] so it was probably mainly as the consequence of changes in farming practices consequent upon enclosure, that such species 'rose from the status of a mild irritant to the farmer to that to that of a major pest'.[85] Their predators may also have increased accordingly, although in this case numbers were also influenced by other factors, especially the activities of gamekeepers, keen to eradicate anything that reduced the numbers of gamebirds available for their employers' guns. The hooded crow (*Corvus coenix*), once common in south Cambridgeshire and north Hertfordshire, was particularly targeted. The local newspaper is still called the *Royston Crow* and has as its letterhead a hooded crow; but the bird is now extinct in the area. Changes in bird populations within the area formerly occupied by the open fields were perhaps affected more by such things, also by the more dramatic changes to the environment resulting from the enclosure of the neighbouring heaths. Nevertheless, in the case of many bird species, the precise pattern of increase or decrease over time will always elude us: 'Most birds adjusted to shifting land-uses and farm methods far too subtly for their fortunes or fate to appear in the patchwork of early ornithological records.'[86]

Enclosure itself probably made little difference to the range of arable weeds to be found in the fields, plants which had developed strategies to compete with the main crop: many, for example, would germinate in winter and flower and set seed by May before the sown crop could offer serious competition.[87] Chemical methods of weed control were not adopted until the twentieth century (it was not until 1892 that the first synthetic pesticide, potassium dinitro-2–cresylate, marketed in Germany, was introduced), but enclosure was often accompanied by more intensive cultivation and agricultural improvers were vocal in their insistence on the need to eradicate common weeds, which they believed could be achieved with some effort. In 1851 Phillip Pusey wrote that together with Charlock and wild flax:

> 'The Corn Marigold I have known a serious nuisance … and have seen it removed by a moderate dressing of lime. Chick weed almost stops cultivation … Tap rooted weeds such as Dock, often to be seen upon slovenly farms proudly waving its banner over the harvest fields … Couch-grass requires Autumn dressing of wheat stubble.'[88]

The eradication of fallows should also have led to some change in the character of weed communities. Nevertheless, there is little in the various descriptions and surveys to suggest that any arable plants became extinct in the district in the course of the nineteenth century, although it is possible that some became rarer. Table 8.15 reveals those plants present before and after enclosure (names in brackets are current names; those marked with an * are now considered rare).

Yet if few weed species disappeared from the fields, biodiversity would have been adversely affected by the fact that the area occupied by the open fields was now universally arable, whereas the pre-enclosure landscape had contained numerous balks, verges, and greens used as pasture, fed off by sheep and cattle from November to April.[89]

Enclosure had a complex impact on the various semi-natural habitats of

Latin name	English name	Before	After	Dates
Whittlesford				
Inula conyza	Plowman's spikenard	√	√	1802, 1991
*Cuscuta epithymum**	Dodder		√	1868
Agrestemma githago (*Lychnis githago*)	Corn cockle		√	1868, 1905
Narcissus pseudonarcissus	Daffodil	√	√	1763, 1939, 1978
Thriplow				
Sheradia arvensis	Little field madder	√	√	1763, 1802, 1988
Shelford				
Consolida orientalis (*Delphinium consolida*)	Field larkspur	√	√	1820, 1987
Mentha arvensis (*Mentha gentiles*)	Corn mint	√	√	1763, 1939
Orobanche elatoir+	Tall broomrape	√	√	1820, 1980

TABLE 8.15. Arable plants recorded before and after enclosure (by parish). Names in brackets are current names. *species now considered rare. + calcareous grassland indicator.

south Cambridgeshire, an impact which, given the nature of the evidence, we can only imperfectly recover. Some of its effects were largely transitory, such as the large-scale fellings of existing plantations to provide revenue and fencing materials. Others were permanent and irreversible, like the ploughing of the heaths, something which completely destroyed the thin layers of sandy soil which had carried the characteristic vegetation of this specialised habitat. The removal of heathland, however, was perhaps the only completely negative aspect of the enclosure process. The effects on wildlife of hedging the open fields were clearly complex and mixed, while the various low-lying 'moors', difficult to cultivate, often survived virtually unchanged, if diminished in extent. The main difficulty in understanding enclosure's impact, however, is that of distinguishing the effects of enclosure itself, and associated changes in land use, from that of other contemporary developments, including new farming methods, and the activities of plant collectors and sportsmen.

Nevertheless, one point is clear. The fact that the destruction of the heaths was so total, and effected so easily, in sharp contrast to the situation regarding the moors, indicates clearly that the heaths had survived up to enclosure not because it had been impossible to plough them, in the sense that they were too infertile to repay cultivation, but rather because they had been a necessary part of the old sheep-corn systems of the pre-enclosure landscape. Ecologists have long argued that particular habitats should not be studied in isolation: 'It is more instructive to consider and connect the woods, meadows and moors etc. of the same area than to draw examples of these from unrelated areas.'[90] In historical terms, similarly, the various environments of an area or region need to be considered in relationship to each other, rather than in isolation.

For most contemporaries, enclosure, of the open fields at least, was a necessary process and one which was both economically and aesthetically desirable. 'Treeless and hedgeless, those very ugly things, common fields, bleak and comfortless', as Cobbett put it. [91] The landscape of enclosed fields, farmed according to modern methods, he found infinitely preferable:

'The fields on the left seem to have been enclosed by act of parliament; they certainly are the most beautiful tract *of fields* that I ever saw. Their extent may be from ten to thirty acres each. Divided by quick-set hedges, exceedingly well planted and raised. The whole tract is nearly a perfect level. The cultivation neat and the stubble heaps, such as remain out, giving proof of great crops of straw, while, on land with a chalk bottom, there is seldom any want of a proportionate quantity of grain.'[92]

Even at the time, as we have seen, not everyone viewed enclosure with equal enthusiasm, but since the nineteenth century the reverence for 'nature', which had been growing steadily in English culture since the seventeenth century, has largely triumphed. Over the past two decades, hedges have been planted where once they were removed and verges are no longer sprayed to kill wild flowers (Figure 8.17).

The Countryside Stewardship scheme has encouraged the planting of wide uncultivated strips in fields to benefit wildlife the reintroduction of once lost birds such as Stone Curlews and Corn Crakes has met with some success, and the Pasque flower is now jealously guarded on Therfield and Royston Heath. Although the Great Bustard has not returned to southern Cambridgeshire, the Dotteril occasionally visits in spring on its way to its nesting grounds in north Britain.[93] Rackham, writing in 1986, mourned the destruction of hedgerows and their accompanying flora but by the 1994 edition he devoted a whole chapter to conservation.[94]

In fact the government is now encouraging farmers to protect wildlife by the introduction of schemes to which farmers can belong and be paid for their efforts.[95] One of the larger farmers in the area has noted an increase in bird species from 40 in 2000 to 57 in 2006. The hedges are cut every three years and then only between November and February to protect nesting birds; the fields are no more than 30 acres (12 ha) in size and are separated with wide 'beetle banks' to encourage wild flowers and insects which, in turn, are fed on by the birds.[96] As well as beetle banks between fields, wide margins are planted with grasses and wild flowers attractive to birds as seen in Figures 8.18 and 8.19.

FIGURE 8.17 Broomrape, *Orobanche elatoir* growing on a Newton verge, 2007.

FIGURE 8.18 *(below left)*. Beetle Bank at College Farm, Duxford, June 2007.

FIGURE 8.19 *(below right)*. Hedge margins designed to attract wildlife, College Farm, Duxford.

It was probably true that farming methods did need to modernise to meet the demands of a growing population but whether the scale of destruction wrought, in particular, on the heathlands of south Cambridgeshire can be entirely justified in such terms is a philosophical question, one rooted in a particular time and place. For it is now appreciated that we live in a fragile eco-system and that while we can control nature with chemicals and technology, the consequences of such interference can be far-reaching and ultimately life-threatening: 'A greater awareness of what is happening today may emphasise how little is known about the agricultural environments of the past.'[97]

Notes

1   C. Levi-Strauss (1966) *From Honey to Ashes* quoted in Mabey (2010), 48. Caltrop is *Tribulus terrestris,* a spiky weed.
2   Chase (1992), 243.
3   Sheail (1986), 1–8.
4   Thomas (1983), 274.
5   Genesis 1.28 quoted in Thomas (1983), 17.
6   *Ibid.,* 17.
7   CRO P156/5/2.
8   Landry (2001), 1.
9   L. Simond (1817) *Journal of a Tour and Residence in Great Britain,* quoted in Thomas (1983), note 5.
10   W. Wordsworth (1814) *The Excursion,* quoted in Thomas (1983), 262.
11   J. Stuart Mill (1848) *Principals of Political Economy,* quoted in Thomas (1983), 268.
12   Ewan and Prime (1975), 22.
13   Forsyth (1803), 27.
14   *Op. cit.* in note 8, 16.
15   Walters (1981), 64.
16   Joint Nature Conservation Committee website. Data provided by G. G. Crompton, D. Wells and P. D. Jones. I am extremely grateful to G. G. Crompton for her advice and help in compiling these databases.
17   Stace (1997); Perring *et al.* (1964).
18   Martyn (1763).
19   J. G. Murrell, Dept of Plant Sciences University of Cambridge, personal communication.
20   Babington (1897), 88.
21   G. Hughes, Curator of Audley End, English Heritage, personal communication.
22   CRO R58/5.
23   Rackham (1993), 179.
24   Cobbett (1830), 74.
25   BPP 30 (1834), question 2.
26   *House of Commons Journal* (1792), 318, quoted in Thomas (1983), 27.
27   *Ibid.,* 371.
28   Pusey (1851), 26.
29   *Ibid.,* 26.
30   Finch (2004), 41.
31   *Cambridge Chronicle,* December 27 1856.

32   *Ibid.*, 334.
33   Rackham (1994), 197.
34   Rackham (1983), 189.
35   Pollard *et al.* (1974), 97.
36   Thriplow Landscape Research Group (2004) *Thriplow Time Trails*, 50. Privately printed.
37   *Op. cit.* in note 33, 94.
38   *Farmers Magazine* (1800) I, 341, 342.
39   *Ibid.*, 165.
40   Forestry Commission (1951).
41   *Op cit.* in note 33, 205–6.
42   NA IR 13652.
43   *VCH* 6, 105–13.
44   Kain and Prince (2000), 24.
45   White (1998).
46   CRO 296/B 661–969.
47   Mitchell (1974), 182–6.
48   *Cambridge Chronicle*, 3 September 1819.
49   *Ibid.* It should be noted that the first date is the date of the advertisement; the second date is that of the sale. Both are for the same sale.
50   CRO R58.5.11/12, Vol 14, 291.
51   Rackham (1994), 283.
52   Cambridgeshire County Council (2003), 1.
53   CUL EDR T.
54   Conybeare (1910), 228.
55   Conversation with Mark Deller, farmer, Thriplow 2005.
56   Babington (1897).
57   Kingston (1890).
58   Godwin (1938), 57.
59   T. James, Plant Recorder for the Hertfordshire Natural History Society, personal communication.
60   Joint Nature Conservation Committee website.
61   Marshall (1815), 613.
62   *Op. cit.*, in note 54, 15.
63   CRO R58/5, Vol. 13, 345.
64   S. Portugal web site www.birdsofbritain.co.uk.
65   Jenyns (1869).
66   Evans (1904), 83P.
67   *Ibid.*, 83.
68   Harrison and Reid-Henry (1998), 104.
69   CRO R58/5, Vol. 4, 17.
70   Vancouver (1794), 66.
71   Rodwell (1991), 41.
72   *Op. cit.* in note 70, 22–72.
73   *Op. cit.* in note 61, 608.
74   CRO R58/5, Vol. 13, 320, 324a.
75   Babington (1897), 195.
76   CRO R85/5, Vol. 12, 302.
77   CRO R58.5.11/12, 301.
78   Compton (1959).

79 CUL EDR T Melbourn and Newton.
80 CRO EDR T Fowlmere 1847.
81 Thriplow Enclosure Award 1845.
82 Lack (1934), 11.
83 *Ibid.*, 119.
84 Cambridge (1845), 35.
85 Jones (1971), 107.
86 Jones (1981), 101.
87 Gilmour and Walters (1969), 85.
88 Pusey (1851), 44.
89 CRO 413/Msrott 1 6 18.
90 *Op. cit.*, in note 51.
91 *Op. cit.*, in note 24, 74
92 *Ibid.*, 22.
93 Conversation with George Dellar, Thriplow Farmer, November 2006.
94 *Op. cit.* in note 51, 27.
95 M. Deller, Rectory Farm, Thriplow. July 2008, personal communication.
96 A. Nottage, farm manager, Russell Smith Farms Duxford, July 2011, personal communication.
97 Sheail (1986).

Conclusion

....

History and nature are the realities which I consider
to be landscape's essential components.
Richard Purslow.[1]

The nineteenth century was a century of radical changes which affected not only Great Britain but the rest of the world. One of these changes was transport – roads changed from ill-kept tracks thick with mud in the winter and choking dust in the summer to smooth tarmacadamed routes by the end of the century. Slow, heavy goods were transported by barge on canals from the mid-eighteenth century until they were superseded by the railways in the mid- to late nineteenth century. The movement of people and goods and the quicker dissemination of news were vastly improved by the advent of the railways resulting in the breaking down of the traditional isolation of many areas in Britain.

Medicine and health also improved; by the middle of the nineteenth century almost half of the patients undergoing major surgery died as a result of post-operative infections. By the end of the nineteenth century this figure was vastly reduced thanks to Joseph Lister's discovery of germ infection and his use of carbolic acid to reduce infection. This acceptance of the need for cleanliness had a dramatic effect on the demography of the country resulting in a rise in the population of England from 8.3 million in 1801 to 16.8 million in 1851, and to nearly double again to 30.5 million by 1901. In addition, attitudes to social welfare and employment, the poor and sick changed radically from mid-eighteenth century to the early nineteenth century, although not always for the better. In place of regarding those less fortunate than themselves as an opportunity to practice care and compassion, attitudes hardened and the poor and unemployed were seen as lazy and indolent. The 1834 *Poor Law Amendment Act* set up Poor Law Unions consisting of several villages which combined to build and run workhouses where the unemployed and old were housed, often separated by gender, parents split from their children and wives from husbands. These buildings sometimes housing over 1000 inmates, were designed to deter people from using them unless really destitute, so much so, that the name workhouse still resonates to this day as a place of last resort.

And finally agriculture on which the country relied for its food. Parliamentary enclosure was the last nail in the coffin in the great shift from public to private use of land that had been underway since before the Reformation. Farming lurched from boom to slump and back again throughout the nineteenth century. During the Napoleonic Wars, 1805–1815, there was a boom, prices of corn were high, wages rose and farmers improved their standard of living. The enclosure movement gained momentum, encouraged by reports made by Vancouver in 1794 and Gooch in 1805, for the Board of Agriculture, on the benefit of consolidation leading to improved productivity and greater profits. From 1815 to 1822 there was a major depression when grain prices fell, taxes rose, and food prices soared. There were bad harvests particularly in 1815, and new machinery was threatening men's livelihoods. Men returning from the Napoleonic wars could not find work and there was much unemployment. Then during the 1850s and 1860s there was a 'Golden Age of Farming' when new farm buildings were erected using concrete for the first time; land was drained and new machinery was bought such as drills, reapers and binders and threshing machines. New inorganic fertilizers including guano from South America and coprolites, from deep in chalk subsoils, were introduced increasing the yield of crops dramatically; this was a period of so called 'High Farming'. By the 1870s there was a further slump, the government did not support local farmers but bought cheap grain from abroad chiefly the United States, and the introduction of refrigeration meant that meat could be brought from Australia and New Zealand. Young able bodied agricultural labourers often with their families emigrated to the growing cities or to the colonies in the hope of a freer and more prosperous life.

The aim of this study has been to examine the enclosure process in the chalk villages of south Cambridgeshire and its effect on the environment of the area. My intention has to been to produce a holistic account, one which considers social, economic, agricultural and environmental change together, as interconnected phenomena. David Grigg reminds us that 'National change is no more than the sum of a number of regional changes; and before the whole can be fully comprehended, the parts must be analysed.'[2] It is hoped that this study of regional change in south Cambridgeshire will add another piece to the jigsaw of national knowledge.

Southern Cambridgeshire was on the edge of the central province as described by Roberts and Wrathmell[3] and was a land of many small landowners; which probably contributed to the late enclosure of the open fields. Its farming practices bridged those of Midland and East Anglian farming as shown in Chapter 3.

The landscape of south Cambridgeshire, although lacking the mountains and lakes of more scenic areas of England, does nevertheless have a local distinctiveness of its own. As the area was never rich and lacked the great estates of some other districts, vernacular architecture overrode the architecture of fashion. The light, easily worked soils, together with a continental climate of warm summers with little rain, meant that from earliest times the area had been particularly suitable for growing grain. The need to keep the soil fertile resulted in a system of farming that utilised the dung of farm animals, particularly sheep, to produce that fertility. So great was the value of the sheep that by the Middle Ages the landowners had appropriated the flocks to themselves and privatised the heaths for this very purpose, allowing only the wet moors, the balks, greens and verges to be shared by the commoners. The sometimes unwilling co-operation between farmers who wished to improve their crops and sheep masters, who wanted to keep the status quo, may have been another reason for the late enclosure of this region. This was reinforced by the comparatively good soils and plentiful water, which enabled many small owners to exist, and which combined with the ecologically sustainable open-field system, resulted in a good living for those who owned the sheep.

The lack of great estates resulted in the principal farmers becoming the village elite and controlling not only the agricultural but also the social and economic life of the parish. These men (and occasionally women) not only controlled the manor courts but held positions of authority in the parish, repeatedly recycling their positions of churchwarden, overseer, constable and surveyor, ensuring that both political and social life remained stable if a little static. Their use of the poor to benefit the village by helping those unable to help themselves, the women caring for the sick and orphaned and laying out and sitting with the dead; the men by performing the menial and routine work within the fields such as ditching and haywarding, resulted in a cohesive and efficient community. Many manors owned by Cambridge colleges were leased for long periods and for food rents resulting in a stable economy and a reluctance to change.

But there were those who were keen to grow the new fodder crops that had already been introduced to a varying but significant extent in the common fields, on a more extensive scale. The rise of the industrial north and the growing population demanding more food, particularly meat, meant that the farmers' desire to improve productivity by growing turnips and the new grasses was one of the driving forces behind enclosure:

> 'But just as a sustainable agriculture had been achieved, the development of chemical fertilisers ... undermined this sustainability. An essentially organic agriculture was gradually replaced by a farming system that relied on energy-intensive inputs dependant on the exploitation of fossil fuels.'[4]

It would seem that this is the price we have to pay to feed the world. Overton points out that, in 1500, 80% of the population was working on the land; by 1850 only 22% were doing the same and despite the growth of the population the majority of farmers were producing more than they needed for themselves and had become businessmen farming for a market.[5]

The privatisation of land caused by Parliamentary enclosure contributed to a loss of the social cohesion of the old order, with the once open fields hedged in and the many footpaths closed. People could no longer walk across the fields as once they had.[6] The great divide between those that owned and those that used the countryside became even wider, as Richard Mabey put it:

> 'The hundreds of miles of new quickset hedges that marked the pattern of enclosure were more than just an indication of a new pattern of agricultural reorganisation. They were symbols of the new barriers which had been created between men and the land.'[7]

The social effects of privatisation, symbolised by the erection of fences and the enclosing and ploughing of the heaths and commons, widened the gap between man and master; the unemployed were seen as almost another species by those whose poor rates seemed to grow yearly.[8] After enclosure, the small common-right owners could no longer rely on the commons to supplement their living with fuel for their fires and fodder for their animals and so were forced to rely on wage labour, sell up or go on the Parish. Although this loss may seem drastic, little is known of the real use to which these commons were put. Some have therefore suggested that the replacement of a somewhat mythical 'freedom' of men, who relied on the commons for a living, with the concrete reliability of a waged job, was more certain.

Moreover, our understanding of the social changes wrought by enclosure, and especially by such late enclosures as those in south Cambridgeshire, is made difficult by the problems of distinguishing the effects of enclosure *per se* from those resulting from wider social, economic and demographic developments. New opportunities were provided for those who had previously assumed that tilling the soil was all there was; the coming of the railways provided work and national schooling enabled previously unlettered labourers to read about actions and opinions of the wider world. Above all, the social and economic environment of south Cambridgeshire in the first half of the nineteenth century was affected by the development of the industrial revolution. Trades and occupations which were carried out locally in homes and small workshops were, by the late eighteenth and early nineteenth centuries, transferring to large factories in the north and midlands of England drawing many workers to them from the countryside. The rise of the small factories in Sawston provided work for many people from the surrounding villages and the growth of consumerism was affecting even the rural parishes of southern Cambridgeshire. The increase in manufactured goods encouraged the newly waged workers to spend what surplus money they could earn.

It is also important to emphasise that if there were those who suffered from enclosure, there were also some individuals who benefited as Chapter 5 illustrates. One would expect the commissioners, surveyors, and large landowners to profit from enclosure but the contractors who dug the ditches, planted the hedges and made the roads also benefited from the process, sometimes to a surprising degree. The commissioners' notebooks also reveal the surprisingly generous spirit shown by the commissioners when they agreed to allot land where it had been requested by the smaller landowners.

The impact of enclosure on the visual appearance of the countryside was as great as that on local society. Enclosure had as profound an effect on the shape of the landscape as the original setting up of the open field system many centuries before, yet to the untutored eye the landscape of Parliamentary Enclosure, with neat fields surrounded by hedges, is seen as 'old England' which had been there from time immemorial instead of for less than 200 years. The commissioners were often professional men working on several enclosures at a time and proficient in their ability to reconcile the division and allocation of the land with the desires and claims of local owners. Their notebooks reveal in minute detail just how the new landscape was designed, how the land was divided, and the fences, ditches and roads made.

But enclosure also contributed to a revolutionary change in the natural world. A range of habitats, sustained by hundreds of years of agricultural activity, were transformed or destroyed with remarkable speed, a topic considered in some detail in the last chapter. The ploughing up of the heaths and wastes and division of the open fields into the privately owned and fenced parcels had a profound effect on the flora and fauna that had previously lived there. A close analysis of the wildlife which flourished both before and after enclosure has been made, and we are fortunate here in having a rich source of nature notebooks written and often published by botany tutors and students from Cambridge University, some dating back to the seventeenth century. The loss of a number of open field and especially heathland species was offset by other species which were now free to colonise the new habitat provided by the hedges and verges of the enclosure roads. Once again, however, it is important to note that the effects of enclosure itself are not always easy to separate from other changes affecting biodiversity, such as the activities of game keepers or the deprivations of the Victorian collectors.

As Richard Purslow has so cogently remarked, 'People, just like every other animal, are organisms who live by exploiting and modifying the resources available to them within a particular habitat'.[9] It is this attitude to human ecology that forms the basis of this study, a detailed account of a small discrete area, predominately rural, undergoing a period of profound change, and examined from a wide variety of perspectives.

Notes

1   Purslow (2006), 105.
2   Grigg (1966), 45.
3   Roberts and Wrathmell (2000).
4   Overton (1996), 4.
5   *Ibid.*, 8.
6   The Journal of the Rev John Wesley 17 July 1759.
7   Mabey (2000), 134.
8   Jefferies (1880).
9   Purslow (2006), 109.

Appendices

Appendix 1. Evidence for manorial sheep flocks before enclosure

Parish	No. sheep	Rights
Duxford	1200	Sheepwalk 2 days a week to Christal farm
Fowlmere	550	2 men claimed right of sheep walk on their land. Lord Dacre claimed right over 'all land of parish'
Foxton	600	300 to Lordship, 100 to Mortimers, 200 to 2 other men. 600 to be kept in 2 flocks 1 for each Manor
Fulbourn	1794–2800	Sheep kept on common 13 Feb to April
Hinxton	500	Three flocks
Harston/Hauxston/ Newton and Lt Shelford	1420	Manor of Butlers – Right of Sheep walk – sheep course & liberty of foldage for 200 sheep (6 score per 100) in, over & upon the fields bounds & commons of Harston, Little Shelford, Hauxton & Newton to the said Manor belonging. Manor of Stonehall – A like right of Sheep walk, sheep course & Liberty of foldage for 200 sheep (6 score per 100). D & C Ely sheep walk for 300 sheep for Newton Rectory. Chas Wale, Lord of Manor of Tiptofts, Harston, sheep walk for 36 score sheep.
GtShelford		Right of common for sheep prevented turnips being grown before enclosure
Lt Shelford		Commonable with Harston/Hauxton & Newton
Pampisford	400	Sheep in winter
Sawston	460	Ferd Huddlestone, Lord of all Manors – Whole sheep walk over common field arable lands and commons according to ancient custom. (Except 30 ewes and ½ share of 1 ram belonging to Brook Farm) 1 moiety Sheep walk 60 ewes & 1ram – Brook farm shared with Richard Robinson
Shepreth	300	Without stint
Stapleford	600	Without stint. Bury has 275a several heath and a sheepwalk for 15 score sheep ADD 6069 Vicar has 2 flocks of 300 in each
Thriplow	1,400	Bury had 500 sheep on 465a. 6 sheep walks, 1 per manor. Sheep on Moor Dec–Feb, on greens and stubble Nov–April
Whittlesford	840	Common, 70a 50a ½ yearly meadow

Appendix 2. Growing Sanfoin 22.1.1789

January 22nd 1789. An agreement made by the inhabitants of the Parish of Thriplow respecting sowing and preserving of sinquefoil, *sanfoin,* as follows.

First, in the HEATHFIELD, from Hurdles Way westward along the top of Towers hill to Farm Lane baulk (excluding the heath Shot) and from the Farm Lane Baulk eastwards to Bush baulk (excluding the shot next Three Acres). and from Bush Baulk (eastwards still) along the top of 20 Acres to Three Acres & so on to Hurdles Way on the southside of the 14 Acres.

Secondly. Every person to have seeds and sow the same quantity of acres with trefoil, in the same field as they have acres of singuefoil, *sanfoin,* & to sow 14 pounds on every acre and to Harrow them in (Dowlage excepted).

Thirdly. The Overseer to buy the seeds at a fair market price, & to produce a bill of the same, Everyman to pay ready money for his seeds. Such lands sown with the aforesaid Trefoil seeds, to lay till harvest is done. Any man not willing to sow them on his own land shall give them to others that will, if such can be found. If not any can be found, then he is freed from this article.

Fourthly. Every time the sainfoin field becomes fallow the trefoil seeds are to be repeated, being sown a sufficient time before hand; in the last year, (that is when the each crop is sown) and to lay as before mentioned.

Fifthly. All cattle to be kept off the young Sanfoin until the first crop is carried, and then none to go on till the Harvest ensuing is finished, (except when the same field is fallow, and then it is common for sheep only after the crop is carried or when the Sanfoin field is cornfield all cattle are to be kept off until harvest is done, & then all cattle are to take it as they do the other stubblefield, except as before excepted upon the young sanfoin.

Sixthly. Every person who feeds any sanfoin contrary to this agreement with any cattle, or that doth not sow seeds in the above manner, & let them lay the time above mentioned, or that in any wise breaketh this article or agreement shall for the first offence forfeit the sum of three shillings & sixpence, for the 2nd, 7 shillings and so on from time to time double; the money arising from such offences to be paid by the owners of the cattle & given to the poor, (first paying the person for his or their troubles). Any person desirous of having a copy of this agreement may at his own expense or trouble have it for his satisfaction.

Seventhly. All cattle to be kept off all the sanfoin at January 5th.

8thly. Every person saving any sanfoin for seed shall pay to the person who receives the Corn tythes the sum of four shillings for every acre that is saved for seed.

9thly. Every person who wilfully trespasseth or breaketh any part of these articles or agreements shall incur the penalty of five pounds to be paid to the overseer & disbursed towards defraying the parish expenses.

Jan 27. 1789

Signed by us

W. Bening	Joseph Ellis	Benj: Prime	Wm Cock
Thos Wallis	Thos Hawes	Bennett Cranwell	Jacob Prime
John Faircloth	Francis Bush		

n.b. a copy of this agreement was sent to Mr Perkins at Chishill 4 May 1822 by J. W. M.

Appendix 3. List of those Assenting, Dissenting or Neutral

ID	surname	first name	freehold	copy	o–10a	11–50a	over 50a	parish	sheepwalk	absentee	dissent	assent	neuter
285	Hagger	Stephen	Yes	Yes	Yes	No	No	Gt Shelford	No		No	No	Yes
274	Chambers	Henry	No	Yes	Yes	No	No	Gt Shelford	No		No	Yes	No
275	Christmas	Sarah	No	Yes	Yes	No	No	Gt Shelford	No		No	Yes	No
276	Coleman	Jon	Yes	Yes	No	Yes	No	Gt Shelford	No		No	No	Yes
277	Collier	Henry	Yes	No	Yes	Yes	No	Gt Shelford	No		No	Yes	No
278	Colliers	Richard love	Yes	No	No	No	No	Gt Shelford	No		No	No	No
279	Dobson	William	No	Yes	Yes	No	No	Gt Shelford	No		Yes	No	No
280	Emson	Robert	No	Yes	No	Yes	No	Gt Shelford	No		No	Yes	No
281	French	Henry rev	No	No	No	No	No	Gt Shelford	No		No	No	No
298	Rawlins	Thomas	Yes	No	Yes	No	No	Gt Shelford	No		No	Yes	No
283	Gell	John	Yes	No	Yes	No	No	Gt Shelford	No		No	No	No
271	Cambridge	William	No	Yes	Yes	Yes	No	Gt Shelford	No		No	No	No
286	Headley	Henry	Yes	Yes	No	No	No	Gt Shelford	No		No	Yes	No
287	Headley	William	No	Yes	No	Yes	No	Gt Shelford	No		No	Yes	No
288	Maris	Allington sen	No	Yes	Yes	No	No	Gt Shelford	No		No	Yes	No
289	Maris	Allington jun	No	No	Yes	No	No	Gt Shelford	No		No	No	No
291	Maris	John	Yes	Yes	Yes	No	No	Gt Shelford	No		No	No	Yes
293	Miller	John	Yes	Yes	Yes	No	No	Gt Shelford	No		Yes	No	No
295	Pamplin	Thomas	No	Yes	Yes	No	No	Gt Shelford	No		No	No	Yes
296	Pearson	Thomas	No	Yes	Yes	No	No	Gt Shelford	No		No	Yes	No
297	Prest	Samuel esq	Yes	Yes	No	No	Yes	Gt Shelford	No		No	Yes	No
282	Foster	Richard	No	Yes	Yes	No	No	Gt Shelford	No		No	Yes	No
262	Wadsworth	Christopher rev	No	Yes	Yes	No	No	Gt Shelford	No		No	Yes	No
247	Jesus	College	Yes	No	No	No	Yes	Gt Shelford	Yes	Cambridge	No	Yes	No
250	Gee	John	No	Yes	Yes	No	No	Gt Shelford	No		Yes	No	No
251	Cotton	Benjamin	Yes	No	Yes	No	No	Gt Shelford	No		No	Yes	No
252	Stacey	Thomas	Yes	No	Yes	No	Yes	Gt Shelford	No		No	Yes	No
253	Smith	E	No	Yes	Yes	No	No	Gt Shelford	Yes		No	Yes	No
254	Caius	College	No	No	No	No	Yes	Gt Shelford	Yes		No	Yes	No
255	Grain	Peter	No	No	No	No	Yes	Gt Shelford	Yes		No	Yes	No
256	Nutter	James	Yes	Yes	Yes	No	Yes	Gt Shelford	No		No	Yes	No
258	St John's	College	No	No	No	No	Yes	Gt Shelford	Yes		No	Yes	No
273	Carter	Sarah	No	No	Yes	No	No	Gt Shelford	No		Yes	No	No
261	Keene	Benjamin	No	Yes	Yes	No	No	Gt Shelford	No		No	No	No
272	Pembroke	Hall	Yes	No	No	No	No	Gt Shelford	No		No	No	Yes
263	Barker	Mary	No	Yes	Yes	No	No	Gt Shelford	No		No	No	Yes
264	Pashley	Robert esq.	No	No	No	No	No	Gt Shelford	No		No	Yes	No
265	Asby	William	Yes	No	Yes	No	No	Gt Shelford	No		No	Yes	No
266	Austin	John	No	No	No	No	No	Gt Shelford	No		Yes	No	No
267	Barker	James	No	Yes	Yes	No	No	Gt Shelford	No	Duxford	No	No	Yes
268	Berry	Rebecca	Yes	Yes	Yes	No	No	Gt Shelford	No		No	Yes	No
269	Betts	Martha	No	Yes	Yes	No	No	Gt Shelford	No		No	Yes	No
270	Betts	Thomas	No	Yes	Yes	No	No	Gt Shelford	No		No	Yes	No

ID	surname	first name	freehold	copy	0–10a	11–50a	over 50a	parish	sheepwalk	absentee	disent	assent	neuter
294	Moore	John	No	Yes	Yes	No	No	Gt Shelford	No		No	No	Yes
259	Green	Edward Humphrey	Yes	No	No	No	Yes	Gt Shelford	Yes		Yes	No	No
491	Elbourn	Thomas	No	Yes	No	No	No	Gt Shelford	No		No	No	No
441	Clark	Elizabeth	No	No	No	No	No	Gt Shelford	No		No	No	No
292	Maris	Richard	Yes	Yes	Yes	No	Yes	Gt Shelford	Yes		Yes	No	No
451	Lockwood	Mr	No	No	No	No	No	Gt Shelford	No		No	No	No
454	Bowrell	Mr	No	No	No	No	No	Gt Shelford	No		No	No	No
459	Moore	William	No	No	No	No	No	Gt Shelford	No		Yes	No	No
461	Wright	Richard	No	No	No	No	No	Gt Shelford	No		No	No	Yes
479	Duce	John	No	No	No	No	No	Gt Shelford	No		No	No	No
486	Hedley	Henry	No	No	No	No	No	Gt Shelford	No		No	Yes	No
299	Rawlins	William	Yes	Yes	Yes	No	No	Gt Shelford	No		Yes	No	No
490	Butler	Phillip	No	No	No	No	No	Gt Shelford	No		No	No	No
500	Hamson	William	Yes	Yes	No	No	No	Gt Shelford	No	Prickwillow	No	No	No
492	Gall	William	No	Yes	No	No	No	Gt Shelford	No		No	No	No
493	Austin	Joseph	No	Yes	No	No	No	Gt Shelford	No		No	No	No
494	Austin	Daniel	No	Yes	No	No	No	Gt Shelford	No		No	No	No
495	Edwards	Robert	No	No	No	No	No	Gt Shelford	No		No	No	No
496	Dear	William	Yes	No	No	No	No	Gt Shelford	No		No	No	No
497	Norfield	John	Yes	Yes	No	No	No	Gt Shelford	No		No	No	No
498	Careless	John	No	Yes	No	No	No	Gt Shelford	No		No	No	No
499	Read	Sarah	No	Yes	No	No	No	Gt Shelford	No	Whittlesford	No	No	No
489	Write	John	No	Yes	Yes	No	No	Gt Shelford	No		No	No	No
306	Willis	William	No	Yes	Yes	No	No	Gt Shelford	No		No	Yes	No
300	Overseers	Ch/wds	No	Yes	Yes	No	No	Gt Shelford	No		No	Yes	No
301	Town	Lands	Yes	No	No	Yes	No	Gt Shelford	No		No	Yes	No
302	Skinner	John	No	Yes	Yes	No	No	Gt Shelford	No	Wilbraham	No	No	No
303	Smith	Rev. doc.	Yes	No	Yes	No	No	Gt Shelford	No		No	No	Yes
304	Tunwell	Henry	Yes	No	Yes	No	No	Gt Shelford	No		No	No	No
445	Barnes	William	No	No	No	No	No	Gt Shelford	No		No	Yes	No
305	Turner	William	Yes	No	Yes	No	No	Gt Shelford	No		No	No	No
51	Northfield	John	Yes	Yes	No	Yes	No	Harston	No		Yes	No	No
36	Hardwick	James	No	No	Yes	No	No	Harston	No		No	No	No
37	Hartley	Thomas	No	Yes	Yes	No	No	Harston	No		Yes	No	No
38	Hayes	Mary	Yes	No	Yes	No	No	Harston	No		Yes	No	No
39	Heffer	Jane	Yes	Yes	Yes	No	No	Harston	No		Yes	No	No
40	Hayes	Allen	Yes	Yes	Yes	No	No	Harston	No		Yes	No	No
41	Hurrell	William	Yes	No	No	No	No	Harston	No	Foxton	No	Yes	No
42	James	Edward	Yes	Yes	Yes	No	No	Harston	No		Yes	No	No
43	Jennings	James	Yes	Yes	Yes	No	No	Harston	No		Yes	No	No
44	Leworthy	William rev.	No	Yes	Yes	No	No	Harston	No		No	Yes	No
60	Whitchurch	William sen.	Yes	Yes	No	No	Yes	Harston	No		No	Yes	No
61	Whitchurch	William jun.	No	Yes	Yes	No	Yes	Harston	No		No	No	Yes
35	Green	Edward esq.	Yes	Yes	No	No	Yes	Harston	Yes		No	Yes	No
63	Whitby	Thomas	Yes	No	Yes	No	No	Harston	No	London	No	Yes	No

ID	surname	first name	freehold	copy	o-soa	tt-soa	over soa	parish	sheepwalk	absentee	dissent	assent	neuter
55	Tuck	Robert	Yes	No	Yes	No	No	Harston	No		No	No	No
65	Whitby	John	No	Yes	Yes	No	No	Harston	No		Yes	No	No
58	Wallis	Swan	Yes	No	No	No	Yes	Harston	Yes		No	Yes	No
56	Wale	Charles esq.	Yes	No	No	No	No	Harston	No	Lt. Shelford	No	Yes	No
59	Widby	Ann	Yes	Yes	Yes	No	Yes	Harston	No		Yes	No	No
45	Littellbridge	J. esq.	Yes	Yes	No	No	No	Harston	Yes		Yes	Yes	No
46	Lyell	Henry esq.	Yes	No	No	Yes	No	Harston	Yes		No	No	No
47	Macer	John	Yes	No	Yes	No	No	Harston	No		Yes	No	No
48	Matthews	Mary	Yes	No	No	Yes	No	Harston	No		Yes	No	No
49	Marshall	Mary	Yes	No	Yes	No	No	Harston	No	Croydon	No	No	Yes
50	Newling	John	Yes	No	Yes	No	No	Harston	No		No	No	Yes
52	Northfield	James	No	Yes	No	Yes	No	Harston	No		Yes	No	No
54	Thompson	Edward	No	Yes	Yes	No	No	Harston	No		Yes	No	No
62	Samuel	Thomas	No	No	No	Yes	No	Harston	No		Yes	No	No
316	Littell	Bridge	No	No	No	No	No	Harston	No		Yes	No	No
23	Amps	Roger	Yes	No	Yes	No	No	Harston	No		No	No	No
34	Gifford	Josiah	Yes	No	Yes	No	No	Harston	No		No	Yes	No
325	Heffer	Jane	No	No	No	No	No	Harston	No		Yes	No	No
53	Rayner	James	Yes	No	Yes	No	No	Harston	No		Yes	No	No
308	Tuck	William	No	No	No	No	No	Harston	No		Yes	No	Yes
25	Beard	James	No	Yes	Yes	No	No	Harston	No	Barley	Yes	No	No
26	Brand	Thomas esq.	No	Yes	No	Yes	No	Harston	No	Meldreth	Yes	No	Yes
32	Flack	John	Yes	No	Yes	No	No	Harston	No		No	No	No
28	Driver	Henry	No	Yes	No	Yes	No	Harston	No		Yes	No	Yes
29	Ellis	David	Yes	No	Yes	Yes	No	Harston	No		Yes	No	No
33	Whitby	Daniel	Yes	No	No	No	No	Harston	No		No	Yes	No
30	Flack	George	No	No	No	No	No	Harston	No		No	No	No
31	Flack	William	Yes	No	Yes	No	No	Harston	No		No	Yes	No
27	Brand	James	No	Yes	No	Yes	Yes	Harston	No		No	No	No
324	Jennings	Thomas	No	No	No	No	No	Harston	No		Yes	No	No
24	Bangle	John	No	No	Yes	No	No	Haslingfield	No	Haslingfield	No	No	No
83	Jepps	Robert	Yes	No	Yes	No	No	Hauxton	No		No	No	No
82	Incarsole	Catherine	No	Yes	No	Yes	No	Hauxton	No	Cambridge	Yes	No	No
81	Halsted	Thomas	Yes	No	No	No	Yes	Hauxton	No	Cambridge	No	Yes	No
77	Gunner	Amy	No	Yes	Yes	No	No	Hauxton	No		No	No	Yes
74	Gardner	Isaac	No	Yes	No	Yes	No	Hauxton	No	Cambridge	No	Yes	No
85	Lilley	Edward	Yes	No	Yes	No	Yes	Hauxton	Yes		No	Yes	No
94	Whitby	Ann	No	No	No	Yes	No	Hauxton	No		Yes	No	No
75	Gillam	Edward	Yes	Yes	Yes	No	No	Hauxton	No		No	No	Yes
86	Lilley	David	No	No	No	No	No	Hauxton	No		No	Yes	No
87	Millbank	Abraham	No	No	Yes	No	No	Hauxton	No	London	No	No	Yes
88	Mitchell	Thomas	Yes	No	No	Yes	No	Hauxton	No		No	No	Yes
89	Morris	Benjamin	No	Yes	Yes	Yes	No	Hauxton	No		No	No	No
90	Morris	Susannah	No	Yes	Yes	Yes	No	Hauxton	No		No	No	No
91	Morris	William	Yes	No	Yes	No	No	Hauxton	No		Yes	No	No

ID	surname	first name	freehold	copy	0–10a	11–50a	over 50a	parish	sheepwalk	absentee	dissent	assent	neuter
73	Finkell	John	No	Yes	Yes	No	No	Hauxton	No	Haslingfield	No	No	No
93	Tuck	Thomas	No	Yes	Yes	No	No	Hauxton	No		No	No	Yes
76	Godfrey	John	Yes	No	Yes	No	No	Hauxton	No	Harston	No	No	No
92	Purchas	John	No	Yes	Yes	No	No	Hauxton	No		No	No	No
72	Finch	Thomas rev.	No	Yes	Yes	No	No	Hauxton	No		No	Yes	No
68	Creek	Sarah	No	Yes	Yes	No	No	Hauxton	No		No	No	No
67	Wale	Charles esq.	No	Yes	Yes	No	No	Hauxton	No	Harston	No	Yes	No
95	Whybury	Abrham	No	Yes	Yes	No	No	Hauxton	No		Yes	No	No
78	Gunner	Thomas	No	Yes	Yes	No	No	Hauxton	No		No	No	No
143	Jeffrey	Benjamin	No	Yes	Yes	No	No	Ickleton	No		Yes	No	No
135	Hailes	William	No	Yes	No	Yes	No	Ickleton	No		No	Yes	No
136	Hammond	William Parker	Yes	No	No	No	Yes	Ickleton	Yes		No	Yes	No
137	Hanchett	John	Yes	Yes	No	Yes	No	Ickleton	No		No	Yes	No
138	Hawkes	Bird, Woodham	Yes	No	Yes	No	No	Ickleton	No	Bishops Stortford	Yes	No	No
139	Hill	John	Yes	Yes	No	Yes	No	Ickleton	No		No	Yes	No
140	Hopwood	Thomas	Yes	No	Yes	No	No	Ickleton	No		No	Yes	No
141	Churchwardens	Ickleton	No	No	Yes	No	No	Ickleton	No		No	Yes	No
114	Amey	Charles	Yes	No	Yes	No	No	Ickleton	No	Fowlmere	No	Yes	No
113	Trinity	College	Yes	No	No	No	Yes	Ickleton	Yes	Cambridge	No	Yes	No
145	Knott	John sen	No	No	Yes	No	No	Ickleton	No	Duxford	Yes	No	No
146	Mumford	Mary	Yes	Yes	Yes	No	No	Ickleton	No		No	No	No
147	Pilgrim	Mary	No	Yes	Yes	No	No	Ickleton	No		No	No	No
148	Nelson	Richard	Yes	No	Yes	No	No	Ickleton	No		No	No	No
149	Pilgrim	Samuel	Yes	Yes	Yes	No	No	Ickleton	No		No	No	No
150	Pytches	Mary	Yes	No	No	No	Yes	Ickleton	No		No	No	No
151	Soole	Richard	No	Yes	Yes	No	No	Ickleton	No		Yes	No	No
152	Pytches	Mary	No	Yes	No	Yes	Yes	Ickleton	Yes		No	Yes	No
142	Charity	Feoffees	Yes	No	No	Yes	No	Ickleton	No		No	Yes	No
125	Clarke	John	No	Yes	Yes	No	No	Ickleton	No		Yes	No	No
130	Gibson	Atkins F.	Yes	Yes	Yes	No	No	Ickleton	No	Saffron Walden	No	Yes	No
129	Gardiner	Isaac	Yes	No	No	Yes	No	Ickleton	No		No	Yes	No
167	Ward	John	No	Yes	Yes	No	No	Ickleton	No		Yes	No	No
153	Ray	Robert	No	Yes	Yes	No	No	Ickleton	No		Yes	No	No
131	Gunning	Henry	Yes	No	Yes	No	Yes	Ickleton	No		No	Yes	No
132	Garner	James	Yes	Yes	No	No	Yes	Ickleton	No		No	Yes	No
128	Creed	Ann	Yes	Yes	No	No	No	Ickleton	No		No	Yes	No
127	Clarke	Alice	No	Yes	Yes	No	No	Ickleton	No		Yes	No	No
116	Clarkson	Townley rev.	Yes	Yes	Yes	No	No	Ickleton	No	Hinxton	No	Yes	No
133	Hagger	Sarah	Yes	No	Yes	No	No	Ickleton	No		Yes	No	No
115	Clare Hall	College	Yes	No	No	No	Yes	ickleton	Yes	Cambridge	No	Yes	No
124	Christle	William	No	Yes	Yes	No	No	Ickleton	No		No	No	No
123	Carder	Barnaby	No	Yes	Yes	No	No	Ickleton	No		Yes	No	No
122	Bull	Nicholas rev	Yes	No	No	Yes	No	Ickleton	No		No	No	No
121	Brook	Susan	Yes	No	No	No	Yes	Ickleton	Yes		No	No	No

ID	surname	first name	freehold	copy	o-toa	1t-soa	over soa	parish	sheepwalk	absentee	dissent	assent	neuter
134	Hailes	John	No	Yes	Yes	No	No	Ickleton	No		No	Yes	No
119	Knight	Jacob	Yes	Yes	No	No	Yes	Ickleton	No		No	Yes	No
118	Spencer	William	Yes	No	Yes	No	No	Ickleton	No		Yes	No	No
117	Houghton	John	Yes	Yes	No	No	Yes	Ickleton	No		No	Yes	No
126	Clarke	Joseph	Yes	No	Yes	No	No	Ickleton	No		Yes	No	No
361	Boose	William	No	No	No	No	No	Ickleton	No		No	No	No
345	Hanchett	Samuel	No	No	No	No	No	Ickleton	No		No	Yes	No
347	Carder	Alice	No	No	No	No	No	Ickleton	No		No	No	No
348	Hopwood	Peter	No	No	No	No	No	Ickleton	No		No	No	No
349	Bird	Elizabeth	No	No	Yes	No	No	Ickleton	No		No	No	No
165	Andrews	Richard	Yes	No	Yes	No	No	Ickleton	No	Hinxton	No	No	No
354	Hubbard	Mrs	No	No	No	No	No	Ickleton	No		No	No	No
154	Rayner	James	No	No	No	No	No	Ickleton	No	Duxford	No	No	No
365	Ellis	Thomas	No	No	No	No	No	Ickleton	No		No	No	No
372	Ellis	Joseph	No	No	No	No	No	Ickleton	No		No	No	No
174	Wiskins	Thomas	Yes	Yes	No	Yes	No	Ickleton	No		No	Yes	No
173	Ray	John	Yes	Yes	No	Yes	No	Ickleton	No		Yes	No	No
172	Matthews	Driver	Yes	Yes	Yes	No	No	Ickleton	No		Yes	No	No
171	Hagger	Stephen	Yes	No	Yes	No	No	Ickleton	No		Yes	No	No
163	Wyndhamhon	Percy Charles	Yes	Yes	No	No	Yes	Ickleton	Yes		No	Yes	No
350	Driver	Edward	No	No	No	No	No	Ickleton	No		No	No	No
170	Fuller	Thomas esq.	No	Yes	No	No	Yes	Ickleton	Yes		No	Yes	No
156	Salmon	Henry	Yes	No	Yes	No	No	Ickleton	No		No	No	No
157	Strange	George	No	Yes	Yes	No	No	Ickleton	No		No	No	No
158	Tofts	James	No	Yes	Yes	No	No	Ickleton	No		No	Yes	No
159	Lofts	Michael	No	Yes	Yes	No	No	Ickleton	No		Yes	No	No
161	Williamson	William	No	No	No	No	Yes	Ickleton	No		Yes	No	No
155	Ripshers	Swan	No	No	No	Yes	No	Ickleton	No		No	Yes	No
164	Foster	Eebeneza	Yes	Yes	Yes	No	No	Ickleton	No		No	No	No
166	Miller	S.	No	Yes	Yes	No	No	Ickleton	No		Yes	No	No
169	Burling	Richard	No	Yes	Yes	No	No	Ickleton	No		Yes	Yes	No
168	Brooke	Susan	Yes	No	No	No	No	Ickleton	No		Yes	No	No
160	Wakefield	Joseph	No	No	No	Yes	No	Ickleton	No		No	Yes	No
107	Hankin	Thomas pate	Yes	Yes	No	No	Yes	Lt Shelford	No		Yes	No	No
106	Wale	Maegaretta	No	No	No	Yes	No	Lt Shelford	No		Yes	No	No
105	Swaine	John rev	Yes	No	No	Yes	No	Lt Shelford	No		No	Yes	No
104	Rust	John	No	Yes	Yes	No	No	Lt Shelford	No		Yes	No	Yes
103	Rider	Joseph	Yes	Yes	Yes	No	No	Lt Shelford	No		Yes	Yes	No
102	Rider	William	No	Yes	Yes	No	No	Lt Shelford	No	Harston	Yes	No	No
97	Finch	William	Yes	No	No	Yes	No	Lt Shelford	Yes		No	Yes	No
98	Gunner	John	No	Yes	Yes	No	No	Lt Shelford	No	Gt Shelford	No	No	Yes
108	Margotts	William	Yes	No	Yes	No	No	Lt Shelford	No		No	No	No
99	Knott	John	Yes	No	Yes	No	No	Lt Shelford	No	Duxford	No	No	Yes
100	Pemberton	Mary	Yes	Yes	Yes	No	No	Lt Shelford	No		No	Yes	No

ID	surname	first name	freehold	copy	0–10a	11–50a	over 50a	parish	sheepwalk	absentee	dissent	assent	neuter
101	Peppins	Edward esq.	No	No	Yes	No	No	No	Lt Shelford	No	? Absentee	No	Yes	No
96	Case	Thomas	Yes	No	Yes	No	No	No	Lt Shelford	No		No	Yes	No
339	Astin	Thomas	No	No	No	No	No	No	Lt Shelford	No		No	No	No
340	Mansfield	William	No	No	No	No	No	No	Lt Shelford	No		No	No	No
57	Wale	Charles esq.	Yes	Yes	Yes	No	Yes	No	Lt Shelford	Yes		No	Yes	No
79	Gunner	Thomas	No	Yes	Yes	No	No	No	Lt Shelford	No	Harston	Yes	No	No
84	Jennings	William	No	Yes	Yes	No	No	No	Lt Shelford	No		Yes	No	No
110	Pemberton	Christopher	No	Yes	No	Yes	No	No	Newton	No	Cambridge	No	Yes	No
111	Sennett	John	Yes	Yes	No	Yes	No	No	Newton	No	Cambridge	No	Yes	No
112	Stevenson	John rev. esq.	No	Yes	Yes	No	No	No	Newton	No		No	Yes	No
318	Wallis	Swan	No	No	No	No	No	No	Newton	No	Harston	No	Yes	No
66	Wale	Charles esq.	Yes	Yes	No	No	Yes	No	Newton	No	Ely	No	Yes	No
69	Ely	Dean and chapter	No	No	No	No	Yes	No	Newton	Yes		No	Yes	No
70	Hurrell	William	Yes	No	No	Yes	No	No	Newton	No		No	Yes	No
80	Grain	Peter	Yes	No	No	Yes	No	No	Newton	No	Trumpington	No	Yes	No
22	Allen	William	Yes	Yes	No	No	No	Yes	Newton	No		Yes	No	No
184	Wards	Charity	Yes	No	No	Yes	No	No	sawston	No		No	No	No
210	Reeder	Thomas	Yes	No	Yes	No	No	No	sawston	No		No	No	No
200	Martindale	Charles	Yes	Yes	No	No	Yes	No	sawston	No		No	No	No
201	Mean	John	No	Yes	Yes	No	No	No	sawston	No		No	No	No
202	Newby	H.	No	No	Yes	No	No	Yes	sawston	No		No	No	No
203	Nash	W.w.	Yes	Yes	Yes	No	No	No	sawston	No	Royston	No	No	No
204	Phillips	John	Yes	No	Yes	No	No	No	sawston	No	Royston	No	No	No
205	Parrott	Jeremiah	No	Yes	Yes	No	No	No	sawston	No		No	No	No
206	Parrott	Thomas	Yes	No	No	No	No	No	sawston	No		No	No	No
207	Robinson	Stephen	No	Yes	Yes	No	No	No	sawston	No		No	No	No
199	Lofts	John	No	Yes	Yes	No	Yes	No	sawston	No		No	No	No
209	Robinson	Richard	No	Yes	No	No	No	No	sawston	No		No	No	No
212	Salmon	Charlotte	Yes	No	Yes	No	No	No	sawston	No		No	No	No
211	Robinson	Richard sen.	Yes	No	Yes	No	No	No	sawston	No		No	No	No
175	Ansell	Elizabeth	No	No	Yes	No	No	No	sawston	No		No	No	No
213	Metcalf	William rev.	Yes	No	Yes	No	No	No	sawston	No	Stapleford	No	No	No
181	Cooper	James	Yes	Yes	Yes	No	No	No	sawston	No		No	No	No
215	Webb	Joseph	No	Yes	Yes	No	No	No	sawston	No		No	No	No
216	Williams	Elizabeth	No	Yes	No	No	No	No	sawston	No		No	No	No
388	Jones	John	No	No	No	No	No	No	sawston	No		No	No	No
400	Hills	Robert	No	No	No	No	No	No	sawston	No		No	No	No
208	Reynolds	William	Yes	Yes	Yes	No	No	No	sawston	No		No	No	No
179	Brown	Simon	Yes	Yes	No	Yes	No	No	sawston	No		No	No	No
214	Wade	Joseph	No	Yes	Yes	No	Yes	No	sawston	No		No	No	No
198	Howell	Stephen	Yes	Yes	Yes	No	No	No	sawston	No		No	No	No
177	Adams	Thomas	No	Yes	No	No	No	No	sawston	No		No	No	No
178	Benning	Ambrose esq.	Yes	No	Yes	Yes	No	No	sawston	No	Thriplow	No	No	No
180	Barnes	George	No	Yes	Yes	No	No	No	sawston	No		No	No	No

ID	surname	first name	freehold	copy	0-10a	11-50a	over 50a	parish	sheepwalk	absentee	dissent	assent	neuter
182	Jesus	College	Yes	No	No	No	Yes	sawston	Yes	Cambridge	No	No	No
185	Duce	Richard	No	Yes	Yes	No	No	sawston	No		No	No	No
186	Fitch	Richard	No	No	Yes	No	No	sawston	No		No	No	No
187	Gibson	A. T.	Yes	No	Yes	No	No	sawston	No		No	No	No
194	Haylock	Ann	Yes	No	Yes	No	No	sawston	No		No	No	No
196	Heffer	Robert	No	Yes	Yes	No	No	sawston	No		No	No	No
176	Atkinson	William	No	Yes	Yes	No	No	sawston	No		No	No	No
188	Gosling	John	Yes	Yes	No	No	No	sawston	No		No	No	No
197	Haylock	John rev.	Yes	Yes	Yes	No	No	sawston	No		No	No	No
195	Huntingdons	Charity	Yes	No	No	Yes	No	sawston	No		No	No	No
193	Huddlestone	Ferdinand	Yes	No	No	No	Yes	sawston	Yes		No	No	No
192	Gibson	A. S.	Yes	No	Yes	No	No	sawston	No	Saffron Walden	No	No	No
191	Gilby	William	No	Yes	Yes	No	No	sawston	No		No	No	No
190	Gregory	James	Yes	Yes	Yes	No	No	sawston	No		No	No	No
189	Guiver	John	No	Yes	Yes	No	No	sawston	No		No	No	No
235	Heffer	Robert	Yes	No	No	Yes	No	stapleford	No		No	No	No
245	Stacey	William	No	Yes	Yes	No	No	stapleford	No		No	No	No
237	Johnson	John	No	Yes	No	Yes	No	stapleford	No		No	No	No
238	Headley	Henry	No	Yes	Yes	No	No	stapleford	No		No	No	No
239	Mulis	Charles rev.	Yes	Yes	No	No	Yes	stapleford	No		No	No	No
236	Heffer	Robert	No	Yes	No	No	Yes	stapleford	No		No	No	No
240	Marshall	John	Yes	No	No	Yes	No	stapleford	No		No	No	No
241	Nutters	John	No	Yes	Yes	No	No	stapleford	No		No	No	No
243	Smith	James	Yes	Yes	No	Yes	No	stapleford	No		No	No	No
246	Willis	Robert	Yes	No	No	Yes	No	stapleford	No		No	No	No
234	Green	Humphrey minor	Yes	No	No	Yes	No	stapleford	No	Sawston	No	No	No
223	Carter	John	Yes	No	No	No	No	stapleford	Yes		No	No	No
242	Osbourne hon	Godolphin J.	No	No	Yes	No	Yes	stapleford	No		No	No	No
226	Collier	Richard	Yes	No	Yes	No	No	stapleford	No	Castle Camps	No	No	No
217	Atkinson	William	No	No	No	No	No	stapleford	No		No	No	No
218	Brand	William	Yes	No	Yes	No	No	stapleford	No		No	No	No
219	Banks	James	Yes	No	No	Yes	No	stapleford	No		No	No	No
220	Collier	Tregonwell	Yes	Yes	Yes	No	No	stapleford	No		No	No	No
221	Cocks	William	Yes	Yes	Yes	Yes	No	stapleford	No		No	No	No
225	Coxall	Mary	Yes	No	Yes	No	No	stapleford	No	Sawston	No	No	No
224	Collier	Richard Love	Yes	No	Yes	No	No	stapleford	No	Castle Camps	No	No	No
233	Gosling	John	Yes	No	No	No	No	stapleford	No	Sawston	No	No	No
227	D and C	Ely	Yes	No	No	No	Yes	stapleford	Yes	Cambridge	No	No	No
228	Allix	Sarah	Yes	No	Yes	Yes	Yes	stapleford	Yes		No	No	No
229	Eades	Joseph	Yes	No	Yes	No	No	stapleford	No	Saffron Walden	No	No	No
230	Freeman	Ann	No	No	Yes	No	No	stapleford	No		No	No	No
231	Grain	Peter jnr	Yes	Yes	Yes	No	No	stapleford	No		No	No	No
232	Grain	Constance	Yes	No	Yes	No	No	stapleford	No		No	No	No
222	Christmas	John	No	Yes	Yes	No	No	stapleford	No		No	No	No

Appendix 4. Size and nature of moors or commons

Parish	Size (acres)	Comments	Ref.
Fowlmere	200	Moorey nature – Bad drainage Cattle without stint, cut sedge and reeds, gather dung and dig clay Spade husbandry	Van. P70 CRO 292/02–36 CRO 292/04B
Hauxton	20	Pasture /commons	*VCH* Vol.8
Hinxston	40	Meadow of moorey nature	Van., p. 68
Ickleton	40 30	Moorey common Half-yearly meadow lands	Van., p. 69
Melbourn	400 100	Meadow covered with bogs and blind wells Balks	PRO IR 13609 tithe files
Pampisford	150 20	Moor, badly drained, cows and horses in summer, sheep in winter Meadow, quote re destruction of hay crop	Van., p. 66
Sawston	100 300	Half yearly meadow land Common – moorey, 'cattle carried off by absolute rot which is communicated by the foulness of the herbage.'	Van., p. 65
Shepreth	100	Common, dry gravel and moorey, Depastures without stint, cows, sheep, horses	Van., p. 71
Stapleford	100 40	Half yearly meadow land Common, without stint	Van., p. 53
Thriplow	180	Moore, loose, spongey black soil abounding in springs, of little value Drained and cultivated on enclosure Baulks grazed	Van., p. 22 St John's Coll. 99/16 PRO IR 13652
Whittlesford		Got Moor, coterminous with Thriplow, similar in nature	Same comments

Van = Vancouver 1794

Appendix 5. CRO 292/02–36 Fowlmere Petition 1845

292/02. Letter dated Jan. 15th 1845 to Samuel Wells Esq, 6 Lincoln Inn, Temple, London

Sir, We are taking great liberties in writing to you but we was advised to do by a great friend in Huntingdonshire on a subject which concerns us as the Labouring class of the inhabitants of the Parish of Foulmire in the county of Cambridge as our landed Proprietors intend applying to Parliament next session for an act to inclose all lands – baulks – wastes & commons pf which commons exclusive of baulks there is upwards of 200 acres – of which we have the privilege of mowing the fodder and gathering dry manure for fuel and of turning cows etc on if we can purchase them – as the poor have the same opportunity of stocking it as the farmers but the farmers are prohibited turning sheep on it. These privileges we have had from generation to generation. There is a rent paid for the commons at Bell & Pymans office No. 6 Gough Square nr Fleet Street – the rent is demanded by the Parish constable but late years has been paid by the Overseer it is called in the demand the Rent for the fee farm – 21s which 21 shillings is paid from the Parish rate which thing we do not understand.

The Rev Mr Metcalf Rector has said the commons belong to Mr Mitchell and himself exclusively as Lords of the Manor of Foulmire.

Sir, you are aware as Labourers chiefly we have not much money but we could collect as small sum for advice and if we can get any land it would seem poor land if it would not pay other expenses by a rent upon it and if you answer us we will pay by post the expenses for enquiring by directing to Mr Wm Dean, Black Horse Inn, Foulmire, Cambs. Feb 14th 1845.

From your humble and obedient servants – the Labourers of the Parish of Fowlmire.

On opposite page 'copy' Fen Office 16th Feb 1845

Mr Dean, I beg you and the poor labourers of the Parish will be assured that I feel both my Duty as well as natural inclination at all times and upon all occasions to stand up and support to the utmost of my power the rights and interests of the labouring poor for whose depressed condition I have always done my utmost for years to prevent. If therefore I can in regards to the Inclosure of Foulmere prevent any wrong done I will cheerfully do it.

Nothing can be done until the Bills presented to the House of Commons and read a first time when we shall see what it contains.

In the mean time I earnestly advise you and your poor neighbours not on any account to sign any paper whatever or give any assent, to any application respecting the Inclosure and you may rely upon me as soon as I obtain a copy of the Bill I will either come down or send for some of you up here to obtain all proper information as the proprietors may not intend to do any injustice and as it is my rule not to prejudice process. You may rely upon my Assistance and that no neglect shall take place.

Your friend

Saml Wells

292/03. Letter dated Feb 8th 1845 to Samuel Wells Esq.

Sir, It was with pleasure we received your kind and condescending letter and according to your letter we did not deem it necessary to write to you immediately but as there are some Lands which we call Town Lands to the amount of 8a 1r open field arable and about 1½a pasture which altogether lets for £22 p.a. which is of late years applied to the repairs of the Church and incidental expenses but formerly was distributed among the poor of the parish and some other things which we think not right which we can appraise you of when we see you – the Proprietors of Lands in Foulmire have had two meetings on the subject of Inclosure and I suppose have presented the petition to Parliament.

Four years since this time they enclosed Thriplow the adjoining parish to us and they have not left a single foot of the extensive commons for the use of the poor with the exception of the recreation ground.

We have about or near 20acres of common land under spade husbandry for the poor to occupy let at from 1¼d to 2d per pole broke up under the 1st and 2nd of William IVth, an act to inclose part of the common for the use of the poor.

When any of us wee you we can inform you more on this and other subjects.

From your humble etc.

Copy 10th Feb. 1845

Mr Dean, The petition for inclosing the Parish of Foulmere is not yet presented nothing is needful to be done until the Bill is presented and I will get a copy of it and take your case. Your case is not neglected.

Saml Wells

292/04.

Sir, According to your requests I have sent a few of the names of the old inhabitants of Foulmere who in common with others have enjoyed the profits arising from our commons both moors and heaths unmolested and they have never heard their forefathers say anything to the contrary. I think I wrote saying there was no right of sheep walk on the moor but there is on the hearth. The undersigned are five of the old inhabitants and from enquiry from the whole which would sign their names if Requisite according to this statement is the same.

The situation of the poors allotment you wish'd me to let you know and distance from the parish are as follows about 6a on the Holmes which is Lammas Ground the Land Lady Mitchells near ¾ mile from parish and about 15a on the old town heath a little over a mile.

Wm Ware aged 76 Born in the Parish
James Runham aged 72 his mark
Edward Harrop aged 70   "
Thomas Smith aged 65   "
James Pearce aged 65   "

The occupiers as under first the Holmes

John Nunn   John Wilkerson
Jas Barker   Chas Course

Thos Wright	Wm Scott
Jas Dean	John Cottredge
Thos Barker	Geo Savil)
Geo Barker	John Bird) 1 rood
Thos Burgess	Jas Scott
Wm Barker	John Smith
John Pluck	Rbt Pearce
Thos Morley	Ed Harrup
Wm Burgess	Thos Scott
Jas Cooper	Benjamin Bright

Are ½a each pd.

Heath	
Ed Ison)	Willshire
Chas Sherwood)1 rood.	Thos Wilkerson
Thos Smith	Joseph Sheldrake
Jos Parkis	an acre & half on
Wm Wilkerson	North Moor
Rbt Lodge	rood
Wm Course	Thos Pearce
Jas Fortune	Jas Hayles
Rich. Warren	Jacob Ward
Wm Smith	Wm Churchman
Jas Perry	Wm Pearce
John Baker	Thos Course
Aaron Harrup	none on the Great Moor
Stephen Ward	which contains
Jos Wallis	180 or 190a
Wk Hayles	

We believe there is more acres of common than at first stated which by estimation should be as follows:

The old town Heath on the sketch map	90a	but encroached upon
Old Norwich Road	7a	"
Great Moor	180a	" a little
North Moor	25a	
Baulks for milch cows not estimated	302a	

I have enclosed a paper which contains the act under which a part of the common was broke up and conditions of tenancy etc.

From Your etc.

20–3–1845

292/04b Notice of Spade Husbandry (see page 78).

292/05.

21–3–1845 – Copy, Mr Dean, The Committee on the Bill meets Monday the 9th. If therefore you wish to have your case on the part of the poor commoners brought before that Committee you have no time to lose, indeed fully expected to have heard from you with the particulars requested when we met at Cambridge.

However I have drawn out a draft of a petition to the House of Commons and my Clerk shall be at the Black Horse Inn at Foulmere on Monday next by the Cambridge coach to meet over the Draft of the petition ??? and get it signed and bring it back with time to present it to the House – you must get the interested parties to attend on Wed. and give every information with the names of 2 witnesses and who will attend to give the statement on the petition who must be upon Sunday 6th April at the latest but Sat. will be better.

I hope you have everybody ready on my clerks arrival.

Can you get the Thriplow Inclosure Act – when is the parish inclosed.

Saml Wells.

292/06. Foulmere April 1st 1845

sir We are very sorry to give you so much trouble in writing to you but our subscriptions being begun by only a few at first for some time we have not raised money enough to cover the expenses at the present – but we have all the poor men joined us now with a very few exceptions we shall not be a great while but the majority have joined of late and have not paid up equal to the first at present as they find it hard to spare a few shillings at once – and as our farmers and most of them in a little trade are very much against us – we cannot borrow any of them for a little while to help us therefore if you could let there is above £20 stand over for a little while we should feel ourselves very much obliged to you and I think give you satisfaction in the Remainder when we come up.

Copy, 2–4–1845

Mr Dean, Twenty pounds will be quite sufficient at present. I don't know that more will be wanted but cannot fully say exactly. I hope you will take care that Wm Hore, Jas Runham, Ed Harrop cometh which will I think be sufficient but some of the parish should come up with them.

I shall want someone to witness as to Thriplow Inclosure,

Saml Wells

292/07. Wm Ward's Deposition, *photocopied.*

"Sur, i am srray to say that i cannot atend threw infirmity but am Ready to take my oath that the Rights of the Commons have bene ingread by all the pore in the parrish and unmolested all my years and i never heard to the contry from my Father or Grandfather or any one else.

Witness my hand this 5 day April 1845.

Wm Weare aged 76 years."

292/09. 3–3–1845 List for Committees on Private Bills – List of counties. Under Cambs is written by hand Lord C.Hamilton, Hon.R.Gore, Mr Greenall, Mr Grimsditch, Major M.Chapman, Mr J.Warren

292/08. 7–4–45 – Hayward and Co. 16 Parliament Street, London

Dear Sir, Foulmire Inclosure,

We are somewhat astonished at your Accusation against us of want of courtesy in not informing you of the postponement of the committee on this Bill, your letter of the 5th Instant in which the accusation is made being the first intimation we had of your having anything to do with the petition against the Bill.

Yours truly

Dorrington Hayward & Co.
To Saml Wells.

292/010. Petition to House of Commons. Draft. Parish has 2111a
292/011. Fair copy

292/012. Notes re amounts of land and practices in other parishes.

1830 About the year 1830 the Parish Officers had potatoes planted upon the North Moor and pay the Labour out of the rates. The potatoes and manure out of the rates – At Michaelmass the parish officers were going to sell them – Three ? men run before the Churchwardens and poor about to buy them and took the potatoes away ? cleared the whole.

The men were taken before Revd. Mr Metcalf a magistrate and Rector of the said parish and pay 1d each the men should be let off but said was waived and the men were discharged.

292/027. Bundle of Foulmere claims and notices of objections.
292/028. Printed list of claims and copy

PETITION Excerpt – 'that your Petitioners have the more reason to fear such results inasmuch as the poor inhabitants of the adjoining parish of Thriplow in the same county having the same rights and privileges on the Commons of the Parish upon the Inclosure without Clauses of protection were utterly and most unjustly deprived thereof upon the Inclosure and every plot of land even the Parish Green was allotted away from the poor parishioners without any compensation whatever except 2 acres as a recreation ground ...'

292/029. Letter to Saml Wells from Parishioners, Wm Wilkerson, Richard Rickard, Ones. Hayles, Jas Barker, Jos Hagger, thanking Mr Wells for appealing on their behalf.

292/034. Jan 7th 1846 To Saml Wells

Sir, We are taking great liberty in writing to you before we discharge our debt but our Recreation ground is set out so very inconvenient for cricketing as it is but 3 acres. It is 11½ chains long and not 3 chains over which it is of very little use for that purpose. We should feel grateful to you if you would let us know whether it could be altered to make it more convenient.

The poor.

292/035. 21–2–1846 To Sam Wells

Sir, Will you be so kind as to send me a note what day you will be at Cambridge as I call'd at the Independent office and they told me you were often in Cambridge as we want to pay you and see you on another subject. I should have come down to Ely but our funds are so low we thought we would meet you at Cambridge when you come up and save us expenses.

292/036 Transcript of all letters by Rev York with notes by Mr Vinter.

Result of Petition – 14½ acres on the Heath to be set aside for Spade Husbandry now to be 28 acres let out to the poor, ditched and fenced from enclosure funds. Income from rent to be allotted to the poor.

Appendix 6. Flora

Authors' initials: JH = J. Henslow; H = G. Henslow; E = Evans; K = Kingston; R = John Ray; Rel = Relhan; Mar = Martyn; B = Babbington, M = Maynard

a) Arable

Latin name	*English name*	*date*	*place*	*author*
aethusa cynapium	fools parsley	1835		JH
aethusa cynapium	fools parsley	1915		H
anthenis arvensis	corn chamomile	1915		H
anthenis arvensis	corn chamomile	1835		JH
antirrhinum orontium	snapdragon	1915		H
brassica alba	white mustard	1835		JH
brassica alba	white mustard	1939	Thriplow	E
brassica arvensis	charlock	1939	Thriplow	E
brassica arvensis	charlock	1835		JH
brassica nigra	black mustard	1835		JH
brassica nigra and alba	mustard	1915		H
brassica sinapsis	charlock	1915		H
campanula specularia	harebell	1835		JH
campanula specularia hybrida	harebell	1915		H
centeurea cynanus	cornflower	1915		H
chrysanthemum segetum	corn marigold	1836	Whittlesford	M
chrysanthemum segetum	corn marigold	1915		H
coriandrum sativum	coriander	1915		H
coriandrum sativum	coriander	1835		JH
cuscutea epithymum	dodder	1868	Whittlesford	M
cuscutea epithymum	dodder	1835		JH
delphinium ajacis	larkspur	1915		H
delphinium consolida	field larkspur	1820	Shelford	Rel
dipsacus fullonum	teasle	1915		H
euphorbia helioscopia	sun spurge	1835		JH
euphorbia helioscopia	sun spurge	1915		H
fumaria officinalis	fumitory	1939	Thriplow	E
fumaria officinallis	fumitory	1835		JH
fumaris macrantha	fumitory	1848	Fulbourn	B
galeopsis ladanum	hemp nettle	1868	Whittlesford	M
galeopsis ladanum	hemp nettle	1835		JH
galeopsis ladanum	hemp nettle	1915		H
galium aparine	cleavers	1915		H
galium aparine	cleavers	1835		JH
githago segetum	corncockle	1915		H
iberis amena	candy tuft	1915	Hitchin	H
iberis amera	candytuft	1939	Shepreth	E
lathrys aphaca	yellow vetchling	1835		JH
lathyrus aphaca	yellow vetchling	1915		H
lithospermum arvensis	gromwell	1915		H
lithospermum officinale	gramwell	1835		JH
lithospermum officinale	gromwell	1939	Thriplow	E
lychnis githago	corn cockle	1939	Newton	E
lychnis githago	corn cockle	1868	Whittlesford	M
lychnis githago	corn cockle	1835		JH

Latin name	English name	date	place	author
lychnis nostiflora	night flowering catchfly	1808	Cherry Hinton	B
mantha gentilis	bushy mont	1763	Shelford	Mar
matricaria chamomilla	wild chamomile	1835		JH
matricaria chamomilla	wild chamomile	1915		H
medicago inula	black medick	1868	Thriplow	M
melamphrym arvensis	cow wheat	1915		H
mentha agrestis	field mint	1820	Pampisford	Rel
mentha arvensis	field mint	1915		H
narcissus biflorus	two flowered narcissus	1835	Garden escape	M
narcissus pseudo-narcessis	daffodil	1877	Dropped by rooks	M
narcissus pseudonarcissis	daffodil	1763	Whittlesford	Mar
narcissus pseudonarcissus	daffodil	1835		JH
narcissus pseudo-narcissus	daffodil	1939	Whittlesford	E
orabanche elatior	tall broomrape	1820	Shelford	Rel
papava rhaeos	poppy	1915		H
papava rhaeos	poppy	1835		JH
polygonum fagaphrum	buckwheat	1873		M
ranunculus acris	buttercup	1915		H
ranunculus acris	meadow buttercup	1835		JH
ranunculus arvensis	buttercup	1915		H
ranunculus arvensis	corn buttercup	1835		JH
rhinanthus crista-galli	yellow rattle	1915		H
rhinanthus crista-galli	yellow rattle	1835		JH
scabiosa arvensis	field scabious	1915		H
scabiosa arvensis	field scabious	1868		M
scabiosa columbaria	small scabious	1868		M
scabiosia arvensis	field scabious	1848	Cherry Hinton	B
scabiosia succisa	davil's bit scabious	1835		JH
scabiosia succisa	devils bit scabious	1842		M
scandix pectin-veneris	shepherds needle	1915		H
scandix pectin-veneris	shepherd's needle	1835		JH
seline otites	catchfly	1915		H
seline otites	catchfly	1835		JH
senecio jacobaea	ragwort			M
senecio jacobaea	ragwort	1835		JH
sheradia arvensis	field madder	1915		H
sheradia arvensis	little field madder	1763	Thriplow	Mar
sheradia arvensis	field madder	1835		JH
sherardia arvensis	field madder	1860		M
sherardia arvensis	little field madder	1820	Thriplow	Rel
silene anglica	small flowered catchfly	1763	Newmarket Heath	Mar
sonchus arvensis	sow thistle	1835		JH
sonchus arvensis	sow thistle	1915		H
thlaspi arvensis	field penny-cress	1835		JH
thlaspi arvensis	field penny cress	1939	Ickleton	E
thlaspi arvensis	penny cress	1915		H
vinca minor	lesser periwinkle	1835		JH
vinca minor	lesser periwinkle	1848	Fulbourn	B
viola lutea	yellow field pansy	1835		JH
viola lutea	yellow field pansy	1915		H
viola tricolour	field violet	1870		M
viola tricolour	field violet	1835		JH

b) Heath

Latin name	English name	date	place	author
agrimonia eupatoria	agrimony	1890	Royston Heath	K
agrimonia eupatoria	agrimony	1835		JH
ajuga chamaepitys	common ground pine	1835		JH
ajuga chamaepitys	common ground pine	1660	Thriplow	R
ajuga chamaepitys	ground pine	1802	Thriplow	Rel
ajuga chamaepitys	ground pine	1763	Thriplow	Mar
alsine tenuifolia		1660	Thriplow	R
anacamtis pyramidalis	purple orchid	1660	Devils Ditch	R
anagalis arvensis	scarlet pimpernel	1835		JH
anagalis arvensis	scarlet pimpernel	1840	Whittlesford	M
anemone pulsatilla	pasque flower	1890	Royston Heath	K
anemone pulsatilla	pasque flower	1840	Devil's Dyke	B
anemone pulsatilla	pasque flower	1848	Fleam Dyke	B
anemone pulsatilla	pasque flower	1842	Whittlesford	M
anemone pulsatilla	pasque flower	1848	Fleam Dyke	B
anemone pulsitilla	pasque flower	1939	Ickleton	E
antennaria dioicia	cat's foot	1763	Newmarket Heath	Mar
antenneria dioica	mountain everlastin	1890	Royston Heath	K
artimisia vulgaris	mugwort	1660	Newmarket Heath	R
asperula cynanchia	squinancywort	1835		JH
asperula cynanchica	squinancy wort	1915	Heath	H
asperula cynanchuca	woodruff	1763	Newmarket Heath	Mar
asperula cynandica	squinancywort	1890	Royston Heath	K
astegalus danicus	purple milk-vetch	1939	Thriplow	E
astragalis arvenarius	milk vetch	1763	Devil's Dyke	Mar
astragalis glycyphyllis	milk vetch	1763	Shelford	Mar
astragalis glycyphyllos	wild licorice	1835	Shelford	JH
astragalus hypoglotti	purple milk-vetch	1840	Devil's Dyke	B
astragalus hypoglottis	purple milk-vetch	1835	Devil's Dyke	JH
astragalus hypoglottis	purple milk-vetch	1890	Royston Heath	K
astragalus hypoglottis	purple mountain milkwort	1802	Shelford	Rel
astregalus glycyphyllos	wild licorice	1939	Thriplow	E
brizia media	quaking grass	1890	Royston Heath	K
calluna vulgaris	ling	1939	Ickleton	E
calluna vulgaris	ling	1835	Royston Heath	JH
campanula glomerata	clustered bellflower	1763	Shelford	Mar
campanula glomerata	clustered bellflower	1763	Newmarket Heath	Mar
campanula glomerate	clustered bell-flower	1890	Royston Heath	K
campanula glomerate	clustered bell-flower	1835		JH
campanula rapunculua	rampion	1915	Heath	H
campanula rotundifolia	herebell	1890	Royston Heath	K
campanula rotundifolia	harebell	1915	Heath	H
carduus nutans	musk thistle	1835		JH
carduus nutans	musk thistle	1890	Royston Heath	K
carex binervis	greenwinged sedge	1802	Shelford	Rel
carlina vulgaris	carline thistle	1763	Newmarket Heath	Mar
carline vulgaris	carline thistle	1835		JH
carline vulgaris	carline thistle	1890	Royston Heath	K
cerastium arvense	mouse-eared chickweed	1763	Newmarket Heath	Mar
cerastium arvense	chickweed	1660	Newmarket Heath	R
cerastium arvense	mouse-eared chickweed	1763	Devil's Ditch	Mar
chelidonium majus	greater celendine	1890	Therfield Heath	K

Latin name	English name	date	place	author
chelidonium majus	greater celendine	1890	Royston Heath	K
chironia centaurium*	common centaury	1802	Shelford	Rel
cineraria campestris	field fleawort	1890	Royston Heath	K
cineraria campestris	field fleawort	1835		JH
cistus helianthemum	dwarf cistus	1802	Thriplow	Rel
conyza squarrosa	plowman's spikenard	1802	Shelford	Rel
conyza squarrosa	plowman's spikenard	1802	Whittlesford	Rel
conyza squarrosa	plowman's spikenard	1802	Stapleford	Rel
crepis foetida	stinking hawkbeard	1802	Whittlesford	Rel
crepis foetida	stinking hawkbeard	1802	Shelford	Rel
cuscuta epithymum	dodder	1915	Heath	H
cystisus scoparius	furze	1835		JH
cytisus scoparius	furze	1915	Heath	H
echium vulgare	viper's bugloss	1890	Royston Heath	K
echium vulgare	viper's bugloss	1835		JH
ergeron aceris	blue fleabane	1835		JH
erica tetralix	cross leaved heather	1835		JH
erica tetralix	cross leaved heather	1859	Thriplow	M
erica vulgaris	common heath	1859	Thriplow	M
erigeron aceris	blue fleabane	1868	Thriplow	M
erigeron acre	blueflowered fleabane	1763	Shelford	Mar
eriophrum polystashion	many headed cotton grass	1842	Thriplow	M
euphrasia officinallis	eyebright	1835		JH
euphrasia offinillis	eyebright	1890	Royston Heath	K
filago germanica	common cudweed	1890	Royston Heath	K
filago germanica	common cud-weed	1835		JH
filago germanica	common cud-weed	1835	Thriplow	M
filago minima	slender cud-weed	1860	Pampisford	M
filago minima	slender cud-weed	1835	Pampisford	JH
filago spathulata	cudweed	1915	Thriplow	H
fumaria parviflora	small leaved fumitory	1938	Royston Heath	E
galium saxatile	bed-straw	1915	Heath	H
galium saxatile	bed-straw	1835		JH
galium uliginosum	fen bedstraw	1915	Meldreth	H
galium uliginosum	fen bedstraw	1835		JH
gentiana amerella	autumn gentian	1890	Royston Heath	K
gentiana amerella	autumn gentian	1835		JH
geranium sanguineum	bloody cranesbill	1660	Newmarket Heath	R
geranium sanguineum	bloody cranesbill	1835		JH
geranium sanguisseum	bloody cranesbill	1763	Devil's Ditch	Mar
gnaphalium dioicum	cat's foot	1802	Shelford	Rel
gnaphalium luteo-album	jersey cudweed	1802	Shelford	Rel
gymnadenia conopsea	scented orchid	1835		JH
gymnadenia conopsea	scented orchid	1660	Newmarket Heath	R
gymnadenia conopsea	scented orchid	1915	Thriplow	H
gymnadenia conopsea	scented orchid	1890	Royston Heath	K
helianthemum	common rock-rose	1890	Royston Heath	K
helianthemum chamaecistus	common rock rose	1915	Shepreth	H
helianthemum vulgare	common rock-rose	1835		JH
hippocrepis comosa	horsechoe vetch	1840	Devil's Dyke	B
hippocrepis comosa	hoeseshoe vetch	1890	Royston Heath	K
hippocrepis comosa	tufted horse-shoe vetch	1763	Devil's Ditch	Mar
hippocrepis comosa	horseshoe vetch	1835		JH

Latin name	English name	date	place	author
hippocrepis comosa	tufted horseshoe vetch	1763	Newmarket Heath	Mar
hippocrepis comosa	horseshoe vetch	1848	Fleam Dyyke	B
hyoscyamus niger	henbane	1835		JH
hyoscyamus niger	henbane	1890	Royston Heath	K
hypericum pulchrum	st John's wort	1835		JH
hypericum pulchrum	St John's wort	1915	Heath	H
hypochaeris maculata	spotted cat's ear	1802	Thriplow	Rel
jasione montana	sheepsbit	1915	Heath	H
jasione montana	sheepsbit	1835		JH
linum catharicum	cathartic flax	1890	Royston Heath	K
linum catharicum	cathartic flax	1835		JH
lotus corniculatus	bird's foot trefoil	1890	Royston Heath	K
melampryum pratense	cow wheat	1915	Heath	H
ophrys apifera	bee orchid	1890	Royston Heath	K
ophrys apifera	bee orchid	1763	Shelford	Mar
ophrys apifera	bee orchid	1835		JH
ophrys aranifera	spider orchid	1802	Shelford	Rel
ophrys muscifera	fly orchid	1763	Devil's Ditch	Mar
ophrys muscifera	fly orchid	1835		JH
ophrys muscifera	fly orchid	1660	Newmarket Heath	R
orchis pyramidalis	pyramidal orchis	1802	Devil's Ditch	Rel
orchis pyramidalis	purple orchid	1763	Devil's Ditch	Mar
orchis ustula	dwarf orchid	1835		JH
orchis ustula	dwarf orchid	1840	Devil's Dyke	B
orchis ustulata	little spotted orchid	1763	Devil's Ditch	Mar
orchis ustulata	dark-winged orchid	1890	Royston Heath	K
orobanche elatior	broom rape	1890	Royston Heath	K
orobranche elatior	knapweed broom rape	1835	Royston Heath	JH
orobranche major	great broomrape	1835	Royston Heath	JH
orobranche major	broom rape	1915	Shepreth	H
polygala vulgans	common milk-wort	1890	Royston Heath	K
polygala vulgans	common milk-wort	1835	Royston Heath	JH
polygala vulgaris	common milk-wort	1915	Sawston	H
potentilla tormentilla	tomentil	1915	Heath	H
potentilla tormentilla	tomentil	1835	Sawston	JH
poterium sanguisorba	burnet	1802	Thriplow	Rel
primula veris	cowslip	1890	Royston Heath	K
primula veris	primrose	1915	Newton	H
pteris aquilina	braken	1915	Heath	H
rumex acetosella	sheep's sorrel	1835	Newmarket Heath	JH
rumex acetosella	sheep's sorrell	1660	Newmarket Heath	R
rumex acetosella	sorrel	1763	Newmarket Heath	Mar
rumex acetosella	sheep's sorrel	1835	Whittlesford	M
rumex acetosella	sheep's sorrel	1915	Heath	H
salix aurita	eared sallow	1915	Heath	H
salix repens	creeping willow	1915	Heath	H
salix repens	creeping willow	1915	Thriplow	H
scabiosa columbaria	small scabious	1890	Royston Heath	K
scabiosia columbaria	small scabious	1915	Thriplow	H
spirea filipendula	dropwort	1835	Thriplow	JH
spirea filipendula	dropwort	1915	Sawston	H
spirea filipendula	dropwort	1890	Royston Heath	K
tencrium scorodonia	wood sage	1915	Royston Heath	H

Latin name	English name	date	place	author
tenucrium scorodonia	wood sage	1835	Royston Heath	JH
thalictrum minus	lesser meadow-rue	1890	Royston Heath	K
thalictrum minus	lesser meadow rue	1915	Sawston	H
thesium linophyllum	bastard toadflax	1802	Thriplow	Rel
thesium linophyllum	bastard toadflax	1763	Thriplow	Mar
thesium linophyllum	bastard toad-flax	1890	Royston Heath	K
thymus calamintha	common calamint	1802	Shelford	Rel
thymus serpyllum	thyme	1915	Heath	H
thymus serpyllum	wild thyme	1890	Royston Heath	K
thymus seryllum	wild thyme	1802	Thriplow	Rel
trifolium glomeratum	clustered clover	1763	Newmarket Heath	Mar
ulex europaeaus	gorse	1835	Newmarket Heath	JH
ulex europaeus	gorse	1660	Newmarket Heath	R
ulex europaeus	gorse	1915	Heath	H
ulex europaeus	gorse	1763	Newmarket Heath	Mar
ulex europaeus	gorse	1915	Ickleton	H
ulex minor	small furze	1939	Thriplow	E
veronica chamaedrys	speedwell	1835	Thriplow	JH
veronica chamaedrys	speedwell	1890	Royston Heath	K
veronica officinalis	speedwell/fluellin	1660	Newmarket Heath	R
veronica officinallis	fluellin	1835	Newmarket Heath	JH
veronica officinallis	fluellin	1763	Newmarket Heath	Mar
veronica spicata	spiked speedwell	1835	Newmarket Heath	JH
veronica spicata	upright speedwell	1660	Newmarket Heath	R
veronica spicata	spiked speedwell	1915	Newmarket Heath	H
veronica spicata	spiked sppedwell	1763	Newmarket Heath	Mar
viola tricolour	wild pansey	1835	Newmarket Heath	JH
viola tricolour	wild pansey	1890	Royston Heath	K
wahlenbergea hederace	ivy-leaved campanula	1915	Royston Heath	H

c) Moor

Latin name	English name	date	place	author
achilla ptarmica	sneezewort	1939	Thriplow	E
achilla ptarmica	sneezewort	1835	Thriplow	JH
alisma plassago	small water plantain	1802	Shelford	Rel
alisma ranunculoides	lesser water plantain	1763	Shelford	Mar
alnus glutinosa	alder	1915	Shelford	H
anagalis tenella	bog pimpernel	1835	Shelford	JH
anagallis tenella	bog pimpernel	1840	Thriplow	M
anagallis tenella	bog pimpernel	1939	Ickleton	E
anagallis tenella	bog pimpernel	1915	Ickleton	H
anemone nemerosa	wood anemone	1847	Nine Wells	M
apium graveoleus	wild celery	1835	Nine Wells	JH
apium graveoleus	wild celery	1867	Old Moat	M
aquiligia vulgaris	columbine	1939	Thriplow	E
butomus umbellatis	flowering rush	1867	Thriplow	M
butomus umbellatis	flowering rush	1835	Thriplow	JH
caltha palustris	marsh marigold	1915		H
caltha palustris	marsh marigold	1835	Thriplow	JH
caltha palustris	marsh marigold	1873		M
cardamine pratensis	cuckoo flower	1835		JH

Latin name	English name	date	place	author
cardamine pratensis	cuckoo flower	1915		H
carduus pratensis	meadow thistle	1802	Shelford	Rel
carex ampullacae	slender beaked bladder carex	1802	Fowlmere	Rel
carex caespitosa	turfy carex	1802	Sawston	Rel
carex diandra	two-stemmed sedge	1939	Thriplow	E
carex elata	tufted sedge	1939	Thriplow	E
carex pseudo-cyperus	bastard carex	1802	Pampisford	Rel
carex pulicaris	flea carex	1802	Shelford	Rel
carex segetum	lesser fox sedge	1939	Melbourn	E
chara polysperma	moss	1850	Nine Wells	B
circaea lutetiana	enchanters nightshade	1868	Shelford	M
circaea lutetiana	enchanter nightshade	1939	Shelford	E
circaea lutetiana	enchanter's nightshade	1835	Shelford	JH
cladium mariscus	mother sedge	1835	Melbourn	JH
cladium mariscus	mother sedge	1939	Melbourn	E
conium maculatum	hemlock	1886	Melbourn	M
conium masculatum	hemlock	1835	Melbourn	JH
denturia bulbifera	ladies smock	1915	Melbourn	H
drosera angelica	great sundew	1835	Melbourn	JH
drosera anglica	great sundew	1802	Sawston	Rel
drosera anglica	great sun dew	1849	Fowlmere	M
drosera longifolia	sundew	1939	Sawston	E
drosera longifolia	long leaved sundew	1802	Sawston	Rel
drosera longufolia	sundew	1835	Sawston	JH
drosera rotundifolia	round leaved sundew	1802	Fowlmere	Rel
drosera rotundifolia	roundleaved sundew	1915	Sawston	H
drosera rotundifolia	round leaved sundew	1835	Sawston	JH
drosera rotundifolia	round-leaved sun dew	1849	Fowlmere	M
epilobium augustifolium	rose bay willow-herb	1939	Sawston	E
epilobium palustre	bog willow-herb	1939	Thriplow	E
epilobium palustre	marsh willow herb	1915	Sawston	H
epilobium palustre	marsh willow-herb	1835	Thriplow	JH
epipactid palustris	marsh helliborine	1860	Nine Wells	B
epipactis grandiflora	white helliborine	1835	Nine Wells	JH
epipactis grandiflora	white helliborine	1867	Nine Wells	M
epipactis latifolia	broad helliborine	1915	Nine Wells	H
epipactis palustris	marsh helliborine	1939	Thriplow	E
epipactis palustris	marsh helliborine	1835	Nine Wells	JH
epipactis palustris	marsh heliborine	1867	Nine Wells	M
equisetum palustre	marsh horsetail	1915	Nine Wells	H
eriophorum angustifolium	common cotton grass	1802	Shelford	Rel
eriophorum augustifolium	cotton grass	1915	Nine Wells	H
eupatorum cannabium	hemp agrimony	1835	Nine Wells	JH
eupatorum cannabium	hemp agrimony	1868	Nine Wells	M
filago apiculata	red tipped cudweed	1860	Nine Wells	B
fumaria macrantha	fumitory	1860	Nine Wells	B
galium palustre	marsh bedstraw	1835	Nine Wells	JH
galium palustre	marsh bedstraw	1915	Nine Wells	H
galium uliginosum	fen bedstraw	1939	Meldreth	E
galium uliginosum	fen bedstraw	1835	Nine Wells	JH
gymnadenia conopsea	sweet sented orchid	1939	Thriplow	E
gymnadenia conopsea	fragrant orchis	1870	Nine Wells	M
gymnadenia conopsea	fragrant orchis	1835		JH

Latin name	English name	date	place	author
hydrocotyle vulgaris	marsh pennywort	1835		JH
hydrocotyle vulgaris	marsh pennywort	1867	Nine Wells	M
hypericum elodes	st John's wort	1835	Nine Wells	JH
hypericum elodes	st John's wort	1915		H
hypericum humifusem	creeping st John's wort	1939	Thriplow	E
inula dypenterica	fleabane	1867	Nine Wells	M
juncus bulbosus	bulbous rush	1802	Shelford	Rel
leontodon palustre	marsh dandilion	1802	Sawston	Rel
libaris loeselii	fen orchid	1915	Nine Wells	H
libaris loeselii	fen orchid	1835	Nine Wells	JH
lychnis flos-cuculi	ragged robin	1868	Nine Wells	M
lychnis flos-cuculi	ragged robin	1835	Nine Wells	JH
lychnis flos-cuculi	ragged robin	1915		H
lycopodium inumdatem	club-moss	1915		H
lysimachia nummularia	moneywort	1835		JH
lysimachia nummularia	moneywort	1868		M
mentha gracilis	narrow leaved mint	1802	Shelford	Rel
mentha hirsuta	hairy mint	1802	Pampisford	Rel
menyanthes trifolia	bogbean	1868		M
menyanthis trifoliata	bog bean	1939	Sawston	E
myosotis caespitosa	tufted forget-me-not	1915	Sawston	H
myosotis repens	marsh forget-me-not	1915	Sawston	H
myrica gale	bog myrtle	1915		H
myrica gale	bog myrtle	1835	Thriplow	JH
myriophyllum verticillatum	whorled water milfoil	1939	Thriplow	E
narthericum ossifragum	bog asphodel	1915		H
nasturtium officinale	watercress	1835		JH
nasturtium offinale	watercress	1939	Fowlmere	E
nymphae alba	white water lily	1763	Thriplow	Mar
nymphaea alba	white water lily	1802	Thriplow	Rel
oenantha crocata	hemlock-leaved dropwort	1868	Thriplow	M
oenanthe crocata	hemlock dropwort	1915	Thriplow	H
oenanthe fistulosa	tubula dropwort	1835	Thriplow	JH
oenanthe fistulosa	tubula dropwort	1915	Thriplow	H
oenanthe lachenalii	parsey water drop wort	1939	Newton	E
ophrys apifera	bee orchid	1837	Abington	B
ophrys apifera	bee orchid	1763	Shelford	Mar
ophrys apifera	bee orchid	1864	Thriplow	M
ophrys arenifera	early spider orchid	1835	Thriplow	JH
ophrys arenifera	early spider orchid	1837	Abington	B
ophrys loeselii	dwarf ophrys	1802	Sawston	Rel
ophrys spiranthus	ladies tresses	1870	Abington	M
orchis anthropoporum	man orchid	1837	Abington	B
orchis conopsea	red handed orchid	1763	Devil's Ditch	Mar
orchis conopsea	fragrant orchid	1885	Nine Wells	M
orchis dactyloris maculata	spotted orchid	1869	Whittlesford	M
orchis dactyloris maculata	spotted orchid	1835	Devil's Ditch	JH
orchis latifolia	early marsh orchid	1915	Nine Wells	H
orchis latifolia	early marsh orchid	1939	Thriplow	E
orchis latifolia	early marsh orchid	1835	Nine Wells	JH
orchis latifolia	march orchid	1870	Nine Wells	M
orchis masculula	early purple orchid	1837	Abington	B
orchis moria	green winged orchid	1870	Nine Wells	M

Latin name	English name	date	place	author
orchis moria	green winged orchid	1835	Nine Wells	JH
orchis morio	green-winged orchid	1837	Abington	B
osmunda regalis	royal fern	1915	Abington	H
parnassia palustris	grass of parnassus	1802	Sawston	Rel
parnassia palustris	grass of parnassus	1802	Shelford	Rel
parnassia palustris	grass of parnassus	1915	Abington	H
parnassia palustris	grass of parnassus		Sawston	M
parnassia palustris	grass of parnassis	1939	Fowlmere	E
parnassia palustris	grass of parnassus	1835	Fowlmere	JH
pedicularis palustris	marsh lousewort	1835	Sawston	JH
pedicularis palustris	marsh lousewort	1939	Sawston	E
pinguicula lusitania	pale butterwort	1915	Sawston	H
pinguicula vulgaris	common butterwort	1849	Sawston	M
pinguicula vulgaris	common butterwort	1835		JH
pinguicula vulgaris	common Butterwort	1802	Sawston	Rel
pinguicula vulgaris	butterwort	1915	Fowlmere	H
pinguicule vulgaris	butterwort	1939	Shelford	E
poa decumbens	decumbent meadow grass	1802	Shelford	Rel
populus canescens	grey poplar	1802	Shelford	Rel
potamogeton heterophyllum	pondweed	1802	Shelford	Rel
primula farinosa	bird's-eye primrose	1915		H
ranunculus ficaria	lesser celendine	1868		M
ranunculus ficaria	lesser celendine	1835		JH
ranunculus trichop	dark heaired crowfoot	1848	Coe Fen	B
rumex domesticus	long leaved dock	1915		H
saponaria officinalis	soapwort	1939	Thriplow	E
saponaria officinallis	soapwort	1763	Shelford	Mar
saponaria officinallis	soapwort	1835		JH
saponaria officinallis	soapwort	1763	Whittlesford	Mar
schoenus compressus		1763	Whittlesford	Mar
schoenus compressus	compressed bog rush	1802	Whittlesford	Rel
schoenus compressus	compressed bog rush	1802	Shelford	Rel
schoenus nigrans	black bog rush	1802	Sawston	Rel
schoenus nigricans	black bog-rush	1939	Sawston	E
scirpus pauciflorus	chocolate headed club rush	1802	Fowlmere	Rel
scirpus setaceus	dwarf club rush	1802	Shelford	Rel
sedum dasyphyllium	stonecrop	1915		H
senecio aquatica	marsh ragwort	1915		H
senecio aquatica	marsh ragwort	1835		JH
serapias palustris	marsh helleborine	1802	Thriplow	Rel
serapias palustris	marsh helleborine	1802	Sawston	Rel
spagamium minimum	small burr-reed	1939	Sawston	E
sparganium natans	floating burr weed	1802	Sawston	Rel
spiraea ulmararia	meadow sweet	1915		H
spiranthes autumnalis	autumn ladies tresses	1915		H
spiranthes oestivalis	spring ladies tresses	1915		H
spirea ulmaria	meadow sweet			M
stellaria aquatica	great chickweed	1939	Sawston	E
taraxacum palustre	little marsh dandelion	1939	Sawston	E
taraxacum palustre	little marsh dandelion	1835	Royston	JH
triticum carness	dog's grass	1869		M
urticularia vulgaris	bladderwort	1835		JH
urticularia vulgaris	bladderwort	1835	Nine Wells	M

Latin name	English name	date	place	author
utricularia minor	lesser bladderwort	1802	Sawston	Rel
utricularia vulgaris	great bladder wort	1763	Thriplow Moor	Mar
utricularia vulgaris	bladderwort	1939	Thriplow	E
utricularia vulgaris	common bladderwort	1802	Thriplow	Rel
valeriana dioica	marsh valerian	1835		JH
valeriana dioica	marsh valerian	1939	Harston	E
verbascum nigrum	black leaved mullein	1763	Shelford	Mar
verbascum nigrum	dark mullein	1939	Harston	E
verbascum nigrum	black mullein	1868	Nine Wells	M
verbascum nigrum	black mullein	1835	Harston	JH
viola grandiflora	yellow violet	1863	Nine Wells	M
viola sylvatica	fen violet	1848	Coe Fen	B

d) Meadows

Latin name	English name	date	Place	author
achilla ptarmica	sneezewort yarrow	1820	Thriplow	Rel
alisma plassago	small water plantain	1802	Shelford	Rel
chlora perfoliata	common yellow centaury	1820	Shelford	Rel
gymnadenis conopsea	scented orchid	1660	Shelford	R
menyanthes trifoliata	buckbean	1820	Thriplow	Rel
orchis conopsea	sweet scented orchis	1820	Thriplow	Rel
polygonum bistorta	great bistort	1763	Shelford	Mar
polygonum bistorta	great bistort	1820	Shelford	Rel
pulicaria dysentrerica	fleabane	1835	Shelford	JH
pulicaria dysentrerica	fleabane	1939	Newton	E
sanguisorba officinallis	great burnet	1820	Shelford	Rel
sanguisorbia officinallis	great burnett	1763	Shelford	Mar
saponaria officinallis	soapwort	1763	Shelford	Mar
spiraea filipendula	dropwort	1820	Thriplow	Rel

e) Roadsides and waste

Latin name	English name	date	place	author
achilla arvensis	corn camomile	1939	Thriplow	E
aectium lappe var. minus	burdock	1915	Thriplow	H
aegopodium podagraria	gout weed	1835	Thriplow	JH
aegopodium podagraria	gout weed	1915	Thriplow	H
aenothera biennis	evening primrose	1915	Thriplow	H
aenothera biennis	evening primrose	1915	Thriplow	H
anagallis arvensis	scarlet pimpernel	1835	Thriplow	JH
anagallis arvensis	scarlet pimpernel	1939	Thriplow	E
antirrhinum minus	least toadflax	1763	Newmarket Heath	Mar
arenaria trinerva	three veined sandwort	1939	Thriplow	E
aristolochia clematis	birthwort	1939	Whittlesford	E
artemisia absinthium	wormwood	1915	Whittlesford	H
artimisia absinthium	wormwood	1835	Whittlesford	JH
arum maculatum	cukoo pint	1835	Whittlesford	JH
arum maculatum	cuckoo pint	1836	Whittlesford	M
atropa belladonna	deadly nightshade	1835	Thriplow	JH
atropa belladonna	deadly nightshade	1915	Thriplow	H
atropa bella-donna	deadly nightshade	1939	Thriplow	E

Latin name	English name	date	place	author
calamintha ascendens	common calamint	1763	Shelford	Mar
campanula rotundifolia	harebell	1836	Newton	M
campanula totundifolia	harebell	1835	Newton	JH
capsella bursa pastoralis	shepherd's purse	1836	Newton	M
capsella bursa-pastoris	shepherd's purse	1939	Thriplow	E
capsella bursa-pastoris	shepherd's purse	1835	Newton	JH
capsella bursa-pastoris	shepherd's purse	1915	Thriplow	H
carum segetum	corn parsley	1939	Ickleton	E
chelidonium majus	celandine	1915	Ickleton	H
chelidonum majus	celandine	1835	Ickleton	JH
chenopodium album	white goosefoot	1835	Ickleton	JH
chenopodium album	white goosefoot	1915	Ickleton	H
convolulus arvensis	bindweed	1835	Ickleton	JH
convolulus arvensis	bindweed	1939	Ickleton	E
crepis foetida	stinking hawksbeard	1763	Shelford	Mar
cricus arvensis	creeping thistle	1915	Shelford	H
doronicum pardalianches	great leopard's bane	1836	Shelford	M
echium vulgare	vipers bugloss	1915	Shelford	H
echium vulgare	vipers bugloss	1835	Shelford	JH
filago jussicei	cudweed	1848	Hills Road	B
fumaria officinalis	fumitory	1835	Thriplow	JH
fumaria offinialis	fumitory	1915	Thriplow	H
gentiana amerella	fellwort	1877	Thriplow	M
geranium circutarium	hemlock-leaved cranesbill	1877	Thriplow	M
geranium colombinum	dove's foot cranesbill	1939	Melbourn	E
geranium robertianum	herb robert	1835	Melbourn	JH
geranium robertianum	herb robert	1939	Melbourn	E
heracleum sphondylium	hogweed	1939	Shelford	E
hyoseyamus niger	henbane	1915	Shelford	H
hyoseyamus niger	henbane	1835	Shelford	JH
hypochaeris maculata	spotted cat's ear	1939	Thriplow	E
hypochaeris maculata	spotted hawkweed	1763	Newmarket Heath	Mar
hypochaeris maculata	spotted hawkweed	1763	Thriplow	Mar
impatiens parviflora	balsam	1939	Duxford	E
inula conyza	ploughman's spikenard	1763	Whittlesford	Mar
inula conyza	ploughman's spikenard	1939	Stapleford	E
inula conyza	ploughman's spikenard	1835	Whittlesford	JH
lactuca muralis	wall lettuce	1915	Whittlesford	H
lactuca muralis	wild lettuce	1835	Whittlesford	JH
lactuca muralis	wild lettuce	1939	Whittlesford	E
lactuca scariola	prickly lettuce	1915	Whittlesford	H
lactuca scariola	prickly lettuce	1835	Whittlesford	JH
lathrys nissolia	grass vetchling	1939	Melbourn	E
lathrys nissolia	grass vetchling	1835	Whittlesford	JH
lepidium campestre	field pepperwort	1939	Ickleton	E
linaria vulgaris	toadflax	1939	Ickleton	E
linaria vulgaris	toadflax	1835	Ickleton	JH
lonicera caprifolium	perfoliate honeysuckle	1847	Thriplow	B
lonicera caprifolium	perfoliate honeysuckle	1835	Ickleton	JH
marribium vulgare	horehound	1835	Thriplow	JH
marribium vulgare	horehound	1915	Thriplow	H
melitotus arvensis	common melilot	1835		JH
melitotus arvensis	common melilot	1848	Hills Road	B

Latin name	English name	date	place	author
mentha longifolia	horsemint	1763	Thriplow	Mar
minuartia tenuifolia	fine-leaved sandwort	1763	Thriplow	Mar
nepeta cararia	catmint	1835	Thriplow	JH
nepeta cataria	catmint	1763	Thriplow	Mar
nepeta cataria	catmint	1915	Thriplow	H
origanum vulgare	common marjoram	1802	Thriplow	Rel
polygonum bistorta	great bistort	1763	Shelford	Mar
potentilla auserina	silverweed	1836		M
potentilla auserina	silverweed	1835	Shelford	JH
ranunculus drouetii	thread leaved crowfoot	1836	Hauxton	B
ranunculus parviflorus	small flowered buttercup	1763	Shelford	Mar
ranunculus repens	creeping buttercup	1915	Shelford	H
reseda lutea	wild mignonette	1835	Shelford	JH
reseda lutea	wild mignonette	1939	Shelford	E
rosa rubiginosa	sweet briar	1939	Whittlesford	E
rosa rubiginosa	sweet briar	1835	Shelford	JH
safina apetala	pearlwort	1835	Whittlesford	JH
sagina apetala pearlwort	pearlwort	1915	Whittlesford	H
scleranthus anuus	knawel	1939	Fowlmere	E
scleranthus anuus	knawel	1835	Fowlmere	JH
sedum acre	wall pepper	1763	Shelford	Mar
senecio jacobaea	ragwort	1835	Shelford	JH
senecio jacobaea	ragwort	1915		H
senecio vulgaris	groundsel	1915	Thriplow	H
senecio vulgaris	groundsel	1835	Thriplow	JH
silybum marianum	milk thistle	1835	Thriplow	JH
silybum marianum	milk thistle	1939	Thriplow	E
sisymbrium officinale	hedge mustard	1939	Thriplow	E
smyrnium olusatrum	alexanders	1939	Fowlmere	E
solanum dulcamera	woody nightshade	1835	Fowlmere	JH
solanum dulcamera	woody nightshade	1915	Fowlmere	H
solanum nigra	black nightshade	1835	Fowlmere	JH
solanum nigrum	black nightshade	1915	Fowlmere	H
thalictrum minus	small meadow rue	1802	Shelford	Rel
urtica urens	annual stinging nettle	1835	Fowlmere	JH
urtica urens	annual stinging nettle	1915	Fowlmere	H
verbascum nigrum	black mullein	1802	Thriplow	Rel
verbascum nigrum	black mullein	1802	Shelford	Rel
verbascum thapsis	great mullein	1835	Thriplow	JH
verbascum thapsis	great mullein	1915	Fowlmere	H
verbena offinialis	verbena	1835	Thriplow	JH
verbena offinialis	verbena	1915	Thriplow	H

f) Trees and hedges

Latin name	English name	date	Place	author
aconitum napellus	monkshood	1836	Ninewells	M
adoxa moschatellina	tuberous moschatell	1802	Shelford	Rel
allium ursinum	ramsons	1915	Whittlesford	H
allium ursinum	garlic	1835	Whittlesford	JH
allium ursinum	garlic	1939	Whittlesford	E
anemone nemerosa	wood anemone	1915	Whittlesford	H
aquiligia vulgaris	common columbine	1802	Thriplow	Rel

Latin name	English name	date	place	author
aristolachia clematis	upright birthwort	1763	Whittlesford	Mar
aristolachia clematis	birthwort	1868	Ninewells	M
aristolochia clematis	climbing birthwort	1802	Whittlesford	Rel
asperula oderata	sweet woodruff	1835	Ninewells	JH
asperula oderata	sweet wood ruff	1915	Ninewells	H
astragalus glycyphyllos	wild liquorice	1802	Shelford	Rel
atropa belladonna	deadly nightshade	1802	Thriplow	Rel
berberis vularis	common barberry	1802	Thriplow	Rel
calamintha clinopodium	wild basil	1915	Ninewells	H
cephalanthera grandiflora	white helleborine	1915	Ninewells	H
convallaria kajalis	lily of the valley	1915	Ninewells	H
corylus avellana	hazel	1915	Ninewells	H
daphne laureola	spurge laurel	1915	Ninewells	H
daphne laureola	spurge laurel	1835	Ninewells	JH
daphne mezerum	daphne	1915	Ninewells	H
digitalis purpurea	foxglove	1915	Ninewells	H
doronicum pardallianches	leopard's bane	1866	Ninewells	M
doronicum plantagineum	plantain leaved leopard's bane	1866	Ninewells	M
epipactis latifolia	helleborine	1835	Ninewells	JH
epipactis latifolia	helleborine	1915		H
eranthis hyemalis	aconite	1866	Whittlesford	M
euonymus europaeus	spindle tree	1763	Whittlesford	Mar
fragaria vesca	wood strawberry	1802	Thriplow	Rel
fragaria vesca	wild strawberry	1915	Whittlesford	H
galathis nivalis	snowdrop	1847	Whittlesford	M
galium verum	ladies bedstraw	1835	Whittlesford	JH
galium verum	ladies bedstraw	1915	Whittlesford	H
hyoscyamus niger	henbane	1847	Ninewells	M
iris foetidissima	stinking iris	1847	Thriplow	B
iris foetidissima	stinking iris	1939	Thriplow	E
iris foetidissima	stinking iris	1915		H
lathraea squamaria	toothwort	1915	Thriplow	H
listera ovata	twayblade	1915	Thriplow	H
listera ovata	twayblade	1835	Thriplow	JH
lonicera caprifolium	perfoliate honeysuckle	1835	Thriplow	JH
lonicera caprifolium	honeysuckle	1939	Thriplow	E
lonicera caprifolium	perfoliate honeysuckle	1847	Thriplow	B
lonicera periclymenum	honeysuckle	1847	Ninewells	M
lonicera periclymenum	honeysuckle	1835		JH
lustera ovata	twayblade	1868	Ninewells	M
lychnis diurna	red campion	1915	Ninewells	H
lysimachia nemorum	yellow pimpernel	1915		H
lysimachia nemorum	yellow pimpernel	1835	Ninewells	JH
lysimachia vulgaris	yellow loosestrife	1939	Hauxton	E
lysmachia vulgaris	yellow loosestrife	1835	Hauxton	JH
mercurialis perennis	dog's mercury	1835	Hauxton	JH
mercurialis perennis	dog's mercury	1915	Hauxton	H
narcissus poeticus	pale daffodil	1763	Whittlesford	Mar
narcissus pseudo narcissus	daffodil	1763	Whittlesford	Mar
narcissus pseudonarcissus	daffodil	1802	Whittlesford	Rel
narcissus pseudonarcissus	daffodil	1915	Whittlesford	H
narcissus pseudonarcissus	daffodil	1939	Whittlesford	E
narcissus pseudonarcissus	daffodil	1835	Whittlesford	JH

Latin name	English name	date	place	author
onithogalum umbellatum	star of bethlehem	1915	Whittlesford	H
orchis mascula	early purple orchid	1867	Ninewells	M
orchis mascula	early purple orchid	1835		JH
oxalis acetosella	wood sorrel	1763	Devil's Ditch	Mar
oxalis acetosella	wood sorrel	1915		H
oxalis acetosella	wood sorrel	1835		JH
paris quadrifolia	herb paris	1835		JH
paris quadrifolia	herb paris	1915		H
pinus sylvestris	scots pine	1915		H
platanthera chlorantha	butterfly orchid	1915	Devil's Ditch	H
polygonatum verticillatu	soloman's seal	1915	Devil's Ditch	H
primula elatior	oxslip	1835		JH
primula elatior	oxslip	1915		H
primula elatior	oxslip	1858	Ninewells	M
primula veris	primrose	1939	Newton	E
primula veris	cowslip	1858	Ninewells	M
primula vulgaris	primrose	1915		H
primula vulgaris	primrose	1836	Whittlesford	M
prunus domestica	plum	1802	Shelford	Rel
ranunculus auricomus	goldilocks	1835	Whittlesford	JH
ranunculus auricomus	goldilocks	1915	Whittlesford	H
rhamnus catharticus	common buckthorn	1835	Whittlesford	JH
rhamnus catharticus	common buckthorn	1915	Whittlesford	H
ribes uva-crispa	smooth gooseberry	1802	Shelford	Rel
rosa rubiginosa	sweet briar rose	1802	Thriplow	Rel
ruscus aculaetus	butchers broom	1915	Whittlesford	H
sanicula europaea	sanicle	1915	Whittlesford	H
sanicula europaea	sanicle	1835	Whittlesford	JH
saponaria officinallis	soapwort	1802	Shelford	Rel
scilla nutans	bluebell	1915	Whittlesford	H
scrophularia aquatica	figwort	1915	Thriplow	E
scrophularia aquatica	figwort	1835		JH
sedum telephium	orchine	1763	Shelford	Mar
sedum teliphium	orphine	1802	Shelford	Rel
stachys betonica	wood betony	1915	Shelford	H
stachys betonica	wood betony	1835	Shelford	JH
tilia platyphylos	large leaved lime	1915	Shelford	H
trollius europaeaus	globe flower	1915	Shelford	H
veronica montana	wood speedwell	1763	Devil's Ditch	Mar
viburmum opulus	guelder rose	1835		JH
viburnum lantana	wayfaring tree	1835		JH
viburnum lantana	wayfaring tree	1915		H
viburnum opulus	guelder rose	1915		H
vinca major	greater periwinkle	1802	Whittlesford	Rel
vinca minor	lesser periwinkle	1802	Thriplow	Rel
vinca minor	periwinkle	1835		JH
vinca minor	periwinkle	1915		H
viola oderata	sweet violet	1835		JH
viola oderata	sweet violet	1836	Whittlesford	M
viola oderata	sweet violet	1939	Thriplow	E
viscum album	mistletoe	1915	Whittlesford	H
viscum album	mistletoe	1835		JH

Appendix 7. Pampisford Hall, date of planting of trees

Enclosure date of Pampisford = 1799

Enclosure map 1799 showing triangular piece of land belonging to W P Hammond, open field, no trees shown.

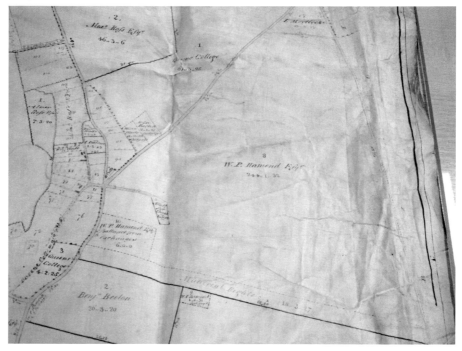

From *VCH*: Pampisford Hall was built by William Parker Hamond *c.* 1830 on former farm land.

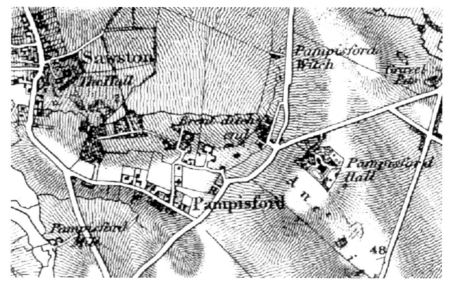

1830 OS 1inch first edition showing Hall and early gardens

From Kelly's *Directory* (1879): 'Remains of formal gardens, pleasure grounds, park *c.*164 acres planted from mid-1840s, mainly to designs by R Marnock, with later planting. Notable collection of conifers'.

Some 40 years after enclosure.

First edition 6 inch OS map 1885 showing pinetum as mature trees.
Note old railway line, bottom right.

Appendix 8. CUL DOC 652–113. Stinting rules

Customs And Manner Of Stocking The Commons In The Parish Of Great Shelford (Draft)

To be entered in the Book of Claims

The Shelford Commons are divided into several districts and are used by the persons intitled to Common Right Houses as follows:-

THE HIGH GREEN – Common all the year for great Cattle and for Pigs in 12th article as agreed at Court Leet and Court Baron held in the Manor of Buristead.

BALKS AND THE BACK MOOR – Common all the year for great Cattle

CROW-LAND & MAY-PASTURE – Common from 12th May for great Cattle every year.

The Sheep Owners are intitled to pasturage over and upon the above districts of common, viz.-

Over all the Open Lands and Grounds, Commons, Commonable places and Meadows within the whole Parish from Old Christmas to Old Lady Day – except on the Lands sown with Wheat, Rye or Turnips.

When NINE WELLS FIELD becomes fallow i.e. once in three years, the Sheep Owners have a right of depasturage upon that part of the Back Moor extending from the Red Cross Road to a line called Waldon Way.

The number of Sheep Commons over this Parish are to:-

Caius College	480 or 24 score sheep
St. John's College	420 or 21 score sheep
E.H.Green Esq	120 or 6 score sheep
Peter Grain	60 or 3 score sheep
The Town Flock	120 or 6 score sheep
TOTAL	1,200 or 60 score sheep

The Folding belongs to:-

Caius College	of their own flock
Caius College	of the Town Flock
St John's College	of their own flock
St John's College	of Peter Grain's flock
E.H.Green Esq	of his own flock

THE SHEEP COMMON AND CABBAGE MOOR – the Sheep Owners have the exclusive right over and upon these two pieces of land at all times of the year.

THE BALKS And Other Commonable Places Within The Open Fields

These parcels of common are stocked as follows:-

In the WHEAT AND BARLEY FIELDS of every year. Cows are led to feed, two by an attendant upon these parcels of Common – From 12th May for fourteen days and when the corn or pulse is cut on each side of any Balk then Horses may be led to graze on such Balks.

In the LEY OR FALLOW FIELDS of every year. Cows and Horses are depastured on these parcels of the Common from 25th day of May until 4th June.

At a meeting on the 16th June of the principal occupiers and proprietors it was agrred that the grass ends from the Cart Balk at Mr Headley's Gate – by Hopham and Hullock Meadow to the Meer Way is part of and belonging to the lands abutting on the same.

The Sheep Owners have a right of pasturage on the fallow fields and Balks from 4th June for the remainder of the season. The ploughing does not commence until nine days after the sheep have taken possession the West fields.

AND

After Harvest the Herd of Great Cattle take the Wheat and Barley fields and have it exclusively for seven days.

The Sheep then take the Wheat and Barley fields along with the great Cattle for the remainder of the season.

COMMON MEADOWS

The Cows and Horses depasture in these Meadows on their being cleared from the Hay every year.

The Sheep Owners have only a right of pasturage from Old Christmas to Old Lady day.

IN THE WEST FIELDS

The going for Great Stock without stint for the space of nine days annually over the three West fields in right of commonable Houses.

INTER COMMON

Common of Pasture over a portion of Hollick meadow situate in Hauxton.

The Cows and Horses depasture here immediately after the Hay is cleared off every year – jointly with Cattle belonging to the owners of the land, Messrs. Hurrell and For the.

The Sheep Owners also have the same right of pasturage from Old Christmas to Old Lady Day on this portion of Meadow Land.

RED MEADOW

Os also divided into districts and used by persons intitled to Common rights as follows:-

From the 26th day of May every year for Great Cattle.

The sheep depasture over this when they take the stubbles.

The Sheep Owners are intitled to pasturage over and upon certain parts only viz:-

On the North when the Causeway West field becomes fallow

On the East when the Church West field becomes fallow

On the South when the Hauxton Mill field becomes fallow.

Say about eight acres every year is Sheep Common.

HOPHAM COMMON

Is generally used as a common for Horses and only this is used by persons intitled to common rights for that purpose, by the general consent of the persons interested.

From 12th May every year until Old Lady Day

The Sheep Owners have a right of pasturage from Old Christmas to Old Lady Day.

Rules regarding stock June 10th 1808

Manor of Buristead, Great Shelford

The presentment of the Jury and Homage at a court Leet and Court Baron held in and for the manor of Buristed in great Shelford on the 10th day of June 1808, who agreed, ordained and ordered as follows.

First – That no Asses, mares, norstoned horses shall be kept on the commons in this parish at any time, on pain of being impounded and the owner to pay to the Lords of this manor one shilling for each and every offence.

2nd – No hogs unrung shall go on the commons after being eight weeks old on pain of being impounded and to pay twopence each.

3rd – No horses to be kept on the balks in the fields, common balks nor cart balks before the corn is cut on both sides, on pain of being impounded and to pay one shilling each.

4th – No horses led on the landsends to be turned loose but kept in hand by the keepers on pain of being impounded and to pay four pence each.

5th – No horses to go on the commons later than ten o'clock at night unless properly staked on pain of being impounded and to pay two pence each, and not to be released from the staking before four of the clock in the morning under the same penalty, and if strayed into the corn one shilling each.

6th – No cows nor cow kine to go on the commons later then ten o'clock at night, on pain of being impounded and to pay two pence each, and if strayed into the corn one shilling each.

7th – No Horses or cows shall be led on the balks or commons (Lanes excepted) before old may day, and no longer than fourteen days on pain of being impounded and to pay two pence each, and if strayed into the corn one shilling each.

8th – No cows nor cow kine to go into the stubblefields before that field is clear of corn, on pain of being impounded and to pay one shilling each.

9th – No sheep to be kept not to go on any of the Cow Commons in this parish, on pain of being impounded and paying one shilling for every score, or an equal proportion for any quantity, for the first offence, and for every after offence Three shillings and four pence per score (or in proportion) from Christmas and Lady Day (both old style) excepted.

10th – No sheep to go into any stubblefield before the cows have been in the same field sevendays under penalty the same as the last article, nor to be kept in any lanes nor bye ways, on pain of being impounded and paying one shilling for every offence.

11 – No cows nor two year old bullocks to of on any commons without having nobs on their horns, on pain of being impounded and top pay two pence each.

12 – No hogs to go on the common further than Townsend pond on one side of the partition ditch, and Granhams corner on the other side of ditch or brook on pain of being impounded and to pay two pence each.

13 – No hogs nor Turkeys shall go into the Stray in any of the fields before ?Heathfield is clear of corn and not without a keeper. Hogs to be impounded and to pay two pence each for every offence, and Turkeys one half penny each for every offence.

14 – No person shall take off from any common Cow or Horse dung before the same is quite dry and fit for fuel. To pay two pence for every offence.

Turn over

15th – No horses shall be turned onto or kept in the homeward meadows till the Hay is cleared off as far as Hark corner, nor in the next meadow till they are clear of Hay as far as Hoppen Water, and to go no further than there before all the meadows are quite clear.

16 – No horse nor horses to be kept in the cornfields before four Clock in the morning, nor after nine at night, the owner to pay for every offence five shillings for each horse.

The last two articles agreed on by the Jury at the last court admitted and confirmed by the court. We present with the foregoing articles as bye laws for the regulation and benefit of the commons of this parish and as our antient rights and customs.

And we do hereby ratify and confirm all former orders made at any court or courts holden for the said manor, and as all other customs and regulations used and observed in the said parish which are hereby not revoked.

In pencil Signed by the Leet Jury.

Appendix 9. Average number of people per house from the censuses

Great Abington

Date	Houses	Population	Average per house
1851	67	331	4.9
1861	62	330	5.3
1871	63	300	4.8
Total	192	961	5.0

Little Abington

Date	Houses	Population	Average per house
1851	63	307	4.9
1861	66	316	4.8
1871	70	339	4.8
Total	199	962	4.8

Duxford

Date	Houses	Population	Average per house
1851	187	844	4.5
1861	184	841	4.5
1871	202	881	4.4
Total	573	2566	4.5

Fowlmere

Date	Houses	Population	Average per house
1851	128	597	4.7
1861	122	560	4.6
1871	129	603	4.7
Total	379	1760	4.6

Foxton

Date	Houses	Population	Average per house
1851	92	459	5.0
1861	90	405	4.5
1871	96	413	4.3
Total	278	1277	4.6

Fulbourn

Date	Houses	Population	Average per house
1851	301	1452	4.8
1861	298	1548	5.2
1871	305	1694	5.6
Total	904	4694	5.2

Great Shelford

Date	Houses	Population	Average per house
1851	196	1038	5.3
1861	221	1006	4.6
1871	213	1005	4.7
Total	630	3049	4.8

Little Shelford

Date	Houses	Population	Average per house
1851	117	580	4.9
1861	102	474	4.6
1871	108	510	4.7
Total	327	1564	4.8

Harston

Date	Houses	Population	Average per house
1851	155	770	5.0
1861	174	782	4.5
1871	187	917	4.9
Total	516	2469	4.8

Hauxton

Date	Houses	Population	Average per house
1851	67	313	4.7
1861	56	262	4.7
1871	59	289	4.9
Total	182	864	4.7

Hinxton

Date	Houses	Population	Average per house
1851	107	465	4.3
1861	95	396	4.2
1871	89	400	4.5
Total	291	1252	4.3

Ickleton

Date	Houses	Population	Average per house
1851	165	813	4.9
1861	159	721	4.5
1871	155	677	4.4
Total	479	2211	4.6

Newton

Date	Houses	Population	Average per house
1851	44	185	4.2
1861	47	216	4.6
1871	54	218	4.0
Total	145	619	4.3

Melbourn

Date	Houses	Population	Average per house
1851	376	1931	5.1
1861	368	1637	4.4
1871	396	1759	4.4
Total	1140	5327	4.7

Meldreth

Date	Houses	Population	Average per house
1851	176	776	4.5
1861	165	735	4.4
1871	170	757	4.5
Total	511	2268	4.4

Pampisford

Date	Houses	Population	Average per house
1851	74	359	4.9
1861	80	347	4.3
1871	79	355	4.5
Total	233	1061	4.6

Sawston

Date	Houses	Population	Average per house
1851	225	1124	5.0
1861	270	1363	5.0
1871	341	1729	5.1
Total	836	4216	5.0

Shepreth

Date	Houses	Population	Average per house
1851	75	321	4.3
1861	78	339	4.3
1871	84	376	4.5
Total	237	1036	4.4

Stapleford

Date	Houses	Population	Average no per house
1851	103	507	4.9
1861	105	465	4.4
1871	125	594	4.7
Total	333	1566	4.7

Thriplow

Date	Houses	Population	Average per house
1851	103	521	5.1
1861	98	502	5.1
1871	107	522	4.9
Total	308	1545	5.0

Whittlesford

Date	Houses	Population	Average per house
1851	135	719	5.3
1861	160	800	5.0
1871	167	821	4.9
Total	462	2340	5.1

Bibliography

Manuscript Sources

CRO 413/M/8 1587 Rental of the manor of Thriplowe belonging to the Bishop of Ely.

CRO 414/04 1789 An Agreement to grow Sanfoin Thriplow.

CRO P62/28/1 1763 Duxford Agreement to grow Cinquefoil.

CRO 413/E8-9 1808 1814 List of crops and stock.

St John's College Archives, Enclosure Papers.

Peterhouse College Archives Enclosure papers.

CRO 1801–1881 Census returns.

CRO 1845 Thriplow Enclosure Award Q/RDc 65.

CRO P171/8/3 1826 Whittlesford Vestry Minute Book.

CRO P72/8/1 1765 Fowlmere Vestry Minutes, September.

CRO P72/8/1.2 1764–1781 Thriplow Overseers' book.

CRO P156/5/2 1732–1831 Thriplow Churchwardens' Accounts.

CRO 413/T27: 4-3-1841 Lease of Ambrose Hope Perkins to Joseph Ellis of Bury Farm, (Bassetts).

CRO Q/Rum/11 1843 Railway Plans.

CRO 296/B: Sale books of Crocket and Nash Royston Auctioneers.

Tithe Files

NA IR 18/13615 Newton 1840.

NA IR 18/13609 Melbourn 1840.

NA IR 18/13652 Thriplow 1840.

NA IR 18/13628 Shepreth 1838.

CUL EDR T Tithe map and schedules for Foxton, Fowlmere, Newton, Melbourn, Shepreth and Thriplow.

Enclosure Commissioners and Other Papers

Fowlmere

CRO P156/12/1,2 Fowlmere Overseers' Accounts.

CRO 317/T1, Tithe papers.

CRO 292/03 1845, Spade Husbandry.

CRO 292/02-36.

CRO Q/RDc 70 Fowlmere Enclosure Award.

CRO EDR T Fowlmere 1847.

Great Shelford

CRO R72/54 1834–1836.

CUL ADD 6067/36. 1834.

CUL DOC 652/1-95. 1833.

CUL DOC 652/2 The Manor of Buristead Great Shelford rules of Stocking 1808.

CUL DOC 652/110 nd.

CRO Q/RDc 50 Gt Shelford Enclosure Award.

Harston

CUL ADD 6011 1798.

CUL ADD 6013 1797–99.

CUL ADD 6048 1800.

CUL DOC 639 nd.

CRO Q/RDc3 Harston Enclosure Award.

Ickleton

CRO 107 1806–17.

CUL DOC 640 1809–14.

CRO Q/RDz27, 129-87 Ickleton Enclosure Award.

CUL DOC/5 1810.

CRO 10, 10 January 1814.

Sawston

CUL ADD 6066 1802.

CUL ADD 6065 1802–11.

CUL DOC 651 1802–15.

CRO P136/12/9 Sawston Overseers' Accounts.

Shepreth

CRO Q/RDz10, Shepreth Enclosure Award.

CRO P139/28/13.

Stapleford

CUL ADD 6068 1801–14.

CUL ADD 6069 1812.

CRO Q/RDz 7, 84-128 Stapleford Enclosure Award.

Thriplow

CRO P156/12/1,2, Thriplow Overseers' Accounts.

CRO 413/F9 Will of Joseph Ellis 1829.

CRO VC 43:251 Will of Grey Purdue, 1779.

CRO Thriplow Poll List 1780.

CRO 413/T21 Lease of Thriplow Rectory 1794.
CRO 413/04, An Agreement to grow Sanfoin, 1789.
CRO VAC 2:4, 1731 and 2:80, 1750 Inventories.
CUL EDR T (1842) Tithe Schedule and Map.
CRO (1845) Thriplow Enclosure Award.
CRO 62/9 1865 Manor Court Rolls of Bacon's Manor.

Trumpington

CRO P158/8/2 Trumpington Overseers' Accounts.

Whittlesford

CRO R58/5 Vols 1–14 George Nathan Maynard Diaries.
CRO P171/8/2 Whittlesford Overseers' Accounts.

General

University of Cambridge Department of Zoology Rev Jenyns,
    L. (1869) *Collections towards a Fauna Cantabrigiensis.*
NA MAF 68 (1867) Abstract of Parish Returns of acreage
    of Crops and Live Stock.

Printed primary sources

Babington, C. C. (1897) *Memorials, Journal and Botanical
    Correspondence.* Macmillan and Bowes, Cambridge.
BPP 30 (1834) *Royal Commission of Inquiry into the
    Administration and Practical Operation of the Poor
    Laws Section B Answers to Rural Questions, County of
    Cambridge.*
BPP 8 (1836) *Select Committee on Agricultural Distress*, Vol. 2.
BPP (various), *Poor Law Returns*, Vols 3, 9, 13, 19.
BPP 81.I (1876) *Returns by County of England and Wales of
    names and addresses of every owner of one acre and above
    and less than one acre.*
BPP 17 (1895) *Royal Commission on Agriculture*, Vol. 4.
CRO (1818) *Rotuli Hundredorem,*f 542 543 1279. Record
    Commission.
Curnock, N. (ed.) (1909–16) *Journal of Rev John Wesley AM
    1703–1791.* Epworth Press, Canterbury.
Denson, J. (1830) *A Peasant's Voice to Landowners* (1991
    reprint). Cambridge Record Society 9.
Martyn, T. (1763) *Plantae Cantabrigienses or a Catalogue
    of Plants which grow wild in the County of Cambridge.*
    Privately printed.
The Hundred Rolls, 1279 (1818) Record Commission 544,
    Thriplow. Translated by Shirley Wittering.
Tomlins, T. E. (ed.) (1804) *Enclosure Act 41 George III 1801.*
    Statutes of the Kingdom of Great Britain and Northern
    Ireland 41 Geo III to 43 Geo III.
Turner, M. E. (ed.) 1982 *Home Office Acreage Returns (HO
    67): List and Analysis.* PRO List and Index Society189,
    Cambridgeshire.
White, J. (1998) *Estimating the Age of Large and Veteran Trees
    in Britain.* Forestry Commission Information Note 12.

Printed works

Books

Allen, R. (1992) *Enclosure and the Yeoman.* Clarendon Press,
    Oxford.
Aston, M. and Rowley, T. (1974) *Landscape Archaeology*
    David and Charles, Newton Abbot.
Babington, C. C. (1897) *Memorials, Journal and Botanical
    Correspondence.* MacMillan and Bowes, Cambridge.
Baker, A. R. H. and Butlin, R. A. (1973) *Field Systems in the
    British Isles.* CUP, Cambridge.
Barrell, J. (1972) *The Idea of Landscape and the Sense of Place
    1730–1840.* CUP, Cambridge.
Bayliss-Smith, T. P. (1982) *The Ecology of Agricultural System.*
    CUP, Cambridge.
Bourne, G. (Sturt) (1912) *Changes in the Village.* Duckworth,
    London.
Caird, J. (1852) *English Agriculture in 1850–51* (1968 reprint).
    Gregg International, Farnborough.
Cambridgeshire County Council (2003) *Cambridgeshire
    Biodiversity Plan. Acid Grassland and Heathland.*
Carter, T. (2003) *The Anatomy of a Victorian Village
    – Whittlesford 1800–1900.* Whittlesford Victorian Group,
    Whittlesford.
Chambers, J. D. and Mingay, G. E. (1966) *The Agricultural
    Revolution 1750–1880.* Batsford, London.
Clare, J. (1986) *The Parish: a satire.* Penguin, Harlow.
Cobbett, W. (1830) *Rural Rides.* T. Nelson and Sons,
    London.
Conway, G. and Pretty, J. (2003) *Unwelcome Harvest:
    Agriculture and Pollution.* Eartscan, London.
Conybeare, Rev. E. (1910) *Highways and Byways in
    Cambridge and Ely.* McMillan, London.
Cunningham, W. D. D. (1909) *The Economic History
    of Cambridgeshire.* Reprinted from *The Ely Diocesan
    Remembrancer.* CUP, Cambridge.
Duffey, E., Morris, M. G., Sheail, J., Ward, L. K., Wells,
    D. A. and Wells, T. C. E. (1974) *Grassland Ecology and
    Grassland Managemen.* Chapman and Hall, London.
Eden, Rev. F. M. (1795) *The State of the Poor* (1928 reprint).
    Routledge, Oxford.
Edlin, H. L. (1944) *British Woodland Trees.* Batsford,
    London.
Engels, F. (1958) *The Condition of the Working Class of
    England* (translated and edited by Henderson, W. O.
    and Chaloner, W. H). Blackwell, Oxford.
Ernle, Lord (1912) *English Farming Past and Present.*
    Longman, London.
Ewan, A. H. and Prime, C. T. (eds) (1975) *Ray's Flora of
    Cambridgeshire.* Wheldon and Wesley, London.
Forestry Commission (1951) *Census Report No. 2 Hedgerow
    and Park Timber and woods under five acres.* HMSO,
    London.

Gilmour, J. and Walters, M. (1969) *Wild Flowers: Botanising in Britain* (4th edn 1954). Collins New Naturalist Series, London.

Gooch, Rev. W. (1813) *General View of the Agriculture of the County of Cambridgeshire.* Board of Agriculture, London.

Grigg, D. (1966) *Agricultural Revolution in South Lincolnshire.* CUP, Cambridge.

Hall, S. and Clutton-Brock, J. (1989) *Two Hundred years of British Livestock.* British Museum Natural History, London.

Hammond, J. and Hammond, B. (1911) *The Village Labourer.* (1995 reprint) Alan Sutton, Stroud.

Harrison, C. and Reid-Henry, D. (1998) *The History of the Birds of Britain.* Collins, London.

Harvey, J. H. (1972) *Early Gardening Catalogues, with complete reprints of lists and accounts of the 16th–19th centuries.* Phillimore, Colchester.

Havinden, M. A. (1961) 'Agricultural progress in open-field Oxfordshire', *Agricultural History Review* 9(2), 73–83.

Henslow, J. S. (1845) *An Address to Landlords on the Advantages to be expected from Spade Tenantry.* H. Hardacre, Cambridge.

Higgs, E. (1996) *A Clearer Sense of the Census.* Public Record Office, London.

Hitch, D. E. (1993) *A Mere Village: a history of Fowlmere, Cambridgeshire.* Privately published.

Hobsbawn, E. and Rudé, G. (2001) *Captain Swing.* Phoenix Press, London.

Hollowell, S. (2000) *Enclosure Records for Historians.* Phillimore, Chichester.

Hoskins, W. G. and Dudley Stamp, L. (1963) *The Common Lands of England and Wales.* Collins New Naturalist Series, Glasgow.

Jeffries, R. (1992) *Hodge and his Masters 1880.* Alan Sutton, Stroud.

Jenyns, Rev L. (1869) *Collections Towards a Fauna Cantabrigiensis.* Manuscript copy, University of Cambridge Zoology Department.

Kain, R. J. P. and Prince, H. C. (2000) *Tithe Surveys for Historians.* Phillimore, Chichester

Kain, R. J. P., Chapman, J. and Oliver, R. R. (2004) *The Enclosure Maps of England and Wales 1596–1918.* CUP, Cambridge.

Kelly's *Directories* (1847, 1864). London.

Kerridge, E. (1992) *The Common Fields of England.* Manchester University Press, Manchester

Kingston, A. (1890) *The Heath and its Wild Flowers* (1961 reprint). Warren Bros, Royston.

Kingston, A. (1893) *Fragments of Two Centuries* (1990 reprint). Royston and District Local History Society, Royston.

Kingston, A. (1904) *The Heath and its Wild Flowers* (1961 reprint). Royston and District Local History Society, Royston.

Lack, D. (1934) *Birds of Cambridgeshire.* Cambridge Bird Club, Cambridge.

Landry, D. (2001) *The Invention of the Countryside.* Palgrave, Basingstoke.

Langland, W. (1905) *The Vision of Piers Plowman* (ed. Skeat). De La More Press, London.

Mabey, R. (1980) *The Common Ground.* Hutchinson, London.

Mabey, R. (2010) *Weeds.* Profile Books, London.

Macfarlane, A. (1978) *The Origins of English Individualism.* Blackwell, Oxford.

Malcolmson, R. (1981) *Life and Labour in England 1700–1780* Hutchinson, London.

Mann, M. (1986) *The Sources of Social Power 1, The History of Power from the Beginning to AD 1760,* CUP, Cambridge.

Marshall, J. D. (1968) *The Old Poor Law 1795–1834.* Macmillan, Oxford.

Marshall, W. (1815) *County Report* Vol. 4 Midlands. (facsimile of 1st edition). Oxford.

Marr, J. E. and Shipley, A. E. (1904) *The Natural History of Cambridgeshire.* CUP, Cambridge.

Mingay, G. E. (1997) *Parliamentary Enclosure in England.* Longman, London.

Mingay, G. E. (ed.) (1989) *The Agrarian History of England and Wales* Vol. 6, 1750–1850. CUP, Cambridge.

Mitchell, A. (1974) *Field Guide to the Trees of Britain and Northern Europe.* Collins, London.

Munby, L. (1996) *How Much is that worth?* British Association for Local History/Phillimore, Chichester.

Neeson, J. (1993) *Commoners, Common Rights, Enclosure and Social Change in England 1700–1820.* CUP, Cambridge.

Nissel, M. (1987) *People Count, a History of the General Register Office.* HMSO, London.

Overton, M. (1996) *Agricultural Revolution in England.* CUP, Cambridge.

Patrick, J. (2001) *The Sawston Story: a history of the village.* Pivately published.

Paxman, J. (1999) *The English: a portrait of a people.* Penguin, London.

Peacock, A. J. (1965) *Bread or Blood: a study of the Agrarian riots in East Anglia in 1816.* Gollancz, London.

Perring, F. H., Sell, P. D. and Walters, S. M. (1964) *A Flora of Cambridgeshire.* CUP, Cambridge.

Phillips, A. D. M. (1989) *The Underdraining of Farmland in England in the Nineteenth Century.* CUP, Cambridge.

Pollard, E., Hooper, M. D. and Moore, N.W. (1974) *Hedges.* Collins, London.

Rackham, O. (1983) *Trees and Woodland in the British Landscape.* Dent, London.

Rackham, O. (1994) *History of the Countryside.* Weidenfield and Nicolson, London.

Relhan, R. (1820) *Flora Cantabrigiensis* (3rd edn). CUP, Cambridge.

Richardson, J. (1993) *The Local Historian's Encyclopedia.* Historical Publications, New Barnet.

Roberts, B. K. and Wrathmell, S. (2000) *An Atlas of Rural Settlement in England.* English Heritage, London.

Robinson, P. (1983) *The Shell Book of Firsts.* Ebury Press, London.

Rodwell, J. S. (ed.) (1991) *British Plant Communities Vol. 2: Mires and Heaths.* CUP, Cambridge.

Saffron Walden Museum (1997) *The Saffron Crocus, History and Cookery.* Saffron Museum leaflet.

Seebohm, M. E. (1952) *The Evolution of the English Farm* (first published 1927). Allen and Unwin, Reading.

Simond, L. (1817) *Journal of a Tour and Residence in Great Britain.* Ballantyne, Edinburgh.

Snell, K. (1985) *Annals of the Labouring Poor, Social Change and Agrarian England 1660–1900.* CUP, Cambridge.

Spufford, M. (1974) *Contrasting Communities: English villagers in the sixteenth and seventeenth centuries.* CUP, Cambridge.

Stace, C. (1997) *New Flora of the British Isles.* CUP, Cambridge.

Tate, W. E. (1946) *The Parish Chest.* Phillimore, Chichester.

Teversham, T. F. (1947) *History of the Village of Sawston.* Privately published.

Tiller, K. (1992) *English Local History: an introduction.* Alan Sutton, Stroud.

Thomas, K. (1983) M*an and the Natural World.* Allan Lane, London.

Thriplow Landscape Research Group (2004) *Thriplow Time Trials.* Privately published.

Trow-Smith, R. (1967) *Life from the Land: the growth of farming in Western Europe.* Longman, London.

Turner, M. (1980) *English Parliamentary Enclosure*: *its historical geography and economic history.* Archon Books, Folkstone.

Turner, M. E., Beckett, J. V. and Afton, B. (2001) *Farm Production in England 1700–1914.* OUP, Oxford.

Vancouver C. (1794) *A General View of the Agriculture of the County of Cambridgeshire.* Board of Agriculture, London.

VCH (1938–2002) *Victoria County History Cambridgeshire* vols 1–10, esp. Vol. 2 (1948), Vol. 6 (1978), Vol. 8 (1982).

Wade-Martins, P. (1993) *Black faces, the History of East Anglian Sheep Breeds.* Norfolk Museum Service, Gressenhall.

Walters, M. G. (1972) *Nature in Cambridgeshire* 15. CUP/Cambridgeshire and Isle of Ely Naturalists Trust, Cambridge.

Walters, S. M. (1981) *The Shaping of Cambridge Botany.* CUP, Cambridge.

Williamson, T. (2003) *Shaping Medieval Landscapes: Settlement, Society, Environment.* Windgather Press, Oxford.

Wright, G. N. (1992) *Turnpike Roads.* Shire, Princes Risborough.

Journals, Articles, Chapters and Papers

Allen, R. (2001) Community and Market in England: Open Fields and Enclosures Revisited. In Aoki, M. and Hayami,Y. (eds) *Communities and Markets in Economic Development*, 42–67. OUP.

Allison, K. J. (1957) The Sheep-Corn Husbandry of Norfolk in the Sixteenth and Seventeenth centuries. *Agricultural History Review* 1, 12–30.

Baker, A. R. H. (1988) Some terminological problems in studies in British Field Systems. *Agricultural History Review* 41.1, 136–40.

Banks, S. (1982) Nineteenth century scandal or twentieth century mode? A new look at 'open' and 'close' parishes. *Economic History Review* 30, 53–73.

Beckett, J. V. (1991) The disappearance of the cottager and the squatter from the English countryside: the Hammonds revisited. In Holderness, B. A. and Turner, M. (eds) *Land, Labour and Agriculture 1700–1920*, 49–69. Hambledon, London.

Beckett, J. V., Turner, M. E. and Cowell, B. (1998) Farming through Enclosure. *Rural History* 9.2, 141–55.

Beresford, M. W. (1946) Ridge and Furrow in the open fields. *Economic History Review* 16 34–45.

Bowie, G. G. S. (1987) New sheep for Old – changes in sheep farming in Hampshire 1792–1879. *Agricultural History Review* 35, 15–24.

Cambridge, W. (1845) On the Advantage of reducing the size and number of hedges. *Journal of Royal Agricultural Society* 6, 333–42.

Cambridge Chronicle (various dates). Cambridgeshire Collection.

Cambridge Independent Press (various dates). Cambridgeshire Collection.

Chapman, J. (1993) Enclosure Commissioners as Landscape Planners. *Landscape History* 15, 51–5.

Chase, M. (1992) Can History be Green? *Rural History* 3.2, 243–51.

Coletta, P. E. (1944) Phillip Pusey, English County Squire. *Agricultural History* 18, 83–91.

Coppock, J. T. (1966–8) Maps as Sources for the Study of Land Use in the Past. *Imago Mundi* 20–2, 37–49.

Crompton, G. G. (1959) The Peat Holes of Triplow. *Nature in Cambridgeshire* 2, 25–34.

Eastwood, D. (1998) The age of uncertainty: Britain in the early nineteenth century. *Transactions of the Royal Historical Society* 7, 91–115.

Evans, A. H. (1904) The Birds of Cambridgeshire. In Marr, J. E. and Shipley, A. E. (eds) *The Natural History of Cambridgeshire*, 75–99 CUP, Cambridge.

Finch, J. (2004) Grass, grass, grass: fox-hunting and the creation of the modern landscape. *Landscapes* 5.2, 41–52.

Godwin, H. (1938) The botany of Cambridgeshire. In

Darby, H. C. (ed.) *A Scientific Survey of the Cambridge District*, 44–59. British Association for the Advancement of Science, London

Goose, N. (2004) Farm service in southern England in the Mid-nineteenth century. *Local Population Studies* 72, 77–82.

Goose, N. (2006) Farm Service, seasonal unemployment and casual labour in mid-nineteenth century England. *Agricultural History Review* 54.2, 274–303.

Hall, C. and Lovatt, R. (1989) The site and foundation of Peterhouse. *Proceedings of Cambridge Antiquarian Society* 68, 5–46.

Havinden, M. A. (1961) Agricultural progress in open-field Oxfordshire, *Agricultural History Review* 9.2 73–83.

Harrison, S. (2002) Open fields and earlier landscapes: six parishes in south-east Cambridgeshire, *Landscapes* 3.1, 35–53.

Holderness, B. A. (1971) Capital formation in agriculture. In Higgins, J. P. P. and Pollard, S. (eds) *Aspects of Capital Investment in Great Britain 1750–1850*, 159–83. Methuen, London.

Holderness, B. A. (1972) 'Open' and 'Close' parishes in England in the eighteenth and nineteenth centuries. *Agricultural History Review* 20, 126–39.

Hoskins, W. G. (1966) English Local History: the Past and the Future. *Inaugural Lecture University of Leicester.* Leicester University Press, Leicester.

Jonas, S. (1847) On farming in Cambridgeshire Prize Report, *Journal of the Royal Agricultural Society* 7, 35–59.

Jones, E. L. (1981) Reconstructing former bird communities. *Forth Naturalist and Historian* 6, 101–6.

Jones, E. L. (1971) Bird pests in recent centuries. *Agricultural History Review* 20, 107–25.

Jones, E. L. (1960) Eighteenth century changes in Hampshire chalkland farming. *Agricultural History Review* 8, 102–19.

Langton, J. (1989) Geographical variations in Poor Relief under the Old Poor Law. mimeo. School of Geography Library, University of Oxford.

Martin, J. M. (1967) The cost of parliamentary enclosure in Warwickshire. In Jones, E. L. (ed.) *Agriculture and Economic Growth in England 1650–1815*. Methuen, London.

Mills, D. (1978) The quality of life in Melbourn, Cambridgeshire, 1800–1850. *Social History Review* 23, 382–404. CUP, Cambridge.

Minchinton, W. E. (1953) Agricultural Returns and the Government during the Napoleonic Wars. *Agricultural History Review* 1, 29–43.

Ottoway, S. and Williams, S. (1998) Reconstructing the life-cycle experience of poverty in the time of the old poor law. *Archives* 23, 19–29.

Overton, M. (1991) The determinants of crop yields in early modern England. In Campbell, B. and Overton, M.

(eds) *Land, Labour and Livestock*, 284–322. Manchester University Press, Manchester.

Presnell, L. S. (1956) *Country Banking in the Industrial Revolution*. Oxford University Press, Oxford.

Purslow, R. (2006) What Landscape means to me. *Landscapes* 7.2, 105–13.

Pusey, P. (1851) What ought Farmers to do? Being a reprint of an article on the progress of Agricultural Knowledge during the last eight years. *Journal of the Royal Agricultural Society Kenilworth.*

Royston Weekly News (1889) 20 December. Cambridgeshire Collection.

Ryder, M. L. (1964) History of sheep breeds in Britain. *Agricultural History Review* 12, 1–82.

Shaw Taylor. L. (2001) Labourers, cows, common rights and Parliamentary Enclosure. *Past and Present* 171, 95–126.

Sheail, J. (1986) Nature conservation and the agricultural historian. *Agricultural History Review* 34.1, 1–11.

Sheail, J. (1993) Green history – the evolving agenda. *Rural History* 4.2, 209–23.

Shiel, R. S. (1991) Improving soil productivity in the pre-fertiliser era. In Campbell, B. S. and Overton, M. (eds) *Land, Labour and Livestock*, 51–77. Manchester University Press, Manchester.

Shurer, K. (2004) Surnames and the search for regions. *Local Population Studies* 72, 50–76.

Simpson, A. (1961) The East Anglian foldcourse, some queries. *Agricultural History Review* 6, 87–96.

Spufford, M. (2000) Enclosure quarrels. *Proceedings of the Cambridge Antiquarian Society* 89, 69–85.

Tate, W. E. (1944) Cambridgeshire field systems, with a hand-list of Cambridgeshire Enclosure Acts and Awards. *Proceedings of the Cambridgeshire Antiquarian Society* 40, 56–87.

Tate, W. E. (1952) The cost of Parliamentary enclosure in England, with special reference to the County of Oxford. *Economic History Review* 2, 263.

Taylor, C. C. (2002) Nucleated settlement: a view from the frontier. *Landscape History* 24, 53–71.

Taylor, C. C. (2006) Landscape history, observation and explanation: the missing houses in Cambridgeshire villages. *Proceedings of the Cambridge Antiquarian Society* 95, 121–32.

Thirsk, J. (1964) The common fields. *Past and Present* 29, 3–25.

Thomson. D. (1994) The welfare of the elderly in the past. In Pelling, M. and Smith, R. M. (eds) *Life, Death and the Elderly*, 194–221. Routledge, London.

Timmer, C. P. (1969) The turnip, the new husbandry, and the English agricultural revolution. *Quarterly Journal of Economics* 83, 375–95.

Turner, M. (1981) Cost, finance and Parliamentary enclosure. *Economic History Review* 34.2, 236–48.

Turner, M. (1986) English open fields and enclosures:

retardation or productivity improvements, *Journal of Economic History* 46.3, 669–92.

Turner, M. (2000) Corporate strategy or individual priority? Land management, income and tenure on Oxbridge agricultural land in the mid-nineteenth century. *Business History* 42.4, 1–26.

Turner, M., Becket, J. and Afton, B. (1996) Taking stock: farmers, farm records and agricultural output in England. *Agricultural History Review* 44.1, 21–34.

Turner, M., Becket, J. and Afton, B. (2003) Agricultural sustainability and open field farming in England. *International Journal of Agricultural Sustainability* 1.2, 124–40.

Wade-Martins, S. (1999) Farming through enclosure – a gentle rejoinder. *Rural History*, 10, 1.

Walters, M. G. (1972) *Nature in Cambridgeshire* 15. Cambridgeshire and Isle of Ely Naturalists' Trust, Cambridge.

Walters, S. M. (1965) Natural History. In Steers, J. A. (ed.) *The Cambridge Region*, 51–67. British Association for the Advancement of Science, London.

Watt, A. S. (1938) The climate of Cambridgeshire. In Darby, E. C. (ed.) *A Scientific Survey of the Cambridge District*, 31–43. The British Association for the Advancement of Science, London.

Way, T. (2000) Open and closed villages. In Kirby, T. and Oosthuizen, S. (eds) *An Atlas of Cambridgeshire and Huntingdonshire History*. Centre for Regional Studies, Cambridge.

Wells, T. C. E. and Wells, D. A. Classification of grassland communities. In Duffey, E., Morris, M. G., Sheail, J., Ward, L., Wells, D. A. and Wells, T. C. E. (eds) (1974) *Grassland Ecology and Wildlife Management*, 42–48. Chapman and Hall, London.

Wrigley, E. A. (1986) Men on the land and men in the countryside. In Bonfield, L., Smith, R. M. and Wrightson, K. (eds) *The World we Have Gained: histories of Population and Social Structure: essays presented to Peter Laslett on his seventieth birthday*, 295–336. Blackwell, Oxford.

Williamson, T. (2000) Understanding enclosure, *Landscapes* 1, 56–79.

Wilson, J. (2001) *The Roads of Thriplow Interim Report.* Thriplow Landscape Research Group, privately published.

Wittering, S. (2000) How reliable are the Government Poor Law Returns? *The Local Historian* 30.3, 160–4.

Wittering, S. (2004) This enclosure business; enclosure commissioners' papers as an historical source. *The Local Historian* 34.2, 104–12.

Unpublished Dissertations and Papers

Birtles, S. A. (2003) *Green Space Beyond Self-Interest: the Evolution of Common Land in Norfolk, c.750–2003.* Unpublished PhD thesis, University of East Anglia.

Hawkins, B. (2005) *Fowlmere Watercress.* Unpublished MA dissertation, University of East Anglia.

Hindle, S. (1999) *Politics of the Vestry*, paper given at Wolfson College, Cambridge.

Postgate, M. R. (1964) *The Open Fields of Cambridgeshire.* Unpublished PhD thesis, University of Cambridge.

Shaw-Taylor, L. (1999) *Proletarianisation, Parliamentary Enclosure and Household Economy of the Labouring Poor 1750–1850.* Unpublished PhD thesis, University of Cambridge.

Turner, M. (1973) *Some Social and Economic Considerations of Parliamentary Enclosure in Buckinghamshire 1738–1865.* Unpublished PhD thesis, University of Sheffield.

Williams, S. (1998) *Poor Relief, Welfare and Medical Provision in Bedfordshire: the Social, Economic and Demographic Context, 1750–1850.* Unpublished PhD thesis, University of Cambridge.

Wittering, S. (1996) *Church and Chapel, a Study of Anglicans and Dissenters in the Nineteenth Century in the South Cambridgeshire village of Thriplow.* Unpublished Dissertation Advanced Certificate in English Local History, University of Cambridge.

Wittering, S. (1999) *Parochial Variation in Poor Relief in Thriplow Hundred, Cambridgeshire 1770–1815.* Unpublished M Studies thesis, University of Cambridge.

Wittering, S. (2008) *Enclosure in South Cambridgeshire: Society, Farming and the Environment, 1798–1850.* Unpublished PhD thesis, University of East Anglia.

Young, A. (1793) *Annals of Agriculture*, London.

Web sites

David, B. and Selby, J. *Dovecotes in South Cambridgeshire*, web site for South Cambridgeshire District Council, nd.

Joint Nature Conservation Committee website, analysed by Cheffings, C. from Preston, Pearman and Dines, (2002). Internet version of England and Wales Rainfall series 1766–1980, and Central England Temperature 1659–1994, (1974) University of East Anglia.

Museum of Rural Life, Reading University, press release (June 2006) www.reading.ac.uk/merl/.

Portugal, S. web site www.birdsofbritain.co.uk

Suffolk Sheep Society web site, www.suffolksheep.org/